The Christian Case
against Contraception

The Christian Case
against Contraception

Making the Case from Historical, Biblical, Systematic,
and Practical Theology & Ethics

BRYAN C. HODGE

WIPF & STOCK · Eugene, Oregon

THE CHRISTIAN CASE AGAINST CONTRACEPTION
Making the Case from Historical, Biblical, Systematic, and Practical Theology & Ethics

Wipf & Stock
An Imprint of Wipf and Stock Publishers
199 W. 8th Ave., Suite 3
Eugene, OR 97401
www.wipfandstock.com

ISBN 13: 978-1-4982-5470-0

Manufactured in the U.S.A.
Scripture quotations have been translated directly from the Hebrew and Greek.

Other Scripture quotations have been taken from the New American Standard Bible, copyright © 1960, 1962, 1963, 1968, 1971, 1972, 1975, 1977, and 1995 by the Lockman Foundation, and are used by permission.

To the glory of God through my children

The Stranger was speaking and pointing at her as he spoke.

She did not understand the words; but Dimble did, and heard Merlin saying in what seemed to him a rather strange kind of Latin:

"Sir, you have in your house the falsest lady of any at this time alive."

And Dimble heard the Director answer him in the same language:

"Sir, you are mistaken. She is doubtless like all of us a sinner; but the woman is chaste."

"Sir," said Merlin, "know well that she has done in Logres a thing of which no less sorrow shall come than came of the stroke that Balinus struck. For, Sir, it was the purpose of God that she and her lord should between them have begotten a child by whom the enemies should have been put out of Logres for a thousand years."

"She is but lately married," said Ransom. "The child may yet be born."

"Sir," said Merlin, "be assured that the child will never be born, for the hour of its begetting is passed. Of their own will they are barren."

—C. S. Lewis,
That Hideous Strength, 278–79

Contents

Preface

THIS BOOK IS DIVIDED into four major arguments, which stem from the four major theological and ethical disciplines of Christianity: historical, biblical, systematic, and practical theology. It will be argued that the practice of contraception is contradictory to the evidence brought about from each of these areas of Christian inquiry. The final two sections consist of answering modern evangelical arguments that attempt to support the practice using the same means. Chapter 7 does this in a traditional format: point-counterpoint, whereas chapter 8 does the same thing but in a more Socratic fashion.

I have purposely fronted the material concerning the Church's view of contraception for a couple of reasons. The first reason is that I wanted to show the evangelical church today that its views of the subject are not the same as the historic Church's position. Whereas evangelicals may not consider this to be a detriment to their position, it does say something toward their limited view of how culture and interpretation work themselves out. If one gains his or her interpretive grid through which all Scripture is evaluated from culture, then the question must ultimately be asked, From which culture is the present Church deriving its interpretive grid concerning this subject—from the culture of the historic Church or from the secular culture in which the current church exists? For this reason, I have presented the material as follows, beginning with our interpretive grids: the historic Church or the culture; continuing with that which we interpret: the Bible; developing that which we derive from both the culture of the historic Church and the Bible as we reason within these: systematics; and seeking to draw out the implications of those things into appropriate applicatory responses in the Christian life: practical theology and ethics.

Such a format I view as essential in understanding the two trajectories of interpretation of the Bible. If a person adopts the interpretive grid of the culture, rather than that of the Church, then of course his or her entire line of reasoning will turn off in that direction. Hence, the importance of understanding that a person begins with presuppositions when interpreting Scripture, and from whence those presuppositions come is vital to understanding the Christian message, both in general and specifically within the subject at hand.

Finally, it is important to note that my line of argumentation has stemmed from authoritative disciplines within Christianity, not from preference, which stems from experience. I cannot express how many times I was told as a young man that I would change my mind when I got married or got older. Such a line of reasoning showed the hand of the evangelicals clearly in that their primary problem with the historic position is not a biblical objection, but an experiential and preferential one. It was surmised, therefore, that when my experience became what theirs was, my position would also become the position that they held. My arguments, however, have never stemmed from how I personally *feel* about the subject, or any experience that led to those feelings. Instead, I have argued from authorities beyond myself, outside of my box, and as such, my position has remained the same even though my circumstances have varied along life's road. I realize, however, that by starting my argument from external authority, rather than personal experience and feeling, I have already set my face against modern evangelicalism, which although it claims the former, is almost exclusively based in the latter. My contention is that if evangelicals exchange the latter for the former, they will be in a better position to evaluate our current issue with an open mind.

Abbreviations

ANF	*Ante-Nicene Fathers*
BDAG	Bauer-Danker-Arndt-Gingrich, *A Greek-English Lexicon of the New Testament and Other Early Christian Literature*
BDB	Brown-Driver-Briggs, *Hebrew and English Lexicon of the Old Testament*
BibSac	*Biblia Sacra*
CAD	*The Assyrian Dictionary of the Oriental Institute of the University of Chicago*
CDA	*Concise Dictionary of Akkadian*
DCH	*Dictionary of Classical Hebrew*
GKC	*Gesenius' Hebrew Grammar*
HALOTSE	*Hebrew and Aramaic Lexicon of the Old Testament,* Study Edition
IBHS	*Introduction to Biblical Hebrew Syntax*
JANES	*Journal of Ancient Near Eastern Studies*
JBL	*Journal of Biblical Literature*
LSJ	Liddel and Scott, *Greek-English Lexicon*
LXX	The Septuagint; specifically, the Greek translation of the Pentateuch
MM	Moulton and Milligan, *Vocabulary of the Greek New Testament*
NIDNTT	*New International Dictionary of New Testament Theology*
NIDOTTE	*New International Dictionary of Old Testament Theology and Exegesis*
NovTest	*Novum Testamentum*
NPNF[1]	*Nicene and Post-Nicene Fathers,* Series 1
NPNF[2]	*Nicene and Post-Nicene Fathers,* Series 2
OG	The Greek translation of the Old Testament, with exception to the Pentateuch
PG	*Patrologiae Cursus Completus, Series Graeca*

PL	*Patrologiae Cursus Completus, Series Latina*
PGL	*Patristic Greek Lexicon*
TDNT	*Theological Dictionary of the New Testament*
TDOT	*Theological Dictionary of the Old Testament*
TLOT	*Theological Lexicon of the Old Testament*
Thayer	*Thayer's Greek-English Lexicon of the New Testament*
TWOT	*Theological Wordbook of the Old Testament*

Acknowledgments

I WOULD LIKE TO thank the various people who took the time to read through the rougher drafts of this manuscript for me, asking questions and playing devil's advocate, which is so vital in a discussion like this one. Among those who took the time to do so were my old college roommate, Craig Maxwell, and his wife, Emily, as well as my old Resident Assistant and roommate, Thad Bergmeier.

I would like to thank Audrey Dorsch for her hard work in copy editing this manuscript, and making it presentable.

I would also like to thank my mother, Michele Bonnée Nichols, whose encouragement and support has not only seen this book to publication, but has also been invaluable to our family throughout life's ups and downs.

I must, of course, give thanks to my wife, Allison Marie Hodge, who has been my advocate and partner throughout the exciting and challenging journey that is childrearing.

And above all, I thank the great God and Father of our Lord Jesus Christ, who, through His Holy Spirit, has poured out His love into our hearts in such a manner that it has overflowed into a love for our children, present and future—a love that has outweighed the pressure to conform to the damaging syncretism of evangelical culture—and reciprocally has taught us to love in a way that we could have never learned otherwise. He has blessed us thus far with four boys, Jonathan Michael, Alexander Charles, Peter Bryan, and Andrew Donald, as well as our little girl, Lily Marie. Our prayer is that they will become the blessings to Him and to His Church that they have been, in this short time upon the earth, to us. *Sola Dei Gloria.*

Introduction

IT WAS IN A college dorm room where our current subject originally caught my attention. Until that point I had never thought ill of the practice of contraception, largely because I never thought of it at all. But when a couple of my fellow freshmen were talking about the subject, I was suddenly brought into the debate, and I had sort of an epiphany. This illumination came when one of my classmates said something to justify the Christian use of contraception, and his line of reasoning struck me as a bit off. I pursued the question, but his answer still didn't address my inquiry adequately. In fact, even though I could not put my finger on it at the time, there was something very unchristian about this Christian's reasoning concerning the issue. I pursued it further and further, and as I did so, I suddenly realized something about an issue I had never thought to be of any relevance to me: I no longer believed the use of contraception to be an acceptable Christian practice. I, like most people, had assumed that there was nothing wrong with the practice. In fact, the assumption was so strong that it took this incident to even put the issue on my ethical radar screen. Not only had I assumed its correctness, I had considered it as relevant a question as asking whether eating bread was acceptable in the sight of God. In others words, it was not a question of whether contraception was morally acceptable because it was not a question for me at all. It was, therefore, quite a shock, to say the least, to discover otherwise. The change of my mind, of course, started out more like a doubt than a dogma. After this conversation, and others that would follow, I simply no longer had the blind faith I once had that this common practice among evangelicals existed among them because it had been well thought out by those who employed it.

It has been many years since that day, but the issue has never left me. The conviction concerning the practice, along with all that it has brought, has followed me every step of the way; and to this day I continue to be humbled by this very Christian idea that eluded my thinking for so much of my early Christian life.

This book is largely the result of two motivating factors: (1) the desire to put forth the Christian case against the practice as a type of smelling salts to a culturally intoxicated Church and (2) the desire to leave behind a Christian witness of the subject to my children. The first led me to think deeply about the subject over the past fifteen years; but it is the second that led me to capture it in writing. As such, this book is not written to cover every topic as thoroughly as I would like. It is written as an introduction to certain Christian arguments against contraception, and it by no means goes into the depths of meaning and implication of our present conclusions—though the riches of such are many and far reaching. The book functions well, however, as an introductory book for Christian ethics courses, as well as for pastors and college-educated laity who may have probing questions concerning our subject matter. It is further my hope that the average layperson will make an effort to digest the book and its subject matter in a thoughtful way, even though the style and language of the book may at first be offputting.

As a preface to this subject, I ought to point out its very controversial nature. It is controversial in that the amount of hostility that arises from the mere claim that there may be something wrong with it pales in comparison to any other subject I have ever encountered.

I must admit that, although my wife and I did not hide our views of the subject from people within the Church, neither were we ecstatic when people found out what we believed. Ironically, believing what the Church has always believed about the subject of contraception in the evangelical Church today is much like being the sole Trinitarian at a Jehovah's Witness convention, or worse yet, a pork vendor at a rally for Islamic jihad. Suffice to say, friendliness and openness have not typically followed the revelation of our beliefs regarding the morality of the issue. Regardless, we have sought to be honest with those who would ask us, and we have tried our best to live out those convictions under the grace and power of God amid a currently closed evangelical Church.

But what are the reasons for such an unwillingness to pursue the subject openly? Perhaps it is that this subject is not some high and lofty idea that has little effect on the life of the listener. Heated discussions may ensue because of egos on any issue, but the fact that this issue demands a complete change in thinking and lifestyle, as well as an admission of guilt for any past practices if deemed wrong, causes an individual to have a gut reaction that seeks to protect the self. This "survival mechanism" is really what separates the discussion surrounding this subject from one in which the individual has nothing to lose by the outcome. It is for this reason that this particular subject has a great value in testing an individual's humility, as well as his or her claim that "Jesus Christ is Lord." If Christ is Lord, then surely the individual who makes that claim will want to know if he or she is following Him in this area of thought and behavior, and perhaps, approach the subject with both greater humility and less enmity.

Nonetheless, the fact that this subject may bring unwanted hostility cannot be our main concern in pursuing it. The prayer and hope of any shepherd of God's people is that they will hear, repent, and have joy in the truth. I present this subject for discussion, then, not for the unbeliever, but for the believer—not for the one who seeks to justify and please him or herself, but for the one who seeks to justify and please God in all things. With that sentiment it will be wise to proceed with the Spirit of God, who commanded us to be "quick to hear, slow to speak and slow to anger; because the anger of man does not bring about the righteousness of God" (Jas 1:19–20). I pray now that we who fear the Lord will enter the discussion accordingly.

WHY THIS DISCUSSION IS IMPORTANT

Of course, it must be stated at the get go that this subject is often neglected largely because most evangelicals assume it is a personal issue and not important, or at least not the business of the Church, to discuss. As one person put it, "The Church should stay out of our bedrooms."[1] Of course, it would be the hope of this author that any dedicated Christian would understand that God should be glorified through the truth He has revealed *even* in the bedroom. In fact, the primary sin that is combined with idolatry in Scripture is that of sexual immorality. If in fact the use of one's sexuality is connected to one's claim that one has a relationship with God, then the bedroom is far from the last place we should evaluate, and indeed, it seems rather to be the first area that God desires us to scrutinize.

---

1. The implication of this statement, of course could be seen as excluding the Christian Church from teaching anything about sexual activity—an idea clearly opposed to the biblical sentiment.

This is often seen as a secondary issue either way, and it is felt that one should not divide the Church over secondary issues. Leaving for another time the discussion of the fact that the Bible does not divide itself up in such a way, the subject should be seen as a primary/essential issue to discuss. I say this because the historic arguments that Christianity has always leveled against birth control carry with them severe consequences for its practitioner if true.

For instance, the first historical argument leveled against the practice is that contraception is a form of murder. The second is that the practice is a type of sexual immorality. The third and fourth arguments perceive the practice to be rebellious acts of idolatry. The unrepentant practice of any one of these individual practices brings about condemnation both from the Bible and consistently by theologians throughout the Church's history.

If someone desires to make the argument that this subject is not important, he or she will have to answer the question, Which one of the sins listed above is not important if one's eternal destiny is on the line? Is the practice of sexual immorality or idolatry, which evidences that a person is going off to eternal punishment (1 Cor 6:9–10; Gal 5:19–21; Rev 21:8), that which we should consider "unimportant"? Or murder, which displays the same non-salvific relationship with God (1 John 3:15; Rev 21:8)? This is not even to mention the host of other arguments brought against it from other avenues that hold the practice of contraception to be a non-Christian one.

One can say that he or she does not believe that the practice of contraception falls under any of those sins, and therefore does not believe that the discussion is important; but that is something he or she will have to prove in discussion of the subject—thus acknowledging the importance of that very discussion. It is easy to say that an issue is not important in order to honor Christ in the Christian life. It is an altogether different thing to prove it as such. Let us therefore move away from the patronizing idea that this is a secondary discussion to have, since if the Church is right on any one of those points, the destiny of the one who fails to heed its warning, according to the Scripture, is in grave peril. Such a prospect ought to lead Christians to acquire a greater enthusiasm for the issue at hand, especially those who have not thoroughly engaged the subject.

IT DOESN'T MATTER,
BECAUSE I'M SAVED BY GRACE ANYWAY

Of course, there are those who feel that the arguments against such a practice don't matter. They are going to live as they see fit, because they are saved by grace, regardless of whether they are committing egregious acts of sin or not. These individuals fail to realize, however, that grace comes through a means. That means is biblical faith.

The type of faith Scripture tells us leads to salvation is the type that seeks to please God in all things and produces actions accordingly. For instance, James states that "faith without works is useless" (2:20). The book that discusses grace and faith proportionately more than any other in the New Testament is Galatians. However, it is in the book of Galatians that we find the closest parallel to the teaching concerning the nature of saving faith in James.[7]

> [7]Do not be deceived, God is not mocked; for whatever a man sows, this he will also reap. [8]For the one who sows to his own flesh will from the flesh reap corruption, but the one who sows to the Spirit will from the Spirit reap eternal life. (Gal 6:7–8)

The Church Father Irenaeus summed it up nicely when he was discussing the reason why Christians pursue obedience to Christ in all areas of their lives:

> The more extensive operation of freedom implies that a more complete subjection and affection towards our Liberator had been implanted within us. For He did not set us free for the purpose that we should depart from Him . . . but that the more we receive His grace the more we should love Him.[2]

Likewise, Calvin long ago stated the biblical and early Church's view of faith reclaimed in the Reformation:

> It is not our doctrine that the faith which justifies is alone; we maintain that it is invariably accompanied by good works; only we contend that faith alone is sufficient for justification. The Papists themselves are accustomed to . . . presenting it out of all shape and unaccompanied by love, and at other times, in its true character.

---

2. Irenaeus, *Against Heresies*, 4.13.3.

> We, again, refuse to admit that, in any case, faith can be separated from the Spirit of regeneration.[3]

Luther, in agreement, stated:

> Instead, faith is God's work in us, that changes us and gives new birth from God (John 1:13). It kills the Old Adam and makes us completely different people. It changes our hearts, our spirits, our thoughts and all our powers. It brings the Holy Spirit with it. Yes, it is a living, creative, active and powerful thing, this faith. Faith cannot help doing good works constantly. It doesn't stop to ask if good works ought to be done, but before anyone asks, it already has done them and continues to do them without ceasing. Anyone who does not do good works in this manner is an unbeliever.[4]

In his *Treatise on Good Works*, Luther interprets a verse in Ecclesiastes 9 as follows: "'Let thy garments be always white,' that is, let all our works be good, whatever they may be, without any distinction." In fact, it was the "easy believism" inherent within the medieval practice of selling indulgences that led Luther to deny the validity of that practice, because he proclaimed that salvific faith was through repentance, not through an easy, ritualistic gesture made to the church. It is through this that we see that the biblical view of faith contains a genuine submissive and loving attitude toward Christ, which then produces acts of grateful submission to Him as Lord. Faith and the desire to do what is pleasing to God go hand in hand. If one were to argue otherwise, one would have to conclude that his gospel is not the biblical one.

The irony, therefore, is that the individual who argues that, since one is saved by grace, what one practices does not matter is in all likelihood the very person not saved by grace at all. Grace comes to the one who seeks the kingdom of God and His righteousness through faith. Apart from such faith there is no grace.

Therefore, if there is even a slight chance that a follower of Christ might be guilty of one of the sins of murder, sexual immorality, or idolatry, that person will surely want to explore the claim of this book's truthfulness in order to worship and seek God's pleasure. The one who casually dismisses the discussion without consideration evidences that he or she has no such desire as that found in the Psalmist when he cried,

---

3. Calvin, *Commentaries on the Epistles*, 152–53.

4. Irmischer, *Martin Luther's Definition of Faith*, 124–25.

"Search me, O God, and know my mind; scrutinize me, and know my assumptions; discover if there is any wicked way in me, and lead me in the everlasting way" (139:23–24).

Therefore, I say again, the importance of this topic cannot be over-estimated. To be concerned about whether one is living in God's pleasure, or in the absence thereof, is to be concerned with either the truth or falsity of the conclusions of our present discussion.

DEFINING THE TERMS

It is important, before we begin, to define our terms, so that there will be little room for confusion. When we speak of "contraception," or the broader term "birth control," certain images of pills may come to mind. However, as we will see, birth control is a mind-set, an intention, more than it is a device that is used. In fact, it will be argued that the use of a device is not necessary for a practice to fall under the category of "birth control," or "contraception."

I have also purposely interchanged the terms "birth control" and "contraception," even though the former terminology is broader than the latter. I have done this mainly to remind the reader that the two familiar terms both have the same ultimate goal: the former "to control whether someone gives birth to a child" (and thus in our present discussion to control whether a child is conceived) and the latter "to counter the con-ception of a child." The goal of both commonly used terms then is to prevent a child, whose existence would normally result from a sexual act, from coming into the world.

DEFINITION

By "birth control," or "contraception," I mean: *Any practice, with or without a device, that is intended to be used by an individual involved in the sexual act, in an effort to prevent the climax of that act from creating an opportunity for God to bring forth a covenant child through the natural, created means of the biological processes that He has set in place.*

BREAKDOWN OF THE DEFINITION

Let us now pursue the meaning and implications of each phrase more closely.

A practice, using a device or not . . .

Many who are adversarial to the use of foreign drugs or mechanisms to prevent conception seem to do so upon the basis of pragmatism. It is argued that such foreign bodies can harm the body in some way, have adverse effects on one's married life, and be financially costly. Some have even argued that what is called "natural family planning" (NFP) is as effective as the most effective form of artificial contraception. Such a practice, however, has as its goal the same outcome of artificial contraception. Hence, it is not for God-centered reasons one refrains from the use of artificial contraception, but from concern of self. It is an ethic of self-survival and self-benefit rather than purely a conviction that one is doing something wrong apart from its pragmatic effects. The contemporary Roman Catholic position, as opposed to the traditional position taken by the historic Christian Church, is to argue that, although it is wrong to try to prevent conception when fertility is at its height, a natural family planning method, employed in order to "naturally" avoid conception, is morally acceptable.

However, as we will see, not only is this position contradictory to the historic Christian position, but also logically there is little difference in the intent when it comes to the method of avoidance, especially when an argument is merely pragmatically concerned about immediate effects upon the self. Any ethic that has its foundation in temporal concerns of mankind rather than eternal concerns of God must be seen as human-made, and produced for the sake of convenience rather than conviction and devotion. Ethics based on a human-centered conception of the world can have nothing in common with genuine Christianity, which by its very nature is God-centered from start to finish.[5]

Of course, the official Roman Catholic position differs from the more popular arguments made for NFP and instead argues from *lex naturalis*, "the law of nature," which the reader will find purposefully absent from the arguments presented in this book due to its numerous logical flaws. However, the critique of the NFP position will be drawn out further in chapter 7.

---

5. This is not to say that all NFP arguments stem from purely pragmatic standpoints, but that this type of reasoning is often present in popular forms of the position. The more "religiously oriented" type of arguments for NFP will be discussed in chapter 7.

. . . intended by those involved . . .

This book is not really about whether or not one has sexual relations and must somehow be omnisciently aware of whether God will bring forth a child through it or not. It is not about accidents that are made during sex, or any other red herring often created to detract from the main issue. This book is about actions with intentions. It is about what one both believes and does acting upon those beliefs to bring about a desired result that is contrary to the desired result set forth in Scripture.[6]

Therefore, the actions with which we are concerned here are more serious than those of Leviticus 15:3, where the spilling of the semen is unintentional and, in that particular text, is simply being used as an instructive picture illustrating the holy and profane and is not seen as an actual crime against God, as opposed to that which is intentional.

. . . in an effort to prevent the opportunity . . .

What is intended is that the opportunity for God to do His work, through the natural processes of the sexual act, be obstructed (other than God having to miraculously bypass the person's obstruction). Now, of course, this is not to say that the person thinks to him or herself, "I hope to thwart God's use of my natural biological processes so He can't give me a baby." Such an idea that people understand and use their depravity in such an exposed manner is absurd. We mask our rebellion with self-deception so as to maintain a standing in both temples of worship: one which is ours and one which is God's. Rather the point is that the person intends to prevent him or herself from having a child, and pretty much doesn't think about what he or she is doing beyond that point. This we may term "willful ignorance." In this popular notion, the practice of contraception is almost always, if not always, seen as a purely natural act, where one is simply stopping a natural process, working independently of God, from producing an unwanted baby as the result of the sexual act. Therefore, the individual is doing nothing in his or her mind against God, but only against his or her individual benefit or lack thereof, which would be gained or lost by one's use of the natural means.

---

6. As Thomas Aquinas (*Summa Theologiae*, 2.2.64, 7) stated, "Moral acts receive their species from what is intended, not by what is outside the scope of one's intention."

. . . for God to bring forth a covenant child . . .

The goal set by God for the sexual act is not simply that a child be *born* into the world but that a child is to be *raised* as a person who worships and devotes him or herself to God and His people. As we will see, sexual acts that may lead to the conception and birth of a child but may also still lead to a child's lack of participation in the covenant community (such as sexual acts like incest, which may lead to health defects, or pagan sacrifice that could end the child's life early) are placed in the same category as our present subject in the Bible. Hence, the intention is for God to bring about a covenant child through the sexual acts of His covenant people.

. . . through the natural, created means of the biological processes which He has set in place.

By "natural means" I do not mean that the process of conception is purely natural as it is understood "atheistically" as it is within the larger, post-Christian culture's definition; my use of this phrase is dualistic, where God uses the natural means, which He created, to bring about a supernatural work of life. In other words, the natural biological process is not the source of the life of a baby but the means used by God to produce one.

Contrary to this, atheism sees the natural biological process as the means for the individual human to create, and therefore it is subject to the desires of the individual, rather than the means of God's work and hence subject to His desires of when and how it is to be used. This presupposition is central to many of those who argue favorably toward the use of contraception among Christians.

However, as we will see, such a mindset is far more the product of our cultural worldview than one gained from Christianity. Ironically then, the justifications supplied as reasons substantiating the use of birth control by Christians aren't Christian at all.

Part ONE

The Historical Argument

It is the peculiar property of the Church that when she is buffeted she is triumphant, when she is assaulted with argument she proves herself in the right, when she is deserted by her supporters she holds the field.

—HILARY OF POITIERS, *ON THE TRINITY*

1

A Brief History of the Use of Contraception within Secular Culture

SOME HAVE ARGUED THAT the historical Christian Church has always condemned the use of contraception because of cultural influences. In other words, people back then just didn't believe in that sort of thing, and so neither did the Church, but now they do and the Church does as well.

A brief history of contraception within secular culture seems appropriate here, as it will give us an understanding that the Christian idea is almost exclusively counter-cultural. The focus of this chapter will be the discussion of secular cultures that surround both the Bible and the Church, and that would have had the strongest influence on Christianity, since they are immediately relevant to any argument that supposes Christianity developed its idea solely from ancient cultural views.

As we will see, nothing could be further from the truth. Contraception is something practiced not only from the beginning of recorded history but even before it.[1] As A. McLaren states, "The ancients did not view the arrival of every child simply as a blessing";[2] and in order to avoid over-population, as Plato and Aristotle suggested, "the proper thing to do is to limit the size of each family."[3] This sentiment is echoed throughout secular culture from the beginning of its recorded history to the present day.

---

1. Riddle, *Contraception and Abortion*, 66 and 69, states that "the idea is older than the [historical] record;" and "the belief that people could control conception through substance use is, therefore, older than the extant records themselves."

2. McLaren, *History of Contraception*, 17.

3. Aristotle, *Politics* 5.1335b.

3

CONTRACEPTION IN EGYPT

Already in the very beginning of civilization there is large amount of evidence recording the widespread employment of contraceptive practices. In Egypt, the papyri (c. 1850 BC) record that "plugs of honey, gum, acacia, and crocodile dung"[4] were used as contraceptive suppositories.

The Ebers Papyrus (c. 1500 BC) records, along with a list of abortifacients, how an individual can regulate the menses, and thus the rhythm cycle, by the use of potions. This was most likely done not only in an effort to ensure fertility to a couple wanting to conceive but also to ensure contraception for a couple who did not.

The Berlin Medical Papyrus (c. 1300 BC) mentions the use of both a suppository "to prevent her receiving the semen"[5] and an oral contraceptive potion "to loosen [or release] semen."[6]

Later, the Egyptians would also employ a magical element in contraception by placing a black fish mixed with various ingredients in a jar and, after ritually preparing it, rubbing it on the male genitals as both a stimulant and a contraceptive.[7] Amulets with the pictograph of Seth, the crocodile god, were also used both to open the womb and to close it.[8]

CONTRACEPTION IN MESOPOTAMIA

In Mesopotamia, herbs were used as contraceptives. R. D. Biggs comments on some of the evidence and notes that "the Babylonian lexical series ḪAR-ra = ḫubullu has entries . . . [such as] ú.nu.peš₄ = [KI.MIN] la [KI.MIN] 'plant for not getting pregnant.'"[9] He further states that "there is evidence in the Babylonian lexical texts for stones thought to . . . prevent childbirth, that is, to prevent pregnancy."[10]

Biggs notes that these stones, apparently in contrast to the plants, were intended as magical rather than oral contraceptives.[11] The *wāšipu/*

---

4. Riddle, *Contraception and Abortion*, 66; McLaren, *A History of Contraception*, 27.

5. Ibid., 72.

6. Ibid.

7. Ibid., 67–69.

8. Ibid., 67.

9. Biggs, "Conception, Contraception and Abortion," 5.

10. Ibid.

11. Biggs (Ibid.) also notes, however, that the Akkadian word for stone (*abnu*) has a wider semantic range that includes glass and seeds. Cf. the many uses in *CDA* 2 and

āšipu, "professional magician" or "exorcist," was usually the "doctor" in ancient culture, and this is where the woman would go to secure these stones as well as other plants and potions.[12] However, he admits that "we cannot exclude the possibility that such stones or minerals were crushed and taken internally with other materials in an attempt to bring about the desired result, but the texts are silent on this."[13]

He does, however, bring out the use of oral contraceptives when listing a host of plants that may have been used in Mesopotamia, one among many being pomegranate skin.[14]

M. Gruber has proposed that women in Mesopotamia used breast-feeding as a form of contraception. It was often either prolonged so that a woman would not conceive, or it was a duty handed over to a wet nurse in order to prepare the woman for the next pregnancy.[15]

Biggs suggests the possibility of an ancient form of the rhythm method, which would advise a person at what times in the day she was more likely to get pregnant.[16] The individuals could thus avoid those times if they wanted to diminish the possibility of pregnancy through the sexual act.

Although *coitus interruptus* is not mentioned as a practice, it would seem logical that this form was used without the need of instructions in Babylonian medical, omen, or incantation texts. These prescriptions are for when semen is released into the woman and the individual does not wish to conceive. Conversely, *coitus interruptus* does not let semen enter into the woman in the first place. If the individual was not successful in attempting *coitus interruptus,* one of the contraceptive "remedies" could be prescribed to accompany, or even to administer after, the sexual act. Furthermore, we see Onan, a descendant of a family that came from

---

CAD 1:54–61.

12. Ibid., 9; the *mašmaššu,* "the incantation priest," may have also played a role in reproductive options.

13. Ibid., 5.

14. Biggs (Ibid., 9) mentions silphium, which was harvested to extinction apparently because of its effectiveness in contraceptive practices, along with other plants such as asafetida, ferujol, rue, and Queen Anne's lace (i.e., wild carrot), Ibid., 7–8. If these were used in Mesopotamia, many of them would have been imported, as some scholars suggest just that (Ibid., 13).

15. Gruber, "Breast-Feeding Practices," 61–83.

16. Biggs, "Conception, Contraception and Abortion," 10.

Mesopotamia, use it in order to avoid giving a child to his brother, so we know it was used in the ancient Near East.

Anal intercourse was a contraceptive method used by the *ēntu* priestesses, and may have been a common practice among the population at large.[17] Homosexual activity was widespread in ancient Mesopotamia, and although there is nothing explicit about its use as a way of avoiding the impregnation of a woman,[18] it may very well be that the Mesopotamian view foreshadowed the Greek practice of that very thing.

The situation in the ancient world, however, is much like our own. There was not only a variety of contraceptive methods available but a culture-wide push to convince people of their moral responsibility to use them.

In one of the three most widely known and influential epics in the Mesopotamian world (and perhaps in the entire Semitic world) there exists an argument that people ought to use contraceptive measures to limit population.

The epic of *Atra-ḫasīs* is actually one large, ancient argument for the use of contraceptive methods to limit children. The epic relates that there was a time when lower gods did all of the cultivating of the land in order to get food. They rebel and complain to one of the supreme gods, Enlil. Because Enlil just wants some sleep, he satisfies their request for work relief by ordering the creation of mankind.

Everything goes as planned, as humans now do the work of the gods, and Enlil can go back to sleep. There is only one problem. Enlil can't sleep because mankind increases its population and is causing too much noise. He becomes angry and sends a plague to reduce the number of humans on the earth, and perhaps even to wipe them out completely. Fortunately, through appealing to the god Namtara, the plague is thwarted.

However, mankind increases again and disturbs Enlil's sleep. He then decides to send forth a famine in order to reduce, or completely annihilate, the number of people on the earth. Through a consistent appeal to Adad, the storm god, rain falls and the famine washes away.

Mankind then increases a third time and disturbs Enlil's sleep. This time Enlil decides to send the flood to wipe out all of mankind. Mankind is preserved only through the Noah figure, named *Atra-ḫasīs*, who is

17. Ibid.
18. Ibid., 11.

warned of the flood by his god Enki. He escapes in a boat made of wood and pitch, together with his family as well as animals, which are brought along for food, sacrifice, and replenishing the earth. Once the flood is over, one of the gods declares a solution to this destructive cycle: bring forth methods with which the bearing of children will be limited.

The text records, in the seventh column of the third tablet, the plan as follows:

1 In addition let there be a third category among the peoples,
2 (Let there be) among the peoples women who bear and women who do not bear.
3 Let there be among the peoples the *Pāššittu*-demon
4 To snatch the baby from the lap of her who bore it
6 Establish *Ugbabtu*-women, *Entu*-women, and *Igiṣītu*-women,
8 And let them be taboo and so stop childbirth.[19]

The solution offered then is to allow some women to have a limited amount of children while preventing others from having them at all. The *Pāššittu*-demon probably exists as a warning to anyone who either was not supposed to have children or had too many. If this was the case, the demon would come and take the life of the child at birth. This is enough of a scare tactic to thwart someone from stepping over the line.

The three groups of women mentioned are all types of priestesses. It was their job to function as temple "prostitutes" and explore different avenues of the sexual act in order both to relieve men of their urges and to curb the conception of children. We have already discussed that there is evidence of the *ēntu*-priestess using anal intercourse as one method in accomplishing this goal. It is not far off to suggest that they would have also sought other contraceptive means as would the other two groups of priestesses.

The epic of *Atra-ḫasīs* then is really one major piece of national propaganda that seeks to convince the society that limiting children through contraceptive means is not simply morally acceptable but it is the responsible duty of the average person. The epic will play a larger role later as we explore what the Bible has to say about the propaganda of *Atra-ḫasīs* when we discuss the Book of Genesis' argument against it.

---

19. Lambert and Millard, *Atra-ḫasīs*, 103.

CONTRACEPTION IN THE GRECO-ROMAN EMPIRE

There is no one reason why birth control is practiced by any given individual today, and the same is true for ancient cultures as well. In Greco-Roman culture, however, one of the main reasons given by various writers was that the number of children needed to be limited for financial reasons. A family's money would go further both in raising a child and in passing on wealth if there were fewer children among whom it was divided.[20] Later, avoiding children was also seen as a good thing because it hindered the evil physical world from continuing. It was the heretic Marcion, in conjunction with common Platonistic/Gnostic thought, who long ago argued the idea that since the world was evil, it would be wrong to bring a child into it.[21] Many individuals, however, argued that the use of birth control was necessary because children, at least too many of them, were just a burden.[22]

Another motivation was that of controlling the population. It was feared that the resources in any given city (or in any given family) would be too thinly spread if the population grew large enough. Early commentaries on Homer's *Iliad* argued that the Trojan War was brought about by the gods in order to reduce population.[23] This story, as portrayed by the ancient commentators, itself has a resonance of the Babylonian propaganda found within the Atra-ḫasīs myth.[24]

Various methods were used as contraceptives. There are a few references to the practice of *coitus interruptus*,[25] but most references are concerned with controlling what happens if semen enters the womb.

A common method, mentioned later by the Church Fathers, is explained by a Hippocratic text that "when a woman has intercourse, if she is not going to conceive, then it is her practice to expel the sperm."[26] If

---

20. McLaren, *History of Contraception*, 17.

21. Noonan, *Contraception*, 88.

22. See Antiphon the Sophist's warning in McLaren, *History of Contraception*, 17.

23. Allen (ed.), *Homeri Opera*, v. 5, 117.

24. Kilmer, "The Mesopotamian Concept of Overpopulation," 160–77; Kikawada and Quinn, *Before Abraham Was*, 36–38.

25. McLaren, *History of Contraception*, 25.

26. Ibid., 26.

she wishes to conceive a child, then the text tells us that "the sperm is not expelled, but stays in the womb."[27]

Both homosexual and heterosexual anal intercourse were encouraged as a contraceptive method. Often Greek men would choose this method of satisfying sexual urges without the burdensome result of the conception of a child.[28]

Women would extend their periods of breastfeeding as well as use "occlusive pessaries, plugs and potions" as forms of contraception.[29] The most common of these were the potions that women would take to avoid conceiving a child. The Greco-Roman culture labeled them with the Greek word *atokia*, "not bearing," and the Latin word *venenum*, "poison."[30] The latter term would become the most common designation employed by the Church when referring to these potions.

Various texts listed many recipes, which included the use of the leaves or bark of hawthorne, ivy, willow, poplar, and misy.[31] Not all contraceptive potions were oral. Juniper berries or cedar gum were to be rubbed on the male genitals to produce temporary sterility. Alum was applied to the female genitals as a contraceptive measure, as was olive oil mixed with oil of cedar, frankincense, or oil of lead.[32]

Magic was also used to prevent conception, as it was and will be throughout other cultures, in the form of talismans and protective amulets.[33]

The rhythm method was also employed by some women. A few ancient texts record that many women were aware of their cycle and believed that conception mainly took place just before or after menses.[34]

Of course, the overwhelming use of birth control by the masses did not lead to population stability as had been argued, but to decline in population. As time went on, the Greeks started to encourage people to have more children, and by the time of the Roman Empire, the problem had become so bad that royal edicts had to be made telling people to have

27. Ibid.
28. Ibid.
29. Ibid.
30. Ibid., 27.
31. Ibid.
32. Ibid.
33. Ibid., 28.
34. Ibid., 27.

children.[35] There was a strong condemnation of sorcery in this period because it was thought that either spouses or enemies would use it on an individual so that she would not conceive—although one could use it on oneself. It was, in any case, within the Roman period where a more "responsible" view of birth control was encouraged.[36]

CONTRACEPTION AMONG SECULAR CULTURES IN THE MIDDLE AGES

Byzantine writers, such as Aetios of Amida (sixth century), recommended that women wear a magical amulet with either a cat's liver or a lioness's womb in order to avoid getting pregnant.[37] Paul of Aegina (seventh century), recorded the contraceptive methods set forth in such early works as Soranos' *Gynaikeia* (second century).[38] In this work, various methods were suggested, including an herbal potion, vaginal suppositories made of wool, "the application of olive oil, honey, cedar resin, alum, balsam gum, or white lead to prevent sperm from passing into the uterus."[39]

In essence, the practices of the Greco-Roman culture extended into the Middle Ages and beyond, even among lay church members and disingenuous clergy,[40] regardless of the genuine Church's condemnation of it. It is clear then that the culture, in which the Church resided, including

35. Such is the case with the edicts of Caesar Augustus in 18 BC and AD 9 (Jones, *The Later Roman Empire*, 284–602). Cf. also the encouragement by Julius Caesar in the giving of land to men with three or more children (McLaren, *History of Contraception*, 42).

36. For a breakdown of the various views concerning the sexual act in Greco-Roman culture see Noonan, *Contraception*, 27–46. It must be stated that Noonan's attempt to undermine the historic position by claiming an adoption of the Stoic idea fails both in the area of the source/genetic fallacy as well as the fact that the Stoic argument is not even close to being identical to the Christian one. (See Appendix D.)

37. Herrin and Kazhdan, "Contraception," 527.

38. E.g., Soranos' advice that "it is safer to prevent conception than to kill the fetus" seems to be the trajectory of the work. See Luneburg, *Die Gynakologie des Soranus von Ephesus*, 43–44.

39. Ibid.

40. It must be remembered that many of the clergy in the Medieval Period were lawyers and businessmen, who were either placed into those positions due to familial connections or entered those positions *via* simony. Many of them were likely Christians in name only. It is not surprising, therefore, to find practices among them mimicking those of the larger culture as opposed to the Church culture. However, all of the evidence from genuinely orthodox Christian teachers and layman leads us to conclude that none of them condoned the practice.

the religious culture, was pro-contraceptive. The only change in this was when the culture was completely influenced by Christianity. Apart from that influence, the culture of the world tends toward the liberty to use contraception on an "as needed" basis. It is no coincidence that modern evangelicalism, which has unleashed itself from the historic voice of the Church, has descended into the same ideological abyss.[41]

41. For further discussion of contraceptive practice within the Middle Ages and the Modern Period, see McLaren, *History of Contraception*, 119–25 and 142–69; as well as Riddle, *Contraception and Abortion*, 118–57.

2

The Teaching of the Historic Christian Church
Concerning Contraception

A CORRECTIVE IS THEN needed if we are to get evangelicalism back on track. Contrasting the Church's teaching on contraception with the world's philosophy is the first step in understanding that Christians ought to be *in* the world but not *of* the world.

Some may ask, "Why should we care what Christian teachers have always believed and taught throughout history when we have Bibles for ourselves and have no need of their contributions to the discussion?" It has become an unfortunate reality among evangelicals in our day that individual and private interpretations of Christianity have replaced the witness of the Holy Spirit through Christian teachers throughout the history of the Church. This concept is no doubt part and parcel of the culture of relativism that has infested modern evangelicalism. Because of this, Christians are left to their own experiences in determining Christian truth and practice. These experiences direct interpretation, selection, and application of Scripture, and are therefore seen as the means through which the Holy Spirit guides the individual.

According to Scripture, however, the teachers of the Church were given as gifts by the Spirit of Christ to Christians "for the equipping of the saints for the work of service, to the building up of the body of Christ; until we all attain to the unity of the faith, and of the knowledge of the Son of God, to a mature man" (Eph 4:12–13). When the Lord Jesus tells us that the Holy Spirit will lead the apostles into all truth, the promise is given to the Church's teachers, and it is only through them that the whole Church is also led into it. Individuals are not promised such directly, and we see both in history and in our own day that individual, private interpretations usually lead to heresy and disunity, among Christians of all ages, instead of orthodoxy and unity.

The conclusion the Apostle Paul makes after stating that "all Scripture is God-breathed and profitable for teaching, for reproof, for correction, for training in righteousness; so that the man of God may be adequate, equipped for every good work" (2 Tim 3:16–17) isn't that each person should then privately lock him or herself in a room and come out with personal opinions of the text, but instead is that *Timothy*, as an apostolic representative, is to "preach the word; be ready in season and out of season; reprove, rebuke, exhort, with great patience and instruction" (2 Tim 4:2).

In other words, because the Scripture is fully sufficient to mature a Christian, the Scripture ought to be taught and proclaimed by the elders of the Church.[1] The rightful heirs of biblical interpretation are the teachers of the Church, and the rightful heirs of receiving that teaching are the whole Church. Due to both the confusion of this order and the unwillingness of post-Enlightenment churchgoers to submit their religious experiences to the ecclesiastical teachers of the Bible, many have turned Christianity into a religion of practical relativism, where even though a Christian claims that there is absolute truth, it is contingent on his or her own personal interpretation and is therefore subject (i.e. , relative) to the individual's experience.

If, therefore, the individual is to have any standard for interpreting Scripture, the teaching of the historic Church should become a necessary guide when one approaches the Bible. This also means that one's maturity rests on whether or not he or she is taught the Scripture by the Church. It means the Church has the authority to interpret the Scripture as well, since that is not only the necessary foundation for preaching it but also the nature of the gifts given to it. This is why Paul calls the Church "the pillar and support of the truth" (1 Tim 3:15). Of course, many people may object to this, but the truth is that a person will gain preconceived ideas from a culture anyway. It is God's set plan therefore that we receive our presuppositions from His covenant community rather than from the world.

This, of course, does not mean that any interpretation given by a single teacher in the Church is infallible, but if an individual Christian, or even an era of Christians, should contradict the theology or morals handed down by the entire collective of historic orthodox Christian

---

1. Hence, Paul describes the elders as those who work hard at preaching and teaching the Scripture (1 Tim 5:17).

teachers before it, then one should have overwhelming biblical evidence, with great theological support, in order to annul such a teaching, and even then do so with fear and trembling. As we will see, such has not been the case with our present issue, and whenever this has been attempted in history, it has always lead to destructive heresy, not a healthy, genuine orthodoxy. It is more the problem, therefore, with modern evangelicalism, that it denies ultimate infallibility to the Church (that is, that it assumes, in the end, the Church will not be able to deliver the message of God accurately and will eventually fail in trying to do so), and therefore denies it any divine authority given to it by the Holy Spirit to teach theology and ethics correctly to the flock of God.[2] Since it is assumed that the Church is incapable of achieving God's goal for it, the modern evangelical must then forge his or her way through the Bible individually in order to experience truth for the self.[3]

In an effort, however, to reclaim the divine insight given to the teachers of the Church, we will now survey their teachings on this particular subject.

THE EARLY CHURCH

To the Church Fathers, marriage and procreation are eminently desirable human goods. But why do the Fathers consider them so? In a culture given to bountiful concepts of the sexual act, the Church had to ask, both biblically and theologically, What, if any, were the divine boundaries set for the sexual act? Aided with their Bibles and the Holy Spirit, who guides His people into all truth, they set their minds to answer that question with the sole purpose to glorify God regardless of the cost that answer might require of them.

The Primary Purpose of the Sexual Act

They concluded that marriage, although capable of fulfilling other secondary functions, was primarily for the purpose of family. Sex, likewise

2. Note the distinction between infallibility (that which cannot fail) and inerrancy (that which is without any error). The historic Church should be seen as holding the former, not necessarily the latter.

3. For an understanding of what I am saying here, as well as a solid argument toward understanding the Reformational view of the historic Christian doctrine of *sola scriptura*—as opposed to the popular evangelical, Enlightenment-oriented view of *solo scriptura*—see Mathison, *The Shape of Sola Scriptura*.

fulfilling other secondary roles, had its primary purpose as the instrument through which God created family. Hence, if one wished to have sex, he or she should get married and have a family. To have sex inside or outside of marriage for any other reason, to the exclusion of the primary reason, is considered a violation of this familial/sexual boundary, which God set in place. Thus, the basic Patristic argument, that the primary purpose of the sexual act is to be procreative, is rooted, not in Greek philosophy or science as some would suggest, but in Genesis 1 and 2. It is in Scripture that the Fathers found their view of the sexual act despite the contrary cultural views presented to them.

Irenaeus (AD 140–202), who was a disciple of Polycarp, a disciple of the Apostle John, stated that "God made the male and female for the propagation of the human race."[4] Note that the terminology used by Irenaeus ("God made male and female" for "propagation") harks back to Genesis 1, where God made them male and female and then gave them the command to be fruitful and multiply.

Justin Martyr (AD 100–165) refers to all Christians when he says, "If we marry it is only so we may bring up children."[5]

Clement of Alexandria (AD 150–215) tells us that "to have coitus other than to procreate children is to do injury to nature."[6] This argument from nature will continue as one of the foundations to the Church's condemnation of contraception. It should be understood that by "nature" the Fathers are not saying that one ought not interfere with blind forces which occur in the natural world. The Fathers neither see nature as a blind force,[7] nor do they seem to be referring to nature as "that which observably occurs in the world according to its observable function."[8]

4. *Haer.*, 1.28.1; *ANF* 1:353.

5. *1 Apol.* 29; *ANF* 1:172.

6. *Paed.* 2.10.95:3.

7. Jaeger, *Early Christianity and Greek Paideia*, 18, "Christian interpreters . . . ought to remember that this Greek concept of nature is not identical with naturalism in our modern sense." I would further argue that no concept in the ancient world is identical with the modern concept of naturalism, Greek or otherwise (with the possible exception of ancient forms of Atheism). Hence, the argument from nature has nothing to do with the modern idea of something "naturally" occurring apart from God's involvement.

8. Hence, the most common patristic argument does not stem from the Aristotelian idea of *lex naturalis/lex naturae*, where moral law is derived from that which is descriptive in nature (i.e., phenomenalogical data derived from what currently occurs), which is primarily from whence the Stoics draw their arguments. See Striker, *Essays,* 209–80.

Instead, the argument from nature (the Greek word *physis*) stems from the creation of male and female in Genesis 1:27–28 interpreted through Paul's argument in Romans 1:26–27, where he calls productive sexual acts *physikos* "natural" and unproductive sexual acts *para physin*, "contrary to nature." This argument from nature is drawn from that which is set in place at creation and therefore "derived its norms of human and social behavior from the divine norms of the universe."[9] These divine norms, for the New Testament and Patristic authors, however, were communicated at creation, prescriptively through special revelation, and as such tell us what we ought to do; whereas, in Greek thought (specifically Stoic), the norms that stem from human experience of the world are descriptive and can tell us only what nature does, not what it should do. The patristic argument is of the former, and there is no trace of the latter within it.

Epiphanius (AD 315-402), remarking on a strange Gnostic cult, commented:

> They exercise genital acts, yet prevent the conceiving of children. Not for the purpose of producing offspring, but for the purpose of satisfying lust, are they eager for corruption. To such an extent has the devil deceived these wretched people that they betray the work of God by perverting it to their own deceits. Moreover, they are so willing to satisfy their carnal desires as to pollute each other with impure seed, by which offspring is not conceived but by their own will evil desires are satisfied.[10]

He cites Romans 1 and 1 Timothy 2:15, as well as Genesis 38,[11] to condemn these acts.[12] He further concludes that their rejection of children in the sexual act is truly the "worst practice and crime."

Cyprian (AD 200–258) conveys to us that the Fathers do not think of procreation as some sort of regrettable, joyless duty. He states rather that "it is a source of joy and glory to humans to have children like themselves."[13]

The argument from *lex naturalis* was not incorporated into a Christian argument until Aquinas, and even then it was not adopted as one of the many arguments given until the sixteenth century and following. The consistent historical line of reasoning against contraception, however, does not follow this line reasoning as its core argument.

9. Jaeger, *Early Christianity and Greek Paideia*, 18.

10. *Pan.* 26.5.2

11. Ibid., 26.11.11.

12. Ibid., 26.16.2–4.

13. *Zel. liv.* 15; ANF 5:495.

It is this joy that brought Marcus Minucius Felix (AD?–250) to discuss the reason that Christians want to get married: "By choice we are bound by the bond of a single marriage with the desire of procreating."[14]

Lactantius (AD 255-320) argues that God does not participate in the sexual act because "the sexes themselves, and the intercourse between them, were given to mortals by God for this reason, that every race might be preserved by a succession of offspring."[15] He further remarks that "there would be no adulteries, debaucheries, and prostitution of women if everyone knew that whatever is sought beyond the desire of procreation is condemned by God."[16]

Such comments, as Lactantius's above, have led some to believe that the Fathers had believed that pleasure in the sexual act was bad in and of itself. It would, of course, be absurd to picture an individual trying not to enjoy the sexual act. The point, however, that is made by the early teachers is not that *desire* is bad, but that *passion/lust*, which intoxicates one's mind like a drug, is bad and ought to be avoided in exchange for a pleasure and desire that is controlled by God's revealed wisdom. (See Appendix D.)

For instance, the very same Lactantius who said the above also said that "sexual desire is given to us for the procreation of offspring." There we have in one sentence that God has given us sexual desire/pleasure, but that it is for the divine purpose of procreation.

Many who have studied the Fathers are often guilty of the false dichotomies that plague modern arguments when analyzing Scripture. (See Chapter 8.) Those same false distinctions are seen when someone comments that, because the Fathers believed that sex was for the purpose of procreation, they did not approve of a person seeking pleasure in the act.[17] However, as we can plainly see by what they have written, pleasure in the sexual act is a given among the Fathers. The condemnation is made against those who would seek *only* pleasure apart from the hope of children.

Furthermore, one must understand the Patristic concept of "the passions." Passion is often seen as opposed to reason. It is that which controls

14. *Oct.* 31.5; *ANF* 4:192.

15. *Epit.* 6; *ANF* 7:226.

16. *Inst.* 5.8; *ANF* 7:143.

17. Or, conversely, if one finds a particular Father who says there is another aspect to the sexual act, that modern reader will often assert that this particular Father doesn't believe the primary purpose of the sexual act must be procreative.

a person so that he or she no longer thinks rationally. It is seen as the natural intoxicant by which a person is pulled off into the domain of the devil.

In contrast to this, the Fathers pick up on the Pauline idea that mankind is to have a rational control of the mind. We are to stay away from anything that would intoxicate us to the point where we no longer think rationally. By "rational" the Fathers are not saying that all Christians should become some sort of Stoic *Star Trek* character, but rather that all Christians are to cultivate a mind that reasons in Christ and seeks to discover the biblical worship of God in all things. The mind must be under control to do so, and true spirituality in the Fathers is exemplified in the individual who accomplishes such.

The point of all of this is that the Fathers are not against the idea that the sexual act is pleasurable. In fact, they even state that the mind that is intoxicated with passion at the point of coitus is a permissible situation, since sex is important to produce children. But they are against the idea that the sexual act should be hedonistically done, seeking pleasure for pleasure's sake. To do so portrays that there is no divine rationale for the sexual act and the individual who treats it this way is giving him or herself over to the devil through the drunken "passions."

Even this, however, seems to be a minor concern in the Fathers. Instead, the two main issues seem to be that (1) the purpose of the sexual act is to be practiced according to the purpose God made for it (conversely, to do otherwise is to be sexually immoral); and connected to that, (2) either it is done to bring forth life or it is done to bring forth death (hence, the immoral act of unproductive sex is also an act of murder).

Titus of Bostra (AD 361[18]–372), in his polemic *Against the Manichees*, described them as those who "contemptuously vituperate the procreation of children and desire that there be bodily intercourse without procreation."[19]

Cyril of Jerusalem (AD 313-386) stated:

> Let those also be of good cheer who are married and use their marriage properly; who enter marriage lawfully, and not out of uncontrolled lust and freedom [to have sex] without boundaries; who recognize periods of continence so that they may give

---

18. This is the date Titus was ordained as bishop of Bostra, not his birth date.

19. *Against the Manichees*, 2.33.

themselves to prayer . . . who have entered into matrimony for the procreation of children and not for the sake of indulgence.[20]

The argument that the sexual act is for the primary purpose of procreation, and therefore to use it otherwise is to commit acts of sexual immorality, is only the first argument leveled against the practice of contraception by the Fathers. The second is equally serious, however; and thus, we turn our attention to the following discussion.

The Condemnation of Contraception

We see then that at the base of the Patristic argument is the natural order set up in Genesis 1 and 2. Since the purpose of the sexual act is procreation, any sort of contraception is seen as a violation of God's intended purpose. The Fathers then draw out Christian reasons as to why procreation is the good that should be sought through the sexual act.

The first reason is that the act of preventing a child that is about to be conceived is the act of preventing a human from living. Hence, to prevent a human from living is considered a form of murder.

Therefore, Hippolytus (AD 170–235) comments on certain women who both take oral contraceptives and practice vaginal exercises aided with a restrictive strap meant to expel the sperm in order to prevent conception:

> Women who were reputed believers began to resort to drugs for producing sterility. They also began to gird themselves around, so as to expel what was being conceived. For they did not wish to have a child by either a slave or by any paltry fellow—for the sake of their family and excessive wealth. Behold, into how great an impiety the lawless one has proceeded: inculcating adultery and murder at the same time![21]

Note the distinction between the sexual act with a person not married (i.e., adultery) from the act of seeking to prevent a child from existing (i.e., murder).

As murder, the use of contraceptives was rejected as a standard Christian response to those who wished to prevent a child from being conceived. Two of the earliest, and most distinguished, works in the early Church, *The Didache* (late second century) and the *Epistle to Barnabas*

20. *Catecheses*, 4.25; NPNF[2] 7:25.
21. *Haer.* 9.7; ANF 5:131.

(early second century) both condemn its use by referring to oral contraceptives, or *pharmakeia* "medicine/potions," as murder.[22] Those who use it are considered "murderers of offspring, corrupters of the mold of God."[23]

Noonan comments that "it may be argued that 'medicine' here means drugs used as abortifacients or contraceptives and that 'destroyers of the work of God' means those committing abortion or contraception."[24]

The Greek word used for "mold" in these texts is *plasma*, which here refers to the stuff from which a human is made. In the Greek translation of Psalm 103:14 the text states "for He knows our *plasma*; He remembers that we are dust." Here the dust is the base material from which man is made. In the Greek translation of Isaiah 29:16, the *plasma* is the unformed clay/material from which God chooses to make something.

The word is used mainly by the Fathers to refer to the physical creation of human beings.[25] Those who corrupt the *plasma* in the *Didache* and the *Epistle to Barnabas* are taking drugs to avoid the possibility of God forming the *plasma* in conception to create a human being. It is therefore most probable that the drugs refer to contraceptives.

Marcus Minucius Felix contrasts Christian women with pagan women who "by drinking drugs extinguish the beginning of a future man, and before they bring forth, commit parricide."[26]

Chrysostom (AD 344–407), in a sermon c. 390, stated the following:

> Why do you sow where the field is eager to destroy the fruit? Where there are drugs of sterility? Where there is murder before birth? You do not even let a harlot remain only a harlot, but you make her a murderess as well. Do you see that from drunkenness comes fornication, from fornication adultery, from adultery murder? Indeed, it is something worse than murder and I do not know what to call it; for she does not kill what is formed but prevents its formation. What then? Do you condemn the gift of God, and fight with His laws? That which is a curse, do you seek as though it were a blessing? Do you make the anteroom of birth the anteroom of slaughter? Do you teach the woman, who is given to you for the

22. *Barn.* 20; *Did.* 5; Holmes, *The Apostolic Fathers*, 256–57, 324–25.

23. Ibid.

24. Noonan, *Contraception*, 120.

25. Cf. the entries in *PGL* 1089, which overwhelmingly favor this use of the word in these particular contexts.

26. *Oct.* 30.2; translation offered by Noonan, *Contraception*, 121.

procreation of offspring, to perpetrate killing? That she may always be beautiful and loveable to her lovers, and that she may rake in more money, she does not refuse to do this, heaping fire on your head; and even if the crime is hers, you are the cause. Hence, also arise idolatries. To look pretty many of these women use incantations, libations, charms, potions and innumerable other things. Yet after such turpitude, after murder, after idolatry, the matter still seems indifferent to many men—even to many men having wives. In this indifference of the married men there is greater evil filth; for then poisons are prepared, not against the womb of a prostitute, but against your injured wife.[27]

Chrysostom tells the congregation at Antioch that the use of contraception is both a form of murder and of idolatry. The idolatry here seems to be connected either to the man's worship of himself through sex or his worship of the woman's body. It is unclear, if they are to be distinguished at all, to which one Chrysostom is referring. Either way, his claim is that God is not the one being worshipped through this kind of sexual act. The murder, as we have seen, is explained as killing what has yet to be formed. It is the intention to wipe out the human person before the human person is ever made.[28]

Chrysostom again states:

In truth, all men know that they who are under the power of this disease [covetousness] are wearied even of their father's old age; and that which is sweet and universally desirable, the having of children, they esteem grievous and unwelcome. Many at least with this view have even paid money to be childless, and have mutilated nature, not only killing the newborn, but even acting to prevent their beginning to live.[29]

---

27. *Hom. Rom.* 24; *NPNF¹* 11:529.

28. The common misconception that the Fathers uniformly believed in the view that held that the seed of the man was a little human embryo itself is clearly contradicted by the wide variety of beliefs held in the Greco-Roman world, and the further statements by Chrysostom concerning the fact that one is preventing a child from living, rather than killing a child already alive. As he states, "She does not kill what is formed, but prevents its formation," speaking of the fact that in the use of contraception nothing is permitted to be brought together, and hence, to create a human being.

29. *Hom. Matt.* 28:5; *NPNF¹* 10:194.

Noonan also points out that the reason given by Chrysostom condemns the use of contraception, whether it is used outside of marriage or "in marriage."[30]

Jerome, when commenting on the virgins of the church, stated that some of them end up pregnant and hide it with certain kinds of dresses, whereas "others, indeed, will drink sterility and murder a man not yet born." He goes on to talk about still others who take drugs to have abortions.[31] Thus, Jerome's comments are yet another example that there was a distinction made between contraception and abortion.

The act of Onan, called *coitus interruptus*, later referred to as "Onanism," was condemned as a type of birth control (whatever reason he practiced it being irrelevant) by a few of the Fathers. Speaking of Onan, Cyril of Alexandria states that "he broke the law of coitus."[32] He is joined by Epiphanius who also condemns the act of Onan as a perversion.

Augustine (AD 354–430) furthers the argument as follows:

> And why has Paul said: "If he cannot control himself, let him marry?" Surely, to prevent incontinence from constraining him to adultery. If, then, he practices continence, neither let him marry nor beget children. However, if he does not control himself, let him enter into lawful wedlock, so that he may not beget children in disgrace or avoid having offspring by a more degraded form of intercourse. There are some lawfully wedded couples who resort to this last, for intercourse, even with one's lawfully wedded spouse, can take place in an unlawful and shameful manner, whenever the conception of offspring is avoided. Onan, the son of Judah, did this very thing, and the Lord slew him on that account. Therefore, the procreation of children is itself the primary, natural, legitimate purpose of marriage.[33] Whence it follows that those who marry because of their inability to remain continent ought not to so temper their vice that they preclude the good of marriage, which is the procreation of children.[34]

---

30. Noonan, *Contraception*, 128.

31. *Epist.* 22:13; *NPNF*[2] 6:27.

32. *violavit legem procreandi* "he violated the law of procreation"; Cyril, *Critical Comments on Genesis* 6. 194; *PG* 69:310.

33. *Propagatio itaque filiorum, ipsa est prima et naturalis et legitima causa nuptiarum.*

34. *Conj. Adult.* 2.12.

Contraception, of course, includes any sexual act that does not provide the opportunity for God to create a covenant child through the natural means He has set in place. Therefore, in the *Epistle to Barnabas*, oral sex is condemned.[35] Justin further condemns unmentioned sexual acts performed by a husband on his wife, which were "against the law of nature and against what is right."[36]

Clement of Alexandria explains that "due to its divine institution for the propagation of man, the seed is not to be vainly ejaculated, nor is it to be damaged, nor is it to be wasted."[37]

What many would call natural family planning today, although slightly different in methodology than the rhythm method, carries the same intent and was also logically condemned by the Fathers' argument. Augustine comments on the use of the rhythm method against a Manichean sect which employed it as follows:

> Is it not you who used to warn us to ardently look for the period following purification of the menses when a woman is likely to conceive, and during that time refrain from intercourse, so that a soul would not be entangled in the flesh? From this it follows that you do not think marriage is to procreate children, but to satisfy carnal pleasure. Marriage, as the marriage tablets themselves proclaim, unites male and female for the procreation of children . . . he [who practices the rhythm method of the Manichees] ceases to make the woman a wife, and turns her into a prostitute, who when she has been given certain gifts, is joined to a man in order to satisfy his lust.[38]

Noonan comments on the irony of Augustine's statement when he says:

> In the history of the thought of theologians on contraception, it is, no doubt, piquant that the first pronouncement on contraception by the most influential theologian teaching on such matters should be such a vigorous attack on the one method of avoiding procreation accepted by twentieth-century Catholic theologians as morally lawful. History has made doctrine take a topsy-turvy course.[39]

35. 10.8; Holmes, *The Apostolic Fathers*, 300–1.

36. *2 Apol.* 1; *ANF* 1:188.

37. *Paed.* 2:10:91:2.

38. *Man.* 18.65.

39. Noonan, *Contraception*, 152; Of course, Noonan wants to argue semantics in stat-

Ironically, we see then that the current intent of the "natural family planning" trend within the modern Roman Catholic Church, as well as that which is adopted by some modern evangelicals, is not the historic Christian position either.[40]

In Augustine's more direct treatment of the issue in his *Marriage and Concupiscence*, he states:

> It is one thing not to have sex except with the sole purpose of producing children: this has no error. It is another to seek carnal pleasure in having sex, even though it is within the limits of marriage: this has some error. I am supposing then that, although you are not intentionally having sex for the purpose of procreating offspring, you are not for the purpose of lust obstructing their procreation by an evil prayer or an evil deed.[41] Those who do this, although they are called husband and wife, are not; nor do they retain any reality of marriage, but with a respectable name cover a shame. . . . Sometimes this lustful cruelty, or cruel lust, comes to this, that they even procure poisons of sterility, and if these do not work, extinguish and destroy the fetus in some way in the womb, preferring that their offspring die before it lives, or if it was already alive in the womb to kill it before it was born.[42]

In the Fathers, the ultimate goal is not that the self is pleased but that God is. Augustine argues that the sexual appetite is like that of the

---

ing that this is the first condemnation of contraception. His attempt to dismiss the legion of statements made by earlier Fathers, which give credence to Augustine's statements here, is denial by technicality; and as such, this particular statement remains unconvincing.

40. For instance, a major issue for the conversion of Scott Hahn to the RCC was this mistaken idea that the historical position and the modern RCC position are the same. He states, "It bothered me just a little that the Roman Catholic Church was the only denomination, the only Church tradition on earth that upheld this age-old Christian teaching rooted in Scripture, because in 1930 the Anglican Church broke from this tradition and began to allow contraception, and shortly thereafter every single mainline denomination on earth practically caved in to the mounting pressure of the sexual revolution" (Hahn, *The Scott Hahn Conversion Story*). Little does Hahn realize, but the Roman Catholic Church "caved in" to a redefinition of the purpose of the sexual act, which eventually led to its break from the historic position to adopt cultural contraceptive practices, centuries before the Anglican Church made its break from historic orthopraxis.

41. Augustine states that some error is in involved when a person does not have in mind God's procreative purpose with the act, but as long as the opportunity for God to naturally bring about His purposes with the act is not intentionally obstructed, the error is more minor.

42. *Nupt.* 1.15.17.

appetite for food. He states that people may use food either in accordance to the will of God, and therefore as a pleasing means to worship God, or in accordance with selfish desires, as a means to worship the self. He states, "And what is considered unlawful food, which is mere pleasure of the belly and the throat, this unlawful intercourse is also in lust which does not seek a family."[43]

Augustine is careful to say that not all desire is bad, but that a desire that is "unreasonable and unlawful" is evil. What he means by "unreasonable and unlawful" is that it does not seek to accord itself with the mandate of God at creation and therefore does not seek to be an act of worship of God, but of the self. It does not take a reasonable direction to fulfill God's purposes through the sexual act but instead seeks only to satisfy a self-worshiping urge and is devoid of any biblical worship or meaning. For this reason, the pagan religions were filled with people who saw sex this way, since the aim of pagan religion is self satisfaction and having sensual experiences in order to attain higher levels of self. In contrast to this, therefore, the Patristic argument is God-centered; it first asks whether God is pleased, and only secondarily concerns itself with whether the self is pleased.

THE CHURCH IN THE MIDDLE AGES

Caesarius, Bishop of Arles (AD 503–543), one of the most important men in the sixth century, mocked the priests under him who would not stand against all sorts of immorality within the Church:

> Who is he who cannot give the warning that no woman is to take a potion for the purpose of rendering her incapable of conceiving or imprison within herself the nature which God willed to be productive. As often as she could have conceived or given birth, of that many homicides she will be held guilty, and unless she undergoes suitable penance, she will be damned by eternal death in hell.[44]

Martin Braga (AD 579), expanding the decrees of the Council of Ancyra, which originally covered only abortion, declared that a woman who kills her baby once born, aborts it before born, or "takes steps so that she may not conceive, either in adultery or in legitimate marriage" was

---

43. *Bon. conj.* 18; *NPNF¹* 3:407.

44. Caesarius, *Sermons*, 1.12; *CC* 103:9.

to do penance for ten years and could only then take communion at her death.[45]

Likewise, the First Council of Braga anathematized anyone who condemns human marriage and the procreation of the newborn.[46]

Gregory the Great (AD 540–604) stated that the married are to be taught that they are to have sex only to produce children.[47]

The Irish Collection of Canons (AD 780) condemned contraception as murder in its quotations and allusions both to Jerome and Caesarius in Chapters 3 and 4.[48]

The *Decretum* of Burchard (AD 1010) repeats earlier condemnations by Regino of Prüm (AD 906) and Halitgar, the Bishop of Cambrai (AD 830) of women using potions and herbs to prevent conception.[49]

A work by Gratian, *Adulterii malum* (AD 1140), quoted by Peter Lombard (AD 1095–1160), while speaking of marital acts which hinder or prevent procreation, states that "the evil of adultery surpasses fornication, but is surpassed by incest; for it is worse to sleep with one's mother than with another man's wife. But the worst of all of these things is what is done contrary to nature, as when a man wishes to use a part of his wife's body not made for this."[50]

Noonan[51] remarks that the two have almost identical headings to the topic: Gratian, "They are Fornicators, Not Spouses, Who Procure Poisons of Sterility,"[52] and Lombard, "Those Who Indeed Procure Poisons of Sterility are not Spouses but Fornicators."

Thomas Aquinas (AD 1225–1274), in his *Summa Theologica*, condemns sex in marriage when "the natural course of the sexual act is not

---

45. Braga, *Opera*, 142, as translated in Noonan, *Contraception*, 186.

46. Ibid.

47. Gregory the Great, *Pastoral Rule* 3.27. "Husbands and wives are to be admonished to remember that they are joined together for the sake of producing offspring; and, when, giving themselves to immoderate intercourse, they transfer the occasion of procreation to the service of pleasure, to consider that, though they go not outside wedlock yet in wedlock itself they exceed the just dues of wedlock" (*NPNF*[2] 12:57).

48. Noonan, *Contraception*, 193.

49. Burchard, *Decretum* 19.5.

50. Gratian, *Adulterii malum*, 2.32.7.11; translated by Noonan, *Contraception*, 215.

51. Ibid., 214–15.

52. Gratian, *Decretum* 2.32.2.7.

kept, either by using an unfit organ or because of using other monstrous and bestial purposes for the sexual act."[53]

Noonan comments that this statement encompasses "anal intercourse, oral intercourse, coitus interruptus, and departure from the normal position."[54] The last description is most likely an overstatement, but it is clear that Aquinas seeks to condemn the first three.[55]

Even Geoffrey Chaucer (AD 1340–1400), in the *Canterbury Tales,* "The Parsons Tale," includes contraception among the seven deadly sins. Among these are a woman "drinking poisonous herbs through which she may not conceive," placing "certain material things in her secret places to slay the child," and unnatural intercourse, which is defined as when a "man or woman sheds her nature in manner or in place so that a child may not be conceived." Noonan points out that all of these refer to contraception and are distinguished from abortion.[56]

St. Bernardino (fifteenth century) argued that contraceptive methods were "against nature," and stated:

> And I say this to women who are the cause that the children that they have conceived are destroyed; worse, who also are among those who arrange that they cannot conceive; and if they have conceived, they destroy them in the body. You (to who this touches, I speak) are more evil than murderers. . . . O cursed by God, when will you repent? Do you not see that you, like the Sodomite, are cause for the shrinking of the world; between you and him there is no difference.[57]

53. Aquinas, *Summa Theologica* 2–2.154.11. Aquinas held this position because he believed that the primary use of the sexual act was to be procreative (*In Libros Sententiarum* 4.31.2.2).

54. Noonan, *Contraception,* 274.

55. Aquinas states that the altering of the sexual position may be due to a wrongful passion, but it is not sin as the others, since it still has the ability to procreate a child (*In Libros Sententiarum,* 4.31.2, 3). He likely makes this argument from his adoption of the argument from *lex naturalis.*

56. Noonan, *Contraception,* 262.

57. As quoted in Herlihy and Klapische-Zuber, *Tuscans and Their Families,* 251.

THE CHURCH OF THE SIXTEENTH-CENTURY REFORMATION

At this point in history, it is interesting to note that the Reformers do not see themselves as starting a new church, but instead as a continuation of the true Church, which is displayed in the Fathers and has always existed as the orthodox thinking preserved from the corrupt sections of the medieval Church, which later became what they refer to as the Romish institution or "the Papists."

I mention this to say how it is interesting that the Roman Catholic Church's path on this issue forks off into a different direction from the earlier Church's view of the sexual act at this point in history, whereas the position of the Protestant Church from this point on continues the earlier Church's view. It is ironic then that the modern Roman Catholic often argues that his continuity with the early Church on this point is proof of the fact that the Roman Catholic Church is the genuine Church. What is ironic is that this argument would essentially prove that the Protestant Church from the sixteenth to twentieth centuries was the true Church, and those Protestants who currently hold the earlier views of the Church, could easily claim the same.[58] I do not wish, of course, to get into Reformed polemics here, but I did want to point out the irony to those Roman Catholics, who often make the claim that the true Church is identified by its faithfulness to the historic position on this subject.[59]

The Reformers, like the Church Fathers before them, see in Scripture the same arguments against contraception.[60]

Martin Luther (AD 1483–1546) saw Onan's sin as an act of sexual immorality, the equivalent of sodomy:

> Onan must have been a malicious and incorrigible scoundrel. This is the most disgraceful sin. It is far more atrocious than incest and

58. This could be applied to the Eastern Orthodox Church as well, since it was of one mind with the Roman Catholic position, and is even beginning to change its stance on the subject toward an acceptance of contraception. See, for instance, Ware, *The Orthodox Church*, 296, and Harakas, *Contemporary Moral Issues*, 78–82.

59. A couple of the works cited (such as Noonan and McLaren) relate that the counter-Reformational view of the RCC began to adopt other views of the sexual act as well as allowing certain contraceptive practices. Noonan (*Contraception*, 84) postulated that the change of attitudes toward the sexual act in the RCC (specifically in Vatican II) will eventually lead to the acceptance of artificial contraception.

60. See Allan Carlson, "The Emptied Quiver."

adultery. We call it unchastity, yes a sodomitic sin. For Onan goes into her; that is, he lies with her and copulates, and when it comes to the point of insemination, spills the semen, lest the woman conceive. . . . Consequently, he deserved to be killed by God. He commited an evil deed. Therefore, God punished him.[61]

Luther argued from Genesis 1:28 that the command to "be fruitful and multiply" was "a divine *ordinance* which it is not our prerogative to hinder or ignore."[62]

Whereas Luther picks up on the argument for distorting God's purpose for sex—thus arguing that contraception is an act of sexual immorality—John Calvin (AD 1509–1564) continued the argument against contraception as an act of murder.

When commenting on the sin of Onan, he writes:

Furthermore, he not only shortchanged his brother of his right, but also would rather spill his seed on the ground, than to bring forth a son in his brother's lineage. . . . I will try to be as brief as propriety allows in discussing this subject. The purposeful spilling of semen outside of intercourse between man and woman is a monstrous thing. Purposely withdrawing from coitus, so that the seed drops on the ground, is twice as horrific. For this is to extinguish the hope of the human family and to kill before he is born the hoped-for offspring. This wickedness is here condemned by the Spirit in the most severe manner possible . . . as though he had, through a violent and premature birth, tore away the seed of his brother out the womb, and had cruelly and shamefully thrown it on the earth. In this way he tried, as far as he was able, to wipe out a part of the human race. When a woman in some way expels the seed out of the womb, using drugs, then this is rightly seen as an unforgivable crime; and Onan rightfully incurred upon himself the same kind of punishment, polluting the earth with his semen, in order that Tamar might not conceive a future human being as an inhabitant of the earth.[63]

61. Luther, *Luther's Works*, vol. 7, 20–21.

62. As quoted in Carlson, "The Emptied Quiver," paragraph 7.

63. Calvin, *Commentaries on Genesis,* 38:8–10, translated from the Latin, since this section, along with any sentence, dealing with the issue in Calvin's "complete" commentary series has been purposely deleted by the editor, an act which seems to be performed by the publisher within the twentieth century. Cf. the similar omission of the text of Genesis 38 within the *Ancient Christian Commentary* series on Genesis 12–50, where the editor clearly did not wish to include any comments by the Fathers on the subject. As we have seen, of course, Epiphanius, Cyril, Jerome, and Augustine would have made

It is Calvin's conclusion, as it was the Patristic and medieval Christian position, that contraception is a type of murder because it prevents a person from living. In this way, contraception is comparable to abortion as a horrible type of murder, a sin from which Calvin proclaims an individual cannot be forgiven. Calvin's statement that it cannot be forgiven is most likely in reference to an individual who does not repent of the deed. The earlier Church's view has always been that one can be forgiven if he or she repents of the sin.

Calvin's view, of course, also stemmed from Genesis 1:28. He commented that this command was still in effect to this very day by stating, "still that pure and lawful method of increase, which God ordained from the beginning, remains firm; this is the law of nature which common sense declares to be inviolable."[64]

THE MODERN CHURCH
(SEVENTEENTH TO THE TWENTIETH CENTURIES)

The Puritan John Trapp (AD 1601–1669) stated of Onan that "the more sinful was this sin of his in spilling his seed."

John Owen (AD 1616–1683), commenting on the purity of the marriage bed in Hebrews 13:4, stated:

> But that marriage is honorable, which is formed on the ground and warrant of divine institution, is a lawful conjunction of one man and one woman, by their just and full consent, into an indissoluble union, whereby they become one flesh, for the procreation of children, and mutual assistance in all things, divine and human. ... For whereas God hath provided such a way and means for the satisfaction of natural inclination, the procreation of children, and comfort of life in mutual society, as are honorable and as such are approved by himself, so as no way to defile the body or mind, or to leave any trouble on the conscience; who can express the detestable wickedness that is in the forsaking of them, in a contempt of

---

great entries. This deliberate omission, where editors feel the need to silence the voice of the Church's greatest teachers on the subject, or where certain authors downplay or even omit the Church's condemnations of contraception in the past, is a trend among the modern reference works which ought to disturb any thinking reader. Cf. further the odd translation of the word *procreationem*, "procreation" in the Augsburg Confession, as "male and female" in *The Creeds of Christendom*, 3:31. It is not known, however, whether Schaff or the revision of his work is to be assigned the translation here.

64. Calvin, *Commentaries on Genesis*, 98.

the authority and wisdom of God, by men seeking the satisfaction of their lust in ways prohibited of God injurious to others, debasing and defiling to themselves, disturbing the whole order of nature, and drowning themselves in everlasting perdition, which the apostle declares in the next words.[65]

The Augsburg Confession stated that "God created men for procreation."[66]

The Annotations of the Synod of Dort (1618–1637) state that Onan's sin is the equivalent of tearing out the fruit from the mother's womb (i.e., that it is murder).

The Westminster Annotations recorded by John Ley in 1657, in commenting upon Onan's sin, bear witness to the Assembly's view as follows:

> There is a seminal vital virtue, which perishes if the seed be spilled; and by doing this to hinder the begetting of a living child, is the first degree of murder that can be committed, and the next unto it is the marring of conception, when it is made and causing of abortion: now such acts are noted in the Scripture as horrible crimes, because, otherwise many might commit them, and not know the evil of them: it is conceived, that his brother Er before, was his brother an evil thus far, that both of them satisfied their sensuality against the order of nature, and therefore the Lord cut them off both alike with sudden vengeance; which may be for terror to those Popish Onanites who condemn marriage, and live in sodomitical impurity, and to those, who, in marriage, care not for the increase of children (which is the principle of the conjugal estate) but for the satisfying of their concupiscence.[67]

Matthew Poole (1624–1679), in his comments on Genesis 38:9 in his Bible commentary, stated that not only was Onan guilty of some sort of hatred for his brother but of far worse a sin "condemned not only by Scripture, but by even by the light of nature." It is deemed a great sin and "a kind of murder." He tells us that this sin is taught to all men by the Holy Spirit here "whereby we may sufficiently understand how wicked and abominable a practice this is amongst Christians."[68]

---

65. Owen, *Hebrews*, 700, 702.

66. Augsburg Confession, "On the Marriage of Priests," *Sec.* 23; see Schaff, *The Creeds of Christendom*, 3:31 in the Latin text provided.

67. Ley, *Westminster Annotations*.

68. Poole, *commentary on Genesis* 38:9.

Cotton Mather (1663–1728) expounding on the act of *coitus interruptus,* stated that "the crime against which I warn you, is that self-pollution, which from the name of the only person who stands forever stigmatized for it in our Holy Bible, bears the name of Onanism."[69]

Matthew Henry (1662–1714), in his well-known commentary, states that the sins (such as Onan's spilling of his seed) "dishonor the body and defile it," and are thus "very displeasing to God."[70] Henry believed Onan's sin to be dishonoring to the body precisely because he viewed God's making of the male and female at creation to be for the purpose of procreation.[71]

John Wesley (1703–1791) had a much harsher criticism of the sin as the following proves:

> Onan, though he consented to marry the widow, yet to the great abuse of his own body, of the wife he had married and the memory of his brother that was gone, he refused to raise up seed unto his brother. Those sins that dishonor the body are very displeasing to God, and the evidence of vile affections. Observe, the thing which he did displeased the Lord—and it is to be feared, thousands, especially of single persons, by this very thing, still displease the Lord, and destroy their own souls.[72]

Wesley believed that any waste of the semen in an unproductive sexual act, whether that should be in the form of masturbation or *coitus interruptus,* as in the case of Onan, destroyed the souls of the individuals who practice it.

Keil and Delitszch comment in their monumental commentary that Onan's act was not merely a covetousness for his brother's inheritance, nor merely a lack of concern for his brother, but also that it was "a sin against the divine institution of marriage and its object, and was therefore punished by Jehovah with sudden death."[73]

Herbert C. Leupold, commenting on Genesis 1:28, writes: "After v. 26 has now given the summary account of the creation of one pair, 'male and female,' v. 27 proceeds to have the divine command laid upon this

69. Mather, *The Pure Nazarite.*

70. Henry, comments on Genesis 38:1–11.

71. See his comments on Genesis 1:26–28.

72. Wesley, *Notes on the First Book of Moses,* comment on 38:7.

73. Keil and Delitszch, *Commentary on the Old Testament,* Genesis 38:8–10.

pair: 'Be fruitful and multiply and fill the earth.' The primary purpose of marriage is here indicated."[74]

A. W. Tozer (1897–1963) bemoaned the fact that Christians no longer sought God's desire and purpose when they used contraception.[75]

John R. Rice (1946) commented:

> The use of contraceptive devices to prevent the conception and birth of children is wrong because it goes against the clear tenor of Bible teaching. . . . The Bible teaches that to have large families is a positive good, a blessing from God. . . . If it is a virtue to have large families, then it is a lack of virtue to limit the family to less than what it would be if God had His way and gave the children that He wants to give to a home. Since married couples are commanded to "multiply and replenish the earth" (Gen 1:28, 9:1), then not to multiply is a sin. . . . It seems also that we may properly infer from the general tenor of the Scripture that to want less children than God would give without human rebellion and contraceptive devices is likewise a sin.[76]

The beloved Christian author and apologist, C. S. Lewis (AD 1898–1963) stated that "the biological purpose of sex is children."[77] In *The Abolition of Man,* he states:

> It is, of course, a commonplace to complain that men have hitherto used badly, and against their fellows, the powers that science here given them. But that is not the point I am trying to make. I am not speaking of particular corruptions and abuses which an increase of moral virtue would cure: I am considering what the thing called 'Man's power over Nature' must always and essentially be. . . . All long-term exercises of power, especially in breeding, must mean the power of earlier generations over later ones.[78]

He furthers his argument by stating:

> As regards contraceptives, there is a paradoxical, negative sense in which all possible future generations are the patients or subjects of a power wielded by those already alive. By contraception simply, they are denied existence; by contraception used as a means of se-

74. Leupold, *Exposition of Genesis*, 96.

75. Tozer, *"The Waning Authority of Christ in the Churches."*

76. Rice, *The Home: Courtship, Marriage and Children.*

77. Lewis, *Mere Christianity,* 89.

78. Lewis, *The Abolition of Man,* 69.

lective breeding, they are, without their concurring voice, made to
be what one generation, for its own reasons, may choose to prefer.
From this point of view, what we call Man's power over Nature
turns out to be a power exercised by some men over other men
with Nature as its instrument. [79]

By these statements, Lewis seeks to charge that the use of birth control is part of humanity's presumptuous ascent in exalting and worshipping himself as God (i.e. , idolatry). An individual who practices such
is taking a position that belongs only to God and seeking control over
whether a future person is allowed to come into existence.

In Lewis, then, we see that the purpose of sex is procreation, and
to use birth control in order to deny the fulfillment of that purpose is to
usurp the authority of God over future people—hence, an idolatry that
can only be described as the type of idolatry practiced by the Anti-Christ
in Scripture: the divine exaltation of the self.

For Lewis, the ultimate goal of using contraception is that the self
has lordship over its own life and the lives of others. In other words, it is a
part of man's sinful desire to seek to be God over himself and over others.
Lewis was able to see this more clearly because of his historical situation
in which so many men (the mafia, the Nazis, etc.) sought power over
others. He saw that this was directly connected to the modern pursuit of
becoming a god through intellect and technology and, more specifically,
through the use of contraception, which he saw as the final step of man's
blasphemy to take over God's position and control even the existence of
future people. Unfortunately, due to our culture's tendency to use the extreme examples (i.e. , limiting labels for such lusts of power to groups like
Nazis, but not applying the same labels to ourselves) as instruments to
justify what are perceived to be milder forms of this deification of the self
as normative, we have failed to learn the lesson Lewis attempted to teach
us, and history continues to repeat itself.

A TASTE OF PERSPECTIVE

Finally, I would like to just list some of the more well known teachers of
the Church, who are representative of the entire Church in their opposition to contraception, so that the reader can gain a perspective on what
I mean when I say the "collective" interpretive voice of the Holy Spirit

79. Ibid., 68–69.

through the Church. This list is by no means exhaustive, but rather representative of the entire Christian Church from the second to the twentieth centuries.

Henry Ainsworth
Henry Alford
Jacob Alting
Thomas Aquinas
The Augsburg Confession
Augustine
Author of the *Epistle of Barnabas*
Christian Gotlob Barth
Richard Baxter
Johann Albrecht Bengel
Samuel Thomas Bloomfield
William Bradford
Martin Braga
Keith Leroy Brooks
John Brown
Johannes Brunneman
Heinrich Bullinger
Martin Bucer
Abraham Calovius
John Calvin
Robert S. Candlish
Joseph Caryl
Geoffrey Chaucer
Adam Clarke
Anthony Comstock
John Chrysostom
Clement of Alexandria
Cyprian
Cyril of Alexandria
Robert Dabney
Conrad Dannhauer
Author of the *Didache*
Daniel Defoe
Franz Delitszch
William Dodd

Philip Doddridge
The Synod of Dort
Alfred Edersheim
Edward Elton
David Engelsma
Epiphanius
Simon Episcopius
Joseph S. Exell
Marcus Minucius Felix
John H. C. Fritz
Ludwig E. Fuerbringer
Thomas Gataker
Annotations of the *Geneva Bible*
Christian Gerber
Johann Gerhard
John Gill
Charles Gore
William Gouge
William Greenhill
Joseph Hall
Robert Hall
Matthew Henry
Hippolytus
George Hughes
Irenaeus
Melancthon W. Jacobus
William Jenkyn
Jerome
Franciscus Junius
Justin Martyr
Johann Karl Friedrich Keil
Richard Kidder
John Knox
Paul E. Kretzmann
Lactantius
Theodore F. K. Laetsch
Johann Peter Lange
Thomas H. Leale

Edward Leigh
Herbert Carl Leupold
C. S. Lewis
Martin Luther
Walter Arthur Maier
Thomas Manton
Cotton Mather
John Mayer
Jean Mercier
James G. Murphy
Wolfgang Musculus
Martin Justus Naumann
Teunis Oldenburger
Johannes Olearius
Lukas Osiander
John Owen
David Paraeus
Simon Patrick
Arthur W. Pink
Edward Pocock
Matthew Poole
Charles Haddon Spurgeon
Franklin P. Ramsay
J. Heinrich Richter
Andre Rivet
John B. Robbins
Richard Rogers
The Saxonian Confession
Sebastian Schmidt
Friedrich W. J. Schroder
Thomas Scott
Titus
John Skinner
Richard Stock
Francis Taylor
Jeremy Taylor
W. H. Griffith Thomas
John Trapp

Johann Christian Friedrich Tuch
Zacharius Ursinus
James Ussher
C. F. Vent
J. F. Walvoord
Richard Watson
John Weemes
John Wesley
The Westminster Divines
William Whittingham
Christopher Wordsworth
Adolph Wuttke

3

How We Got Here

IF THE CHRISTIAN STANCE on the subject was so strong throughout Church history, as we have seen, how did modern Christians come to practice the very thing condemned so vehemently by those Christians of the past? What identifiable changes took place that brought about such a turnabout of praxis?

Three main transitions in thought occurred that led to the modern assumption that the use of contraception is morally acceptable. The first was that the two views of hedonism (i.e., pleasure for pleasure's sake) and romanticism (i.e., spirituality as mystical emotion) became a part of how Westerners gauge their moral actions in the world. The relationship between a man and a woman was painted solely in these terms, and family was seen as a result of the sexual union but not the primary purpose of it. A less-than-critical church then adopted these viewpoints when it came to the relationship of men and women within the church. The redefinition of the primary purpose of sex, then, directly opposed the historic Christian view that the sexual act is primarily for the purpose of procreation.

Secondly, the worldview of naturalism became a part of how Westerners see the world. God was involved in the world only to sustain it and (if a person was more religious) to perform occasional miracles, which were seen as abnormal behavior for God. Along these lines, a false dichotomy was drawn between what is natural and what is supernatural, with supernatural elements discernible only through an individual's existential experience.[1] Since supernatural involvement cannot be verified,

1. The physical world was divorced from, and put in contrast to, the metaphysical world. Hence, rather than seeing the physical world as a means through which God worked in the metaphysical realm, people started to contrast the two and believe that if one found a physical cause for such and such an event, then a metaphysical cause was automatically excluded from the explanation. For example, one often hears the statement

one had to function from what was naturally known, and any religious convictions, which cannot be physically verified, were then seen as relative to the person.

These ideas flooded into our culture's view of sex through the vehicle of popular feminism, which used these presuppositions to cut a path for the acceptance of birth control, not only in the form of contraception but eventually in the form of abortion as well.[2]

IDENTIFYING THE GLASSES THROUGH WHICH WE SEE

A further defining of terms may help the reader see the distinctions between the views held historically by Christians *versus* the views held by modern evangelicals.

Hedonism

Hedonism is a mind-set that seeks to have pleasure for pleasure's sake. In other words, the only purpose in pleasure is that one has pleasure. The purpose of the hedonist, then, is solely to stimulate and worship the self. At the foundation of hedonism is really an atheism, which assumes "since there is no God to whom I owe worship, I will use all things to please myself."

One need only take a survey of why someone goes to the movies, why he or she dates a certain individual, why he or she goes dancing, or dresses up, or goes shopping, or watches football, etc. The most assured reply by everyone in our society will be, "Because I enjoy it; it makes me

---

that people in the Middle Ages believed the plague to be caused by the supernatural hand of God, but we now know that it was caused by the natural feces of rodents. This *either/ or* fallacy pervades our modern thinking.

2. Popular feminism's argument centered on the woman being equal to the man even though it essentially argued that in order to gain equality the woman had to become like the man. This "equality through sameness" was radically opposed to historic Christianity's complementarian view, which taught equality through a heavenly status before God in Christ, expressed differently on earth through gender, thus retaining both equality and gender uniqueness. Hence, in the Feminist view, the woman had to be capable of treating sex the way a man was able to do so (i.e., engaging in it without the repercussions of pregnancy). This disguised misogyny, where the woman must minimize or even reject her biological womanhood (either generally or in specific instances), has been the primary instrument used to introduce the many sexual distortions and types of gender confusion within our culture today. It, furthermore, perpetuates the ancient Gnostic view that the woman must become like the man in order to be of equal value to him. (See for instance, *Gos. Thom.* 1:114.)

happy." Although we may not like the term hedonist applied to us, ultimately, it is not only at our core belief system in the West, but is an essential force in our fallen nature as human beings.

Of course, there is nothing wrong with enjoying something, and despite the caricatures of the historical Church, made by those who seek to undermine its credibility, no one ever said it was wrong. What Christians have always condemned is the idea that has now taken over the modern Church itself: that one should partake in something *only*, or even *primarily*, because he or she enjoys it. The primary purpose for partaking in anything should be to seek God's purposes through it, and the pleasure of the thing should be seen as a subsequent result, not the primary reason for doing it.

Most advocates of contraception don't realize that when they argue that sex can be used for the purpose of pleasure for pleasure's sake, apart from any procreative purpose God may have for it, they are adopting an atheistic point of view. It is atheistic primarily because it ignores the existence of God and His purpose for a particular action and aims the goal of that act solely toward the pleasing of the self. Similarly, to say that God is pleased because we are pleased and that is sufficient enough to perform a self-loving act ignores that God has an *eternal* purpose for all things; and to assume that His purpose is simply the temporal satisfaction of a fleeting urge is to turn God Himself into a hedonist.

Romanticism

Romanticism is really the way Westerners view spirituality in general. For those not satisfied with the atheistic mindset of hedonism, romanticism offers the individual a more meaningful encounter with life. Since Romanticism is such a broad category and can encompass a much larger scope than that which we will discuss here, I will limit our definition to the area of relationships.

Romanticism in the area of relationship is seen as a spiritual connection with another individual. The idea is that one is not merely connecting to another person on a surface level but in a psychologically deeper, mystically in-depth way. The connection need not be explained, since it is a mystical experience, where one is bonded to another existentially (i.e., an emotional, rather than logical, connection).

The adoption in how we view relationships is a direct result of the natural/supernatural divide created from the Enlightenment, which is really a resurgence of a type of Gnosticism that divides the spiritual world from the physical world. What is physical is known through the mind, but what is spiritual can be known only through emotion. It is no coincidence that many people attempt to pit their feelings as an authority against the divine revelation of the Scripture whenever they may conflict.

For instance, where a Christian of the Reformation once believed that one must be connected to God by being of the same mind with Him (hence, believing revealed truth creates a relational connection with God), one now believes that intimacy with God occurs through a mystical bond, often expressed through emotion. If a person is emotionally connected to another individual, then this is often seen as a *spiritual* event (and thus it is a deeper experience than one gained through mere hedonistic connections).

Likewise, if a person accomplishes this romantic connection through the sexual act, then the sexual act has reached a divine/spiritual purpose. Procreation need not be a part of the act, since a spiritual purpose has been thought to have been supplied.[3] Romanticism, then, which also seeks to create a deeper experience for the individual(s) involved in the sexual act, also stems from an atheistic self-worship which assumes the absence of another God beyond the self worthy to have its desires (spiritual or otherwise) fulfilled. This self-worship, of course, is shared with the other person. Unfortunately, however, God is once again left with having to be pleased with the satisfaction (physical or emotional) of the humans involved in the sexual act apart from any fruitfulness offered to Him through it.

---

3. This is made evident in reinterpretations of Genesis 2:18–24, where the man is said to be lonely and then is spiritually fulfilled in the two flesh union. Sex itself is then viewed as a fulfillment of intimacy. Of course, it escapes the notice of these interpreters that the two flesh union is of the "flesh," not spirit, and is broken at the event of one partner's death (1 Cor 7:39). If there was a spiritual union, no such union could be broken; nor would it just be referred to as the union of the flesh. Hence, the union is physical, not spiritual.

Naturalism

Naturalism,[4] as we will define it here, is the idea that whatever is *in* nature is *by* nature, whether a deity stands by to sustain its abilities or not. Phillip Johnson sums up this worldview as follows:

> This philosophy assumes that in the beginning were the fundamental particles that compose matter, energy and the impersonal laws of nature and adds nothing to them. To put it negatively, there was no personal God who created the cosmos and governs it as an act of free will. If God exists at all, he acts only through inviolable laws of nature and adds nothing to them. In consequence, all the creating had to be done by the laws and the particles, which is to say by some combination of random chance and lawlike regularity.[5]

This view came part and parcel with the Enlightenment in that it was argued that one could know only what he or she could verify through the senses (i.e., empiricism), and therefore, to say anything beyond what can be known empirically is to make an individual religious claim. This religious claim comes through an individual's personal existential experience, and therefore, cannot be binding over anyone else unless universally experienced by everyone. Hence, moral relativism is created by philosophic naturalism, which assumes atheism.

This dichotomy between what is universally verifiable (and therefore the rule) and what is relatively true for the individual (and therefore a personal opinion) became a staple belief of modern society and the evangelical Church as we know it today.

Relativism

Relativism, the idea that since truth must be experienced through subjective means it cannot be known with certainty, is a result of philosophic naturalism. If God does not aid people in knowing the objective truth, which only He can know with certainty, then mankind is left to its own opinions. These opinions are largely based on culture and are, therefore, incapable of providing boundaries for the beliefs and actions of others. One can only subjectively believe and do what seems right to oneself.

---

4. To be more specific, the type of naturalism with which we are concerned here is ontological naturalism, otherwise known as philosophic materialism or physicalism.

5. Johnson, *Wedge of Truth*, 13.

As mentioned before, however, having the Scripture does not necessarily provide a bulwark against relativism, since if every individual is left to personal interpretation, selection, and application of what he or she thinks is important within Scripture, then a religious form of relativism results.

Unfortunately, this has resulted in the assumption of relativism—the subject of much scrutiny among modern evangelicals when condemning the larger culture's immersion in it—being adopted almost without opposition into the thinking of the modern Church when it comes to the issue of the sexual act *within* marriage.

A Very Brief Analysis

Let us now take note of the presumption of the above views found within arguments that favor the use of birth control among Christians. First, we need to keep in mind the application of the above ideas to the conception event.

1. *Naturalism* supposes the conception of a child to be a mere God-given ability instead of a supernatural event.

2. *Hedonism* is the pursuit of pleasure of the self for pleasure's sake.[6]

3. *Romanticism* is based on non-Christian assumptions of spirituality and seeks fulfillment of the sexual act through feeling rather than through the purpose revealed in the special revelation of Scripture.

4. *Relativism* bases itself on naturalism and leaves what one does in the sexual act to the whims of the individual's experience.

With these definitions in mind, the reader should take a look at some popular religious arguments in favor of the use of contraception, and see if he or she can identify any of the above presuppositions within these arguments.

A. We must be good stewards of the abilities God has given us.

B. God made sex for uses other than procreation. Pleasure and intimacy can be the sole purpose for the sexual act as well.

C. Individual Christians need to decide when and if having children is right for them. They must also decide how many children they are going to have.

---

6. I would classify pleasure for the sake of the other person as a form of paganism, where self is sacrificed or has joy in the pleasure of an object or person of worship other than the self (hedonism proper) and other than the one true God.

D. Sex is a beautiful thing between a man and a woman, which bonds them together spiritually and makes them whole. It need not have a procreative aspect to it, since it is a spiritual event between man and wife.

E. We're going to have sex, and if God wants to give us children, then He can miraculously override our decision to use birth control.

Naturalism	Relativism	Hedonism	Romanticism
A, C, E	A, B, C, D, E	B, E	B, D, E

After modern evangelicals adopted naturalism, the child was no longer seen as a creation of God brought about by the divine knitting of the material of the human parents into a new being, but became instead like a chemistry set given to children by their parents, a sole product of a natural biological process, where individuals could simply choose to put together a child through the sexual act as they saw fit.

After adopting hedonism and romanticism, both products of an adoption of the secular humanism that stems from philosophic naturalism, the sexual act itself was redefined so that it was primarily for the pleasure of one or more of the individuals involved. In other words, the moral success of the sexual act was gauged by how well it pleased the humans involved. God was nowhere in sight. If a single individual could be pleased through the satisfaction of urges (*per* hedonism), a more lofty goal was the pursuit of the emotional satisfaction a couple gained as they grew closer in intimacy through the sexual act (*per* romanticism). Either way, the new use of sex practiced *by* Christians was primarily *for* Christians, and the sexual act had as only much generic intent to please God as someone enjoying an ice-cream cone.

Whereas, at one time, the Christian motto may have been "Let us participate in the sexual act to worship God through His divine purpose of our being fruitful and multiplying His covenant children," a sentiment reflecting Christ's lordship over these individuals, the new motto is "Let us have sex and hope that God is just happy with what we do because we're happy with what we do," reflecting the man-centered service of the self.

With the further adoption of relativism, the assignment of purpose to the sexual act was up to the individual who used it. The individual evangelical closed the bedroom doors to the voice of God through the expositional preaching of the historic Christian Church and instead began to find it an easier pursuit to judge the lost world on sexual matters rather than seeking to take the log out of his or her own eye.[7]

THE LAMBETH CONFERENCE

The Lambeth Conference was the central conference for the Anglican Church in deciding which direction to take on important moral issues of the day. The conference was the first major church body to rule that contraception was morally acceptable in certain circumstances. This ruling came in 1930, but the conference had held quite a different view just a few years before.

In 1908 the conference held a meeting and advocated a similar view to that of the current Roman Catholic Church.[8] When speaking of the subject of birth control, the conference concluded:

> The Conference, while declining to lay down rules which will meet the needs of every abnormal case, regards with grave concern the spread in modern society of theories and practices hostile to the family. We utter an emphatic warning against the use of unnatural means for the avoidance of conception, together with the grave dangers—physical, moral and religious—thereby incurred, and against the evils with which the extension of such use threatens the race. In opposition to the teaching which, under the name of science and religion, encourages married people in the deliberate cultivation of sexual union as an end in itself, we steadfastly uphold what must always be regarded as the governing considerations of Christian marriage. One is the primary purpose for which marriage exists, namely the continuation of the race through the gift

---

7. There have been attempts by some evangelicals to show how these views of the sexual act are contradictory to the Christian view. Cf. for instance, Daniel R. Heimbach (*True Sexual Morality: Recovering Biblical Standards for a Culture in Crisis* [Wheaton: Crossway, 2004] 253–310), who breaks up non-Christian/pagan views of sex in our culture into four categories: Romantic Sexual Morality: Sex as Affection; Playboy Sexual Morality: Sex as Pleasure; Therapeutic Sexual Morality: Sex as Wholeness; and Pagan Sexual Morality: Sex as Spiritual Life. I, of course, have combined the first with the latter two under the general view of Romanticism and the second under that of Hedonism. The book is a helpful analysis of why these views are not Biblical. The problem, however, with Heimbach's assessment is that it ends up proving what it seeks to disprove by not setting the procreative aspect of the sexual act as primary.

8. Resolution 41, "The Conference regards with alarm the growing practice of the artificial restriction of the family, and earnestly calls upon all Christian people to discountenance the use of all artificial means of restriction as demoralising to character and hostile to national welfare."

and heritage of children; the other is the paramount importance in married life of deliberate and thoughtful self-control.[9]

Notice that the view of sex, even at this time, is not that of the earlier Church, but instead a transitional position between the earlier view and the view it will later come to adopt. The conference condemns the use of artificial birth control and the overuse of any type of birth control method. They stated that it holds "grave dangers—physical, moral and religious;" it "threatens the race;" it is "in opposition to the teaching" (i.e., to the Church's official doctrine); it fails to recognize the primary purpose for marriage in procreation; and it lacks self-control. This decision was not simply a convention constructed as a preference for the Anglican Church alone. The bishops clearly meant it to be binding upon all Christians when they stated: "We desire solemnly to commend what we have said to Christian people and to all who will hear."

The conference further places the sin of contraception within the context of other sexually immoral, but not necessarily biblically explicit, practices. In this condemnation, the conference urges the removal of "such incentives to vice as indecent literature, suggestive plays and films, the open or secret sale of contraceptives, and the continued existence of brothels."[10]

However, by the time of the Conference's meeting in 1930, the view of sex, marriage, and therefore birth control, had taken the full turn.

> The Conference emphasizes the truth that sexual instinct is a holy thing implanted by God in human nature. It acknowledges that intercourse between husband and wife as the consummation of marriage has a value of its own within that sacrament, and that thereby married love is enhanced and its character strengthened. Further, seeing that the primary purpose for which marriage exists is the procreation of children, it believes that this purpose as well as the paramount importance in married life of deliberate and thoughtful self-control should be the governing considerations in that intercourse.[11]

The Conference now claimed that the sexual act did not need to be procreative. Instead, it stated that "intercourse between husband and wife

9. Resolution 68.

10. Resolution 70.

11. Resolution 13.

as the consummation of marriage has a value of its own." What value does it have? The Conference answered that it enhances love by strengthening its character. In this vague and seemingly contradictory notion, the Conference began to argue, in the terms of the day, that the sexual act could be performed for the sake of intimacy absent of its procreative purpose.[12] The conference, of course, did not annul its previous statements on the primary purpose of marriage, but instead, it redefined the sexual act, which it originally saw as inherent within the statement, as the sexual experience within marriage in general. In other words, somewhere within marriage, the individuals ought to try to have children, but every sexual act need not comply with the procreative ideal.

There is no doubt that this definition of the purpose of the sexual act still plagues the modern Church and has contributed to the church's indistinguishable character from secular culture. In essence, when one argues for atheistic purposes of the sexual act, one also receives the atheistic practices and consequences that come with it.

Nonetheless, an argument from pragmatics will not be made here. Instead, it is simply important to see that the cause, which led the way for modern evangelicals to assume that the use of birth control is morally acceptable, was the redefinition of the purpose of the sexual act from the Christian theocentric concept (i.e., centered on God's purposes) to the romantic anthropocentric concept (centered on man's purposes) of our atheistic and naturalistic culture.

Due to this redefinition, then, the Conference concluded what was inevitable:

> Where there is clearly felt moral obligation to limit or avoid parenthood, the method must be decided on Christian principles. The primary and obvious method is complete abstinence from inter-

12. cf. conversation between Anne Kennedy, secretary of the American Birth Control League (what would become Planned Parenthood) in 1926, and Patrick Ward, where Kennedy asserted that, aside from the propagation of children, the sexual act has an intrinsic spiritual and uplifting value which God intended for it. Ward responded by saying, "the so called spiritual value she was putting on the sexual act was a purely emotional and sensual one. The spirituality of the act lay *solely* in the knowledge and in the disposition at the moment of conception that a human being was brought into existence endowed with a soul in God's image and likeness, and which it was God's intention should one day return to Him to enjoy eternal bliss" (John A. Ryan, "Family Limitation," *Ecclesiastical Review* 54.6 [June 1926], 684-85, as related in Leslie Woodcock Tentler, *Catholics and Contraception: An American History* (Ithaca: Cornell University Press, 2004), 46.

course (as far as may be necessary) in a life of discipline and self-control lived in the power of the Holy Spirit. Nevertheless in those cases where there is such a clearly felt moral obligation to limit or avoid parenthood, and where there is a morally sound reason for avoiding complete abstinence, the Conference agrees that other methods may be used, provided that this is done in the light of the same Christian principles. The Conference records its strong condemnation of the use of any methods of conception control from motives of selfishness, luxury, or mere convenience.[13]

Here in the Lambeth decision we see the vestiges of the historical position with a small exception based not on the historical understanding but on modern, redefined definitions for the purpose of the sexual act. It would seem then that the conference sought to retain historical Christian language and boundaries without retaining the historical Christian understanding of that language and those boundaries.

But what is really interesting is that this turn was taken within ten years of the conference's decrying of any use of contraception whatsoever. The adoption of a secular view of sex, which was certainly more conservative and more Christian sounding than the views adopted by secular culture in the "anything goes" Roaring '20s, was all that was needed to bring down the wall that had been protected so vigorously by the community of God from the penning of Genesis to the early twentieth century.[14]

The adoption of the idea that the use of birth control could be permissible in some circumstances was, of course, the only logical conclusion once the presuppositional shift was made. In fact, due to this shift, the use of birth control was seen not only as acceptable but as a moral obligation in some circumstances. Three of the four presuppositions (naturalism, romanticism, hedonism, and relativism) about the sexual act can be seen within the decision. The three presuppositions about the sexual act it adopted were as follows:

1. Naturalism, where the conception process was purely a human event and thus could be controlled by the human without any fear of rebelling against an act of God;

13. Resolution 15. There were some who voted against the decision, but in the end, the vote came down to 193 for and 67 against.

14. See Tentler, *Catholics and Contraception,* 45–47.

2. Romanticism, where the sexual act was given another primary purpose (strengthening love through an abstract intimacy), which could replace the procreative as perceived need dictated;

3. Relativism, where the individual is left with the decision, as he or she sees fit, according to the individual's perception of Christian principles, when and for what purposes the procreative goal of the sexual act can be thwarted.

Once these ideas were adopted, any suggestion that the use of birth control was morally unacceptable was seen as absurd. Hence, as other denominations adopted these presuppositions, which were those adopted in the Lambeth decision, they inevitably fell to the same conclusion that those presuppositions dictated. However, take these three presuppositions, along with that of hedonism, away from the argument and the contrary (i.e., the use of birth control by Christians) will be seen as absurd. Let us now, therefore, turn and explore the contrary.

PART TWO

The Biblical Argument

And they were bringing children to Him so that He might hold them; but the disciples rebuked them. But when Jesus saw this, He was indignant and said to them, 'Permit the children to come to Me; do not hinder them; for the kingdom of God belongs to such as these.'

—MARK 10:13–14

4

The Hebrew Bible

THERE IS A COMMON assumption that the Bible has nothing to say concerning the issue of contraception. It will be the purpose of this section to show that this assumption is a false one. We'll begin where any argument concerning sexual ethics should: at the beginning.

THE ARGUMENT OF GENESIS

Although most people read the book of Genesis on the surface and never see past the creation–evolution controversies, at the underpinnings of the theology of Genesis is a polemical message that argues against the idea of using the sexual act in a non-procreative way. Scholars have argued for some time now that Genesis 1–11 is meant to counter the ancient Near Eastern ideology of population control found within the Mesopotamian text of *Atra-ḫasīs*.[1]

Whereas, *Atra-ḫasīs* starts out with humans being created to provide labor for the lower gods, nothing more than work horses who should be limited if they become too numerous, Genesis starts out with mankind as God's representative over creation, His representative who subdues it by having children and filling it up (Gen 1:26–28). He creates a woman, also royalty, and not to be confused with the lowliness of work animals[2]

1. Batto, *Slaying the Dragon*, 44–72; Hamilton, *The Book of Genesis 1–17*, 274; Frymer-Kensky, "The Atrahasis Epic 1–9," 147–55; Kilmer, "The Mesopotamian Concept of Overpopulation," 160–77; Kikawada and Quinn, *Before Abraham Was*, 36–53; Wenham, *Genesis 1–15*, xxxix, xlvii–xlix.

2. 2:18–22: [18]"Then the Lord God said, 'It is not good for the man to be by himself; I will make him a helper equal to his nature.' [19]From the ground the Lord God formed every wild animal and every bird of the sky, and brought [them] to the man to see what he would call them; and whatever the man called a living creature, that was its name. [20]The man gave names to all the domestic animals, and to the birds of the sky, and to

53

as humans are in *Atra-ḫasīs*, to help the man accomplish this procreative goal. Since this is the case, in Genesis, God desires people to engage joyfully in the sexual act to increase and "fill up the earth." Evil comes in because of choices people make, starting from the Fall of Man in Genesis 3, continuing through the decision of Cain to the judgment of that evil in the flood narrative in Genesis 6 and 7. Whereas in *Atra-ḫasīs*, evil exists in the world because there are too many people and the god Enlil sends the flood to silence the racket of so much noise, Genesis teaches that evil is in the world because of decisions people make, not because there are too many of them, and God sends the flood because "every crafting of the thoughts of his [i.e., mankind's] mind were evil" (6:5).

Whereas in *Atra-ḫasīs*, in an effort to scare people from having too many children, a warning is given after the flood that women should use contraceptive methods in order to limit their children or a she-demon would cause miscarriages, in Genesis, God repeats His desire for humans to "be fruitful and increase in number and fill up the earth" (9:1). In order to emphasize this, God repeats it twice to Noah, the second time with emphasis: "be fruitful and multiply; populate the earth abundantly and multiply in it" (9:7). The word *šāraṣ* "populate," here literally means "to swarm," and the translated Hebrew reads: "Be fruitful and increase in number, swarm upon the earth and increase in number upon it." This is a clear and direct attack upon the pro-contraceptive argument of *Atra-ḫasīs*, which seeks to communicate the exact opposite. As T. Frymer-Kensky sums up:

> Unlike *Atra-ḫasīs*, the flood story in Genesis is emphatically not about overpopulation. On the contrary, God's first action after the flood was to command Noah and his sons to "be fruitful and multiply and fill the earth" (Gen 9:1). This echoes the original command to Adam (1:28) and seems to be an explicit rejection of the idea that the flood came as a result of attempts to decrease man's population. The repetition of this commandment in emphatic terms in Gen 9:7, "and you be fruitful and multiply, swarm over the earth and multiply in it," makes it probable that the Bible consciously rejected the underlying theme of the Atrahasis Epic,

---

every wild animal, but for Adam there was not found a helper equal to his nature. [21]So the Lord God caused a deep sleep to fall upon the man, and he slept; then He took one of his ribs and closed up the flesh at that place. [22]The Lord God fashioned into a woman the rib which He had taken from the man, and brought her to the man."

that the fertility of man before the flood was the reason for his near destruction.[3]

The conclusion, therefore, is that Genesis rejects not only the reason for the flood provided by *Atra-ḥasīs* but its provided solution as well. It does so because God's purpose in creation was that the earth be filled up with humans.

Overview of Genesis 1–11

A brief summary of the subject matter in Genesis will aid in the illumination of this polemic within the book. Chapters 1–11 are particularly of interest due to the fact that the major motifs within this section parallel those within the *Atra-ḥasīs* epic. The section begins with the creation of man and ends with the message God has for His people coming out of the flood ("be fruitful and swarm over the earth") and spreading out from overcrowded Babel (i.e., Babylon, from whence the epic of *Atra-ḥasīs* comes). *Atra-ḥasīs*, of course, begins with the creation and ends with the opposite message coming out of the flood (i.e., let contraceptive measures be taken to stop childbearing). As we will see, God will counter this message in the very first book of Scripture.

GENESIS 1

In Genesis 1, the earth is not capable of supporting the habitation of humans (v. 2).[4] This constitutes the first threat, in the Book of Genesis, to God's purpose of filling up the earth with covenant children. The earth is then made capable of supporting a population of humans (vv. 3–25), and therefore God makes humans male and female and commands them to fill it up (vv. 26–31). These humans are His image (i.e., the representatives

---

3. Frymer-Kensky, "The Atrahasis Epic," 150.

4. The statement in v. 2 is that the earth was *tōhû wābōhû*, "uninhabitable and uninhabited," two terms that describe the background for why creation has come about. The earth is uninhabitable, and therefore, uninhabited. This interpretation of the two terms in Genesis 1:2 is also noted by Young in *Studies in Genesis One*, 33: "an earth of וֹבֹהוּ תֹהוּ, therefore is an earth that cannot be inhabited." In the Hebrew Bible, the word *bōhû* "uninhabited" (used only three times—Gen 1:2; Isa 34:11; Jer 4:23) refers to people, not animals. This is made explicit in God's judgment against the Israelites' rebellion in that the land will be made *bōhû*, "uninhabited," but all sorts of animals will remain there (Isa 34:10ff). Therefore, the problem is that the current state of the uninhabitable earth poses a problem to the existence of mankind. See also Tsumura, *The Earth and the Waters in Genesis 1 and 2*.

of His rule over the earth) and are to multiply, so that the picture of God's sovereignty is spread over the entire earth through the creation of images (covenant children), who subdue and cultivate (i.e., make habitable) the entire earth. The threat of an "uninhabitable" earth, therefore, is thwarted by God making one that is habitable; and the uninhabited earth is (and continues to be) thwarted when God makes mankind and commands him to be fruitful, multiply, and fill it up.

GENESIS 2

Because God made the earth to be filled by humans, it is not good for a man to be alone, i.e., a single unit (v. 18). The word for "alone" here is used to refer to someone who is supposed to have a family/household but doesn't. It speaks of someone who has been separated from a group (in this case, Adam has been separated from all of the offspring he would have, i.e., humankind).[5] God creates the woman after He makes the animals in order to convey the idea that only the human female can help (vv. 19–23). The "helping" in context has to do with making the man more than a single unit. It therefore has to do with helping procreate.[6] Only she can help him become more than a single human and be fruitful and multiply and fill up the earth, so they join together as two persons in order to become one flesh through the procreation of a child (v. 24).[7] The "one flesh" in context here mainly refers to the child, which would come about through the sexual act, and is extended later in the interpretation of the New Testament, which fills out the doctrine nicely according to Christ's hermeneutic, where the man and woman are also physically bonded together in unity through the sexual event. The original meaning in the context of Genesis, however, refers to the making of a human child

5. The uses in Genesis alone display this concept: 21:28–29; 30:40; 32:16–17, 24–25; 42:38; 43:32; 44:20; 46:26; 47:26.

6. Although Ellen van Wolde (*Words Become Worlds,* 18–19) falls prey to the idea that the man is lonely, she also notes the major reason for the woman's creation as ʿēzer, "helper," is the perpetuation and survival of humanity through procreation. She further notes (18 n. 7) the study by J. Ska, "'Je vais lui faire allié qui soit son homologue' (Gen 2, 18). A propos du terme ʿēzer—ʾaide'" (*Biblica* 65, 188–204), which concludes that the "help" is to counter a mortal threat (i.e., the threat of non-life). This, of course, is consistent with what we have concluded here (i.e., that the man needs help to multiply, turning the dead, uninhabited earth into a human-filled earth).

7. Verse 24 is progressive, not parallel. Therefore, the man leaves his parents, then he cleaves to his wife in the sexual act, then they become one flesh by having a child, who is the product of that sexual act. Hence, they fulfill the mandate in Genesis 1:28.

through the cleaving together (i.e., the sexual act) of the two persons.[8] The bond between the couple, therefore, is through the making of a child.

However, any idea expressing loneliness is nowhere in the context. Instead, the word in Genesis 2:18 should be seen as God's displeasure that the man be separated primarily from his offspring (i.e., his human family of mankind), and only to a smaller degree from the woman, who is one member of that larger family. Hence, this second problematic threat to God's desire, to fill up the earth *via* procreation, is resolved by the creation of the woman, where the two become joined in one flesh, and make a third. The term, therefore, may speak more about God's sexual, and thus social, purpose for the male and female relationship than it does about a psychological, emotional, or existential one. The man is no longer separated from the other human (his wife) or the other humans (mankind which will fill up the earth) as a result of the two flesh union.

8. We see in the creation of the woman, that God first makes the statement as to why He is going to provide a "helper" for the man. He states that it is not good for man to be *l^ebad,* "alone." Unfortunately, in our overly romanticized culture, this text is read through the lens of our current cultural filter, and when one reads the word "alone," what he or she sees is the word "lonely." It is the context, however, that brings us back to the intended purpose of God's statement. God goes on to state that He will make for the man a "helper." Is she really a helper for his loneliness? And why was God not enough for the man's feeling of loneliness? What will men and women ever do in the new creation when there is no such relationship? How will they solve their loneliness then? Why exactly would the all-sufficient God not be good enough to solve any sense of loneliness? We see the resolution of this conundrum by looking further into the text to see what God means by "alone" and "helper." God then does something that the reader in any generation would find as odd, but it is to express an important point. He brings all of the animals to the man, who names them, but they are then rejected as to being a suitable helper for the man: "But for Adam there was not found a helper equal to his nature." The phrase, "according to his side," is meant to express that none of the animals are human. They are unfit to "help" the man. Once again, this is read through the lens of romanticism (often expressed through a hermeneutic gained from modern psychology), where the woman is able to be intellectually intimate with the man in a way the animals are not (and thus cure his loneliness). However, the purpose of all of this is seen in a statement made in the preceding text of 1:28, and the result of this union (2:24) displayed in the text that follows in 4:1 (despite its interruption by the Fall in Chapter 3).

The result of the union, and its displayed purpose, is found in 4:1. Thus, it is not good for man to be alone because he cannot "be fruitful and multiply" on his own. The statement has nothing to do with him being lonely. God is the source of our ultimate companionship and therefore cure for loneliness. One of the problems of our culture is that we give that job to the opposite sex, much to the failure of the desired goal, and create an idolatrous relationship with the individual. The text is not supporting such an idolatrous way of thinking despite its many modern supporters.

Procreation is the means through which the woman functions as the man's helper. The man cannot have children by himself. He cannot have children with the animals. God therefore makes the woman as the answer to this problem. She helps him solve the problem. As a result of her creation, the two can become one flesh. The purpose of that union would have been expressed when the man and the woman completed the act for which their sexes were created. Instead, the text is interrupted by the Fall of Man in Genesis 3. It picks up again, outside the garden, in 4:1, where the man has sexual relations with his wife and God creates a person through her—hence, the two have become one flesh, both temporarily with each other and eternally in a child.

In summary, then, the second threat to God's purpose of filling up the earth with humans is presented as man's singleness. The resolution to this threat is brought about by the creation of the woman, who is another type of human, with whom the man can now multiply.

GENESIS 3

It is interesting to note in Genesis 3 that the very purpose for which the man and woman are created is the very thing that will now become more difficult outside the garden. The man was created for work in Genesis 2, and therefore, the man's work is made more difficult in Genesis 3. Likewise, the woman was created for childbirth in Genesis 2, and thus, the woman's childbirth is made more difficult in Genesis 3.[9] This is yet another indication that the purpose of her creation was not to fill the loneliness of the man, but instead to fulfill the procreative mandate, making humans many rather than one.[10] In fact, the harsh fallen world will now increase the difficulty to fulfill the creation mandate in that both children and the resources (specifically fruit-bearing land) will be harder to come by. God promises, however, that the devil will not win by thwarting God's goal. The woman will have offspring (i.e., covenant children

9. Cf. The blessing given to these curses when the individual follows the Lord in Psalm 128.

10. It should be stated that no one is suggesting that the woman is created to be a female *only* for that purpose any more than anyone is suggesting that the man is made male solely to perform male-oriented duties. What is being suggested is that the text makes it clear that the creation of the sexes (not the individual humans, who could have been made by God into any sex and even androgynous for that matter) is for the purpose of procreation. The creation of gender is seen to have other purposes as well, but the *primary* purpose is taught here in the early chapters of Genesis.

culminating in the person of Jesus Christ) who will destroy Satan and the chaos of an uninhabitable and uninhabited world. Thus, even in the Fall, God declares that He will still accomplish His goal and fill up the earth with covenant children.

GENESIS 4

The man and the woman have sexual relations, and God shows His purpose in the sexual act by creating a child through it. Eve proclaims that "together with the Lord" she has "created a man" (v. 1).[11] A third threat to God's purpose of filling up the earth with humans, who represent His rule over it, comes when Cain kills Abel (vv. 2–8). A fourth threat comes when Cain himself may be killed for the murder he has committed (vv. 9–14). In reverse order, the fourth threat (i.e., the possible execution of Cain) is thwarted by God's placement of His royal protection over Cain, from whom springs a line of humans who begin to fill up the earth (vv. 15–24). The third threat (i.e., the murder of Abel) is then thwarted when

---

11. In early poetic texts, like those found within the Pentateuch and Psalms, the word Eve uses, *qānā(h)*, often translated as "acquire," actually means "to create" (McCarthy, "Creation Motifs," 78). In fact, the West-Semitic word (such is found in Ugaritic literature) often means "to create" (cf. Deuteronomy 32:6, where the word is in parallel to other words of creating: *Is He not your father, your Creator [qānā(h)], who made you and formed you?*). Thus, here in the early Genesis account, which scholars have always seen as a text filled with archaic words, the passage retains the common poetic tendencies of ANE accounts concerning origins. If so, the word must indisputably mean "to create." This is not even to mention the fact that the idea that she has "bought" the man doesn't make sense in this context. The word does not mean "to acquire" something in the sense that someone gave it within poetry or narrative, but in the sense that it is purchased (the word is used to acquire something in the former sense in wisdom literature, such as Proverbs). Hence, Eve's statement here is "I have created a man together with the LORD." See Tigay, *Deuteronomy,* 402 n. 38; Christensen, *Deuteronomy 21:10–34:12,* 795; and some further poetic texts which favor the archaic meaning of *qānā(h)*: Exodus 15:16; Psalm 78:54; Psalm 139:13: "Through the sexual act, you created [qānā(h)] my inward parts."

This statement becomes highly significant for two reasons:

    1.   Eve is involved in the creation of a human being—hence the last place on earth where God is still creating is inside the woman when the divinely ordained purpose of the sexual act takes place.

    2.   God is intimately involved in this act of creation. Eve has not created a man because YHWH gave her the ability at her creation to do so, and now stands from afar as she makes a child with that ability. Instead, she makes this child "together with YHWH ," and thus shows us that the child is not made only by divinely bestowed natural abilities anymore than the world created itself using the divine ability given to it.

God replaces Abel with Seth, from whom a line of humans, who begin to fill up the earth, also springs (vv. 25–26).

GENESIS 5

Chapter 5 is a genealogy that relates the filling up of the earth with humans from Adam through the line of Seth to Noah. The word often translated in v. 1 as "generations" is the Hebrew word *tôleḏôth*, which literally means "births."[12] Only Seth's line is said to be Adam's "image," as they represent God's rule more accurately by their godliness than Cain's wicked line (contrast the climax of Cain's line with Lamech, who takes life, as opposed to the climax of Seth's with Noah, who preserves life upon the earth). Seth's line is more God's intended purpose in filling the earth, as His intent is to fill it with covenant people. The two seeds in Genesis 3:15 can be seen through the line of Seth, who are the preservers of life, and the line of Cain, who are the destroyers of life.

GENESIS 6–10

Some commentators have seen the "sons of God" in 6:2 as angels, who mixed their nature with that of man's; others have seen it as an allusion to the murderous and pagan line of Cain mixing with the covenant children of Seth; and still others have seen it to refer to oppressive kings, like Gilgamesh, who took the wives (betrothed or married) from his community and thus prevented pure sexual relations between married couples.

Whichever view of vv. 1–4 is adopted, the text indicates that God's filling up the earth with humans who represent Him is threatened by the event mentioned.[13] This is a fifth threat against God's filling up the earth with humans who represent Him in Genesis.

12. All scholars acknowledge that the very structure of the book is fit together with the *tôleḏôth* sections, which display the author's intended subject. The word *tôleḏôth* is a noun derived from the verb *yālad*, which means "to give birth." The word *tôleḏôth* at its basic use in the book means "births," and it appears in the birth of the heavens and the earth (2:4); the births of man through the line of Seth (5:1); the generations of Noah (6:9); the sons of Noah (10:1, 32); the births of man through the line of Shem (11:10), Terah (v. 27); the line of Abraham through Ishmael (25:12, 13); the births of Abraham through the line of Isaac (25:19); births from Esau (36:1, 9); and finally through Jacob (37:2). With each section comes a threat to God's purpose in filling up the earth with His covenant people; but each section also provides God's solution. His solution, of course, is always to preserve, and never to hinder the filling up of the earth.

13. In all three of the main views concerning the "sons of God" and the "daughters of men," there is a threat presented that hinders God's purpose of filling up the earth

Genesis counters the pro-birth control propaganda of the Babylonian epic *Atra-ḫasīs* by stating that God sent the flood because mankind was evil (vv. 5–7), not because humans are filling up the earth and are numerous (what Genesis says God wants to happen).

God's solution then to the fifth threat (i.e., the marrying of the daughters of men by whomever) is to send the flood in 120 years from the time He pronounced judgment (v. 3), and thus He thwarts that threat with the deluge.

However, His judgment of man's evil with the flood, which He must deal out, becomes the book's sixth threat set against God's filling up the earth with humans who represent Him. God states that He will blot out mankind from the face of the earth (v. 7) by sending a flood.

The terminology used in the flood narrative is the same used in creation (seven days, breath of life, etc.), only this time it is a reversal of creation, so that it once again becomes covered with the waters and is incapable of supporting a human-filled earth.

This threat is then solved by God finding favor in Noah, preserving him along with his family in the ark, and commanding the humans again to be "fruitful and multiply and swarm upon the earth." God then promises that He will never again send this type of flood upon the earth, even though mankind's thoughts are evil from his youth.

Another point can be made about this passage. God also states that He sent the flood because the earth was "corrupt" and it was filled with violence. The word translated as "corrupt" (*šāḥat*) here is used in Genesis only when it refers to the sexual sins of an individual or the reciprocal judgment for those sins returned upon them by God (with the word then having the connotation of destroying something). The word is used here, in the episode of Sodom and Gomorrah, and in the case of Onan in Genesis 38. In the case of the latter two, the parties are guilty of distorting the purpose of the sexual act, where the sexual activity performed threatens the procreative purpose God designed for it.

There is, therefore, good reason to conclude that, given the polemic in Genesis against the pro-contraceptive propaganda of *Atra-ḫasīs*, and the connection of the word used only in these contexts within the book, that the word here in the flood narrative also refers to a distortion of the

---

through births.

purpose of the sexual act.[14] This would then imply that the wickedness that brought about the cataclysmic judgment of the deluge included non-procreative sexual activity. If this is true, the polemic has set forth a great irony in that the solution suggested to please the high god, Enlil, in *Atra-ḥasīs* is the very sin that brought about God's wrath in the first place.

GENESIS 11

We are then told that humans have accumulated in one place and begun to build a city with a tower that would reach into the sky. The tower itself is a representation of power, and if it is indeed a Sumerian ziggurat, erected as a monument reflecting human power in usurpation of God's power as displayed in the creation of man, then the power sought is divine.[15] However, there is more in this passage that reflects the idea that the people here were pursuing divine power of a specific kind.

In 11:6, God makes the statement that literally reads "Now there will be no holding back from them anything they devise to do." The idea of being able to accomplish whatever one plans to accomplish is an aspect of divinity. It displays one to be divine, since only the divine can devise and execute a plan without interference from the supernatural. If a mere mortal devises a plan, he or she can expect that plan to be thwarted if the gods should decide to do so; but a god devises and accomplishes what he has planned to do. God is now declaring, therefore, that the humans, in congregating to one place and seeking divine power, will now wield that power to their own demise.

There is a connection between this statement and that found in 18:14, which displays that nothing is so beyond YHWH's authority that He cannot bring it about. Given the context, there may be an idea within these two statements that reflects the power of divinity over childbirth. The rhetorical question, "Is a matter too much for YHWH to accomplish?"

14. Cf. Frymer-Kensky's analysis of *ḥāmās* (6:11, 13), normally translated as "violence," and its contextual semantic inclusion of sexual immorality, murder and idolatry ("The Atrahasis Epic," 154)

15. Cf. Strong ("Shattering the Image of God," 632), who makes numerous astute observations toward the traditional understanding of this text: "Thus, when the humans state that their motive for building the city and the tall tower is 'to make a name for ourselves' (Gen 11:4, ונעשה לנו שם), it would be clear to an ancient reader that the humans were defacing the image of God and were, in essence, scratching off the name of God and replacing it with their own name. This was not a neutral act, though this may be lost on modern readers; it was an act of hybris."

(18:14) refers to the power of childbirth that YHWH wields according to His wishes.

Likewise, God makes a statement, which most likely refers to the overpopulation of the city, and the subsequent uses of power to control childbirth that will follow. This would make sense within the polemic of the book, against the city of Babylon, stating, "And now nothing they plan to do will be withheld from them." It must be remembered that the backdrop of this passage is the *Atra-ḫasīs* epic, which hails from Babylon and premises its argument upon the idea that the land is overpopulated. Hence, the "wise" god, Enki, devises a plan to keep Enlil from destroying all of humanity. His solution, of course, is to control, specifically to devise ways to stop, childbearing. It seems likely, given the author of Genesis' polemic, that the "Tower of Babel" episode is meant to make one final direct attack upon the Babylonian epic and its central city by displaying the two misguided ideas in the epic: (1) that God wants people to congregate in one place instead of spreading out and filling up the earth; and (2) that humans should pursue divine power over procreation in an effort to "close the womb" when such is purely reserved as a divine right.

Hence, the builders of the city with a tower are viewed as the serpent's seed, who attempt to be "like God," where those of the woman's seed, throughout the book, attempt instead to fulfill the procreative mandate as His representatives and fill up the earth with those who are "in His image" and "like His likeness." The former seek equality with God and to wield His power as though it were their own, and the latter seek to submit to God as His images, who seek to have His divine spirit and power work through them but do not seek to take hold of that power themselves.

This threat is thwarted, of course, when God "goes down" to disperse them. The three times this type of terminology is employed is always in the context of judgment for unfavorable deeds. In the garden, God came and conducted a trial to judge the perpetrators. Likewise, in the Sodom and Gomorrah pericope, He came down to evaluate the sins of the city that had come up before Him. Here, He goes down to judge their actions, showing that what they are seeking does not meet divine approval. The ultimate irony of both the passage and God's statement is that, although they seek to be gods, there is still one more powerful who is able to judge and thwart their evil plans if He so chooses.

The Polemic Continues

Since *Atra-ḥasīs* places its literary setting upon the backdrop of creation and flood, Genesis directly counters it only in Chapters 1–11. However, further statements throughout the patriarchal section of the book of Genesis will continue to promote the idea that God is the one who should decide when and if a child is created through the sexual act, and that this decision does not ultimately belong to the man and woman. Likewise, the *tôlᵉdōth* "births" passages will appear throughout the rest of the book to communicate that the author's intended polemic is not yet complete.[16] Therefore, whereas the motifs no longer parallel the *Atra-ḥasīs* epic, the polemic set against its propagandistic message, which attempts to argue that people should limit how many children they have, continues all the way to the end of the book.[17]

OVERVIEW OF GENESIS 12–50

As we move along into the patriarchal section of Genesis, we first encounter a man, Abraham (Chapters 12–25), who is called out by God to become a father of many nations but has no children. Although we see at the very beginning of the story that he acknowledges that he has no child because God has not given him one, the long narrative will take us through a journey where it is clear he believes that procreation is mainly a human choice and endeavor. We follow this man through one human attempt after another as he tries to accomplish this on his own (e.g., having sex with his wife's handmaid because perhaps "she's more fertile" than his wife and since procreation is natural, God couldn't give him a child through his wife who was old; laughing at God for suggesting otherwise; etc.).

---

16. It is probable that the city of Babel (11:1–9) is a sub-polemic against the congregating of people in one place when God wants them to spread out and fill up the earth. The city itself becomes a potential threat to filling up the earth, not only because it fails to do so but because it becomes the primary place where overpopulation arguments originate. In cities, the overpopulation argument seems viable, since there are so many people in one place. In wide open country, however, the argument seems absurd. This may explain the slight shunning of the city and the exaltation of nomadic life by the author of Genesis throughout the book. See Kikawada, *Before Abraham Was*.

17. Note that, even in the end of the book, God seeks to preserve the masses rather than let a famine wipe them out, contrary to Enlil, who sends a famine to wipe them out in the *Atra-ḥasīs* epic.

We are told of the incident when he lied to Abimelech, saying that Sarah was his sister, in order to save his life. He may have reasoned, "Surely God cannot give me a child if I am dead." Abraham must bring about his own safety and preserve his posterity this way. We are told that God, who creates children, closed the wombs of all of Abimelech's wives in order to get him out of the mess—a two-fold lesson showing us that God should be the one who both brings about the creation of children without the interference of men by opening the womb as He sees fit and chooses to prevent their creation by closing the womb.

By the end of this painful lesson in humility we are finally taught by the birth of Isaac that "nothing is impossible" for God and that He gives children whenever and to whomever He wishes.[18]

The next scene (Chapter 26) concerns Abraham's son Isaac, who finds himself in the same predicament in which his father had entangled himself. After God gives him the same promise of offspring that He gave to his father, Isaac lies by telling Abimelech's men that Rebecca is his sister. Like his father Abraham, it is clear that he too thinks that he must accomplish this on his own, for certainly God could not give him offspring if he were dead. This, of course, only puts God's promise in jeopardy rather than helping it. God delivers him from this mess when He causes Abimelech to catch them in the act.

Then we are brought to Jacob and his wives (Chapters 29–30). We first might mention the acknowledgement on the part of both the narrator and Leah that God is the one who has given her children. The text reads as follows:

> [31]Now *the Lord saw* that Leah was unloved, and *He opened her womb*, but Rachel was barren. [32]*Leah conceived and bore a son* and named him *Reuben*, for she said, *"Because the Lord has seen my affliction*; surely now my husband will love me." [33]Then *she conceived again and bore a son* and said, *"Because the Lord has heard that I am unloved, He has therefore given me this [son] also."* So she named him *Simeon*. [34]*She conceived again and bore a son* and said,

18. It should not be assumed, however, that God will thwart birth control attempts in order to give the practitioner a child anymore than it should be assumed that if a Christian is bitten while playing with a viper, God will heal him without medical care. These biblical instances, concerning God's thwarting of man's missteps in the area of procreation, should be seen as the exception rather than the norm. Furthermore, Abraham's missteps are attempting to fulfill God's procreative purposes. Birth control, on the other hand, attempts the contrary.

> "Now this time my husband will become attached to me, because I have borne him three sons." Therefore he was named Levi. [35]And *she conceived again and bore a son* and said, *"This time I will praise the Lord."* Therefore she named him *Judah.* Then she stopped bearing. (29:31–35, italics added)

Leah's response toward the conception of her children is an interesting continuance of the theme concerning God's involvement in conception event. Notice that Leah gives credit to the Lord the first two times. By the third child, Levi, she seems to forget to acknowledge God's hand in the event. The book, however, tells us that she corrects this mistake in naming her fourth child, and says, "This time I will praise the Lord."

Then the text tells us of Rachel's barrenness and her frustrations with Jacob. At first, Rachel evidences a common way of thinking among modern evangelicals; namely, that "people make children." Her statement to Jacob in 30:1 evidences as much: "Now when Rachel saw that she bore Jacob no children, she became jealous of her sister; and she said to Jacob, 'Give me[19] children, or else I die.'"

Jacob's demeanor, as well as his answer, is also God's answer throughout the book of Genesis: "Then Jacob's anger burned against Rachel, and he said, 'Am I in the place of God, who has withheld from you the fruit of the womb?'" (v. 2)

Jacob gives the rightful place to God, whereas Rachel gives that place to humans. She is rebuked accordingly. She now turns, however, and acknowledges this error to a degree in that she sees God giving her handmaid a child for her:

> [5]Bilhah conceived and bore Jacob a son. [6]Then Rachel said, "God has rendered judgment in my favor, and has indeed heard my voice and has given me a son." Therefore she named him Dan. (vv. 5–6)

Of course, this is still not an acknowledgement that God can give her a child anytime He wishes, but she seems now to acknowledge that God is the one withholding a child from her and that He has caused her handmaid to give birth.

Leah likewise will acknowledge this when she gives her handmaid to Jacob and she bears Jacob two more sons. However, the text continues to tell us that even though Leah saw that she was no longer giving birth,

---

19. The Hebrew actually states, "Bring about for me children," or even "cause children to come forth for me."

and naturally thought from a human perspective that her time was done, the text again tells us that "God gave heed to Leah, and she conceived and bore Jacob a fifth son" (v. 17).

Leah once again acknowledges the work of God by stating: "God has given me my wages because I gave my maid to my husband." But she wasn't done yet. Leah conceived again and bore a sixth son to Jacob and proclaimed, "God has endowed me with a good gift; now my husband will dwell with me, because I have borne him six sons." Afterward she bore a daughter and named her Dinah. God gave her three children after, supposedly, according to our finite view of life, she was done having children.

Rachel then is blessed by God:

> ²²Then God remembered Rachel, and God gave heed to her and opened her womb. ²³So she conceived and bore a son and said, "God has taken away my reproach." ²⁴She named him Joseph, saying, "May the Lord give me another son." (vv. 22–24)

Note that it is God who receives the credit for the primary responsibility in the act of Rachel conceiving a child. God remembered her. God gave heed to her. God opened her womb. God took away her reproach. If she has another child, God will be the one who gives her that child.

Other threats to God's filling up the earth with covenant children continue throughout the Jacob cycle: Esau's coming, which threatens Jacob's entire family; Dinah's rape, which threatens the possibility of covenant children, since a Canaanite seeks to marry her; the damaging of Jacob's "loins" by God in a wrestling match; the dangerous, and ultimately fatal, labor of Rachel; the incest between Reuben and Jacob's concubine; the intent of Joseph's brothers to murder him; the famine, which has the potential of destroying a massive number of people (including Jacob's family); etc.[20] Space does not permit me, however, to go into detail with each of these, nor does it permit me to mention the other threats to God's procreative purpose to fill up the earth with His covenant children found throughout the book. Those mentioned should suffice for now. Instead, I wish to pursue only one more event in further detail.

---

20. Even the Book of Exodus continues this idea with Israel in Pharaoh's killing of the firstborn sons and the preservation of the Israelites through the Exodus event itself.

ONAN, THE BARBARIAN

We come then to a controversial passage in Scripture that is often interpreted apart from the context of the book's argument. The text is as follows:

> [6]Now Judah took a wife for Er his firstborn, and her name was Tamar. [7]But Er, Judah's firstborn, was evil in the sight of the YHWH, so YHWH put him to death. [8]Then Judah said to Onan, "Go into your brother's wife, and perform your duty as a brother-in-law to her, and raise up offspring for your brother." [9]But Onan knew that the offspring would not be his; so when he went into his brother's wife, he wasted his seed on the ground in order not to give offspring to his brother. [10]But it was evil in the eyes of YHWH, that which he did, so He put him to death as well. (38:6–10)

Birth control proponents argue that the act God condemns here is either the failure to complete the levirate marriage contract; the taking of Tamar but then denying her offspring; the rebellion of Onan against Judah, his father; or a combination of two or three of these options.

It should first be noted that the attempt to identify the sin as anything other than what is explicitly stated as the sin in the text is a modern innovation not shared with most scholars and theologians past and present.[21]

1. Death is not the penalty for not fulfilling the levirate marriage law (Deut 25:5–10). Although one could argue that what is evil is that Onan goes into her and doesn't fulfill the law, neither sin would bring death upon a man. Onan would simply have to undergo the shame ritual and pay a fine to his father for doing so.

2. Whereas one might argue that God is harsher here in Genesis because He wishes to set a standard for later times, God is actually portrayed in Genesis as more lenient due to the lack of revelation given at that time. For instance, Cain murders his brother and should be executed, but God protects him and allows him to live instead. Whatever the sin of Onan, it was considered to be so grievous that God killed him on the spot for it in order to show all generations that the sin he committed was worthy of death.[22] The law broken then is not merely that of the levirate marriage.

21. See Chapter 2 for some of their comments.

22. Contra GKC (§112e and §159) and Driver (*The Book of Genesis,* 328, as well as the host of modern commentators who have uncritically followed this remark [Alter, 218; Hamilton, 436; Kidner, 188]), the Hebrew verb does not carry a "tense" with a frequenta-

3. The text states that what was evil in the eyes of the Lord was what he did, not what he failed to do. What he did was to "waste his seed" in the sexual act with the intention of doing so. He purposely distorted the use of the sexual act, instead of using it for God's purpose of making a child.

4. One could likewise argue that "what he did" refers to what he did not do in the sense that he intended not to give his offspring to his brother. However, because the text is so explicit, and unlike any other pronouncement of sin in the book, the emphasis is really on the explicit act that he did (i.e., he wasted his semen in order to avoid the conception of a child). The act is described in such detail that it would be unlikely that the action of wasting the semen would not be the explicit sin committed.[23] As B. Harrison comments:

> Indeed, a further problem faces this conventional modern reading of the passage. If simple refusal to give legal offspring to his deceased brother were, according to Genesis 38, Onan's only offense, it seems extremely unlikely that the text would have spelt out the crass physical details of his contraceptive act (cf. v. 9). The delicacy and modesty of devout ancient Hebrews in referring to morally upright sexual activity helps us to see this. As is well known, Scripture always refers to licit (married) intercourse only in an oblique way: "going in to" one's wife, (i.e., entering her tent or bedchamber, cf. vv. 8 and 9 in the Genesis text cited above, as well as Gen. 6:4; 2 Sam. 16:22; 1 Chron. 23:7) or "knowing" one's spouse (e.g., Gen. 4:17; Luke 1:34). When language becomes somewhat more explicit—"lying with" someone, or "uncovering [his/her] nakedness"—the reference is without exception to sinful,

tive sense or otherwise. Nor do the uses of the perfect in collocation with ʾim bōʾ/ô ʾ bear this out. Any frequency of time must be gained from the larger context, since the Hebrew verb is aspectual and does not indicate time. When GKC makes this remark, using its supporting passages, it is clear that there is confusion between what is indicated by the verb and what is indicated by the context. The context here is not in such a position as to indicate, one way or the other, how often, whether many times or only once, Onan had sexual relations with Tamar. It is, of course, not an essential component of the argument being made here either way; but I did want to note the attempt by commentators to try and make Onan's refusal to perform the levirate duty worse than the standard refusal in order to justify God's harsh response. If one accepts the text within the larger literary context and argument of the book, no such justification is needed. The misuse of the sexual act is a rebellion against creation, and advocacy for the reversal of such, and runs counter to God's purposes of filling up the earth with covenant children. Onan works against God and His purposes in the world. He is thus severely punished for it.

23. *Genesis Rabba* 55:5–6.

shameful sexual acts. And apart from the verse we are considering, the Bible's only fully explicit mention of a genital act (the voluntary emission of seed) is in a prophetical and allegorical context wherein Israel's infidelity to Yahweh is being denounced scathingly in terms of the shameless lust of a harlot (Ezek. 23:20).[24]

5. Although the levirate marriage law is clearly referred to, the larger context shows why Onan was put to death: because God viewed his action as a rebellious, non-procreative use of the sexual act. To say then that the text is concerned *only* with the levirate marriage law is:

   (a) to take it out of the contextual argument of Genesis and

   (b) to create a false dichotomy, where *either* it is speaking of the levirate marriage law *or* it is speaking about sexual immorality. One could take the stance that "the sin is not sexual immorality, but rebellion against the levirate marriage law" only if the two sins cancelled each other out. However, the two are not exclusive to one another. Hence, interpreters throughout the history of the Church have always included the one with the other (i.e., he refused to provide offspring for his brother by committing the egregious sin of purposefully wasting his semen). The levirate law provided the occasion for the sin, where the sexual act was to be productive for the brother; but the sin itself was the intent of Onan to engage in a non-productive sexual act.

6. The red herring of contraception advocates, as to whether this is about Onan wiping out the life of a child before it is made for his brother or extinguishing the existence of a child before it is made alone, misses the point. Everyone agrees that the sin Onan committed was an act that would prevent the child from coming into existence. Hence, the sin is using the sexual act in a way so as to not let a covenant child, which would be conceived, begin to live. For what purpose the child was being brought into the world is, therefore, irrelevant.

7. In regard to point six, there is, therefore, an inherent connection between the levirate law and the correct use of the sexual act (i.e., to bring forth covenant children). The two, therefore, should not be distinguished so broadly. Onan could have refused to perform the duty without partaking in the sexual act with Tamar, but instead he took part in an unproductive sexual act and refused to let it bring forth a covenant child in the process.

24. Harrison, "The Sin of Onan Revisited," 1.

Wenham, in the Word Biblical Commentary series, further observes the following in these verses:

> "Evil" is Er [עֵר] spelled backwards (רַע), and I have attempted to capture the pun by translating "Er erred." The nature of his sin is not divulged, "But the completely similar sentence and fate suggest a very similar sin" to Onan's (Jacob, 712). Lev 20:10–20 prescribes death or cutting off, i.e., death at God's hand, for a variety of sexual offenses. The main point though is that Er deserved to die: it was not Tamar's fault. Note that nothing is said about Judah mourning the loss of his firstborn, in contrast to Jacob (37:34–35).[25]

If Wenham is right here, then it becomes a strong argument against those who would label Onan's sin as anything other than *coitus interruptus*, since Er does not fall into any of the sins that birth control advocates usually level against Onan in order to avoid the explicit sin the text says he commits.[26]

Wenham continues:

> Onan has to obey his father's injunction but is unwilling to give "descendants to his brother," so he practices *coitus interruptus* whenever they come together. . . . "What he did offended the Lord." The terminology is very similar to v 7. Why was God offended by Onan's contraceptive methods? In the light of passages such as 1:28; 8:17; 9:1, 7; Pss 127, 128, it seems unlikely that the Old Testament would approve of systematic contraception, for it frustrates God's purpose in creating mankind in two sexes. But in Onan's case it is specially reprehensible, for God's repeated promise to the patriarchs was that he would make them fruitful and multiply (17:6, 20; 28:3; 35:11; cf. 15:5; 22:17; 26:4; 32:13 [12]). Onan is thus deliberately frustrating the fulfillment of those promises. The threefold reference to "descendants" in 38:8–9 must allude to these promises, and Onan's action demonstrates his opposition to the divine agenda. For this reason, the Lord "let him die" (cf. Num 14:27–35).[27]

Finally, the text fits well into the polemical context of Genesis if interpreted as a sexual distortion. If, however, it is interpreted as a condem-

---

25. Wenham, *Genesis 16–50*, 366.

26. He is not under obligation to provide a child by the levirate marriage code, and all other arguments (that Onan rebels or takes Tamar without giving the child) are wrapped around the *solo* levirate marriage view.

27. Wenham, *Genesis 16–50*, 367.

nation of the failure to fulfill the levirate marriage law alone, the text has little or no connection with the subject matter of the rest of the book.

One could say that these were simply the impressions of ancient peoples and that the book is merely descriptive of their ideas of conception. However, this argument fails on two counts:

1. The ancients in the Near East are universal in their beliefs that conception is a human decision (given by the gods sometimes, if asked for) but largely a human act to be influenced only through a miraculous intervention, not a normative one. The ancient Israelite view is completely foreign to, and even polemical against, the ancient Near Eastern mind-set on the subject.

2. The characters in the story are not the only ones making statements such as these. The narrator himself, and therefore God through him, makes the same claims and he has made the same argument throughout the entire book.

LEVITICUS 18

Scholars have noted that the passage appearing in Leviticus 18:1–30 deals with sexual relations, and is framed in the same type of apodictic law that exists in the Ten Commandments.[28]

> [1]Then the Lord spoke to Moses, saying, [2]"Speak to the sons of Israel and say to them, 'I am the Lord your God. [3]"You shall not do what is done in the land of Egypt where you lived, nor are you to do what is done in the land of Canaan where I am bringing you; you shall not walk in their statutes. [4]"You are to perform My judgments and keep My statutes, to live in accord with them; I am the Lord your God. [5]"So you shall keep My statutes and My judgments, by which a man may live if he does them; I am the Lord." (1–5)

First we see that viewing sexuality above and beyond the aspects of pleasure and intimacy is countercultural. The ancient Near Eastern view of the sexual act's purpose was that of pleasure, intimacy, and procreation—only one of which was necessary to seek through the sexual act at any given time. This view is identical to the view throughout the history of Western civilization, excepting only devoted adherents to one of the

---

28. Noth, *Leviticus,* 134.

three main religions influenced by the Bible: Judaism, Christianity, and Islam (largely due to the influence of the former two on the latter).[29]

The Levitical text above indicates that God does not want sex to be used in particular ways. But in what ways are cultural views of sex contradictory to God's thinking about sex and why? How are the views of the Egyptians and Canaanites any different than that which is advocated by God? We have a list given to us, which should not be seen as exhaustive, but as a list of examples from which the people of God can build an idea of what constitutes sexual immorality.

In v. 6 we find the following summary statement of the incest prohibitions: "No one among you is to approach any blood relative of his to uncover nakedness; I am the Lord." The rest of the verses in the section on incest (vv. 7–18) specify instances of incest that are prohibited—once again, they are not meant to be exhaustive, but only examples.

One has to wonder why God prohibited incest when so many cultures practiced it for various reasons. In Egypt, certain Pharaohs would intermarry with their sisters in order to keep the bloodline pure. As we see in the case of Lot and his two daughters, they are concerned for procreation (Gen 19:30–38), but this is placed in an evil light precisely because their act could counter this goal.[30] In the case of David's son, Amnon, the misguided brother "loves" his half sister, Tamar (2 Sam 13:10–33). However, all of these examples would be condemned by this passage. The problem one encounters, however, is the case of Abram and Sarai. Did not Abram marry Sarai his half sister? Why are the above examples condemned and not Abram for marrying his half sister, Sarai? God states that Abraham actually walked in His statutes (Gen 26:5). The example of Lot and his daughters, presented in a much worse light than that of Abram and Sarai, would especially be of interest as he and Abraham are contemporaneous to one another. So what is the difference?

I would suggest that it has to do with the high rate of birth defects and infant deaths that ancients observed when such a union took place. The bloodline between half brother and sister by the time of the patriarchs would not have been as corrupted as the bloodline between parent

---

29. We must note, however, that Judaism's acceptance of contraception, as reflected in the Talmud (Yebam. 12b), takes place around the time Christianity comes on the scene. At this point, Christianity takes up the banner opposing the practice.

30. Their actions eventually create two of the major nations at odds with God's people.

and child. Hence, the action of Lot's daughters is placed in a bad light, whereas the union of Abram and Sarai is blessed at that point.

However, as time went on, the bloodlines became more impure and the high rate of birth defects and infant mortality led God to prohibit the sexual act with "either your father's daughter or your mother's daughter" (v. 9).

This view is not purely scientific on the part of the Israelites, but it reflects the theology of the Genesis 2 passage, where one could connect two people who became one flesh through a child as a single person. This then would expand the prohibition to any to whom a blood relative was enjoined through marriage. To have sex with an in-law then is to have sex with the blood relative with whom he or she is united. Such a union should not be violated, and to do so would bring upon the individual a curse, which would be placed upon any offspring produced from it.

Therefore, the text's concern with incest is that it can deform, or worse, kill a child brought forth from such a union. Since the *primary* purpose of the sexual act, as we have seen in Genesis, from which Leviticus draws, is to create an opportunity for God to bring forth a child to be raised in His community, incest—as a threat to this very thing—is prohibited.

We see the continuation of this type of thought in v. 19: "Neither are you to approach a woman to uncover her nakedness during her menstrual impurity."

Whereas, some associate this with the ritual uncleanness, which simply paints a picture of that which is holy *versus* that which is profane, found in the ritual section of the book, it is clear that in this section of the book, called the Holiness Code, these prohibitions are moral, not ritual. These condemnations bring about not a temporary ritual banishment from the camp, as do the ritually unclean violations, but instead, one who practices them is cut off from the people (i.e., executed). When speaking about this act, as well as the rest of this discourse, God declares, "Do not defile yourselves by *any* of these things" (v. 24); and "But as for you ... you will not do any of these abominations" (v. 26). Hence, according to this text, there is something about the sexual act with a woman who is menstruating that is unholy, sexually immoral, corrupt, and an abomination.

If we understand that God is primarily concerned about the right use of the sexual act as a natural vehicle through which He can bring up offspring for Himself, then we immediately see how such an act would bring about such a condemnation in vv. 24–30.[31]

Note as well that the failure to obey the procreative command, spoken in Genesis 1:28, also forfeits the blessing of the land and its subjugation to God's people as a providential source of sustenance (i.e., the reversal of one element of the command in Genesis 1:28–30 brings about the reversal of the entire blessing). Hence, the failure to be fruitful and multiply leads to being "cut off" from the land.

Some have commented that the woman can still get pregnant during menses, so this text does not really prohibit an unproductive sexual act. However, even if one were to interpret this text as referring just to the period of blood flow, it would have to be acknowledged that the chances of the woman to conceive are very limited.

This mistaken objection also fails to realize that the period of menses may include the seven days of purity which follow it (15:19); and as such would be prohibiting the sexual act, not only during the flow of blood, but seven days after it has stopped.[32]

In any case, however, whether sex with a woman during menses threatens/limits the possibility of a child being born or is only believed to do so, God is still seeking to give the Israelites a lesson concerning the right use of the sexual act.

The next statement in v. 20 concerns adultery: "You are not to have intercourse with your neighbor's wife, to be defiled with her."

Now, at first glance, one might think that the subject matter here is different. However, the text states that this would defile both of them, not simply rob the husband. In fact, the actual phrase in the Hebrew states: "You are not to give your semen to plant seed/offspring into your neighbor's wife, becoming sexually corrupted with her." The emphasis here, then, is on a child that might come about through the affair. It is not of the coveting aspect of the sin of adultery, which deals primarily with ownership issues, but instead is concerned with the implications for the child that may be conceived as the result of this type of sexual act.

---

31. This interpretation makes sense, since the period of uncleanness for all other bodily defilements occurs not during but after the act has taken place.

32. This is the primary rabbinical interpretation of the text. See *b. Nid.* 57b, 69a; Jacob, *Leviticus 1–16*, 935, also notes this interpretation among the Ethiopian Jews who have no contact with rabbinic literature.

Together with the phrase that they will be polluted (and hence must be cut off from the community, i.e., put to death), it is clear that God is concerned for what happens to the child. The prohibition here, then, is not a repeat of the eighth commandment, but is one that now frames adultery as not only the sin of coveting another man's wife but also one of sexual immorality.

Adulterers are executed at this time in the wilderness wanderings. Unlike the later practice we see among the Puritans of sparing the mother's life until the child is born (because it was thought that the child is innocent and should not be killed along with the mother for a crime), in ancient Israel (along with the ancient Near East in general) the woman is killed regardless of whether she is pregnant or not; and if the child by another man does survive, that child is killed as well.[33]

This execution would, of course, destroy any possibility for the child to be brought up to the Lord within the community. The sexual act of adultery then is not just an act of desire for a neighbor's wife, but also an act of sexual immorality in that it threatens the opportunity for God to create a child for the purpose of being raised up to Him.

Suddenly, in v. 21, we have a very odd phrase, which seems like it does not fit the context very well: "You shall not give any of your offspring to offer them to Molech, nor shall you profane the name of your God; I am the Lord."

This seemingly misplaced verse, however, fits very well within the context if one understands the true subject matter of the text. If one supposes that the subject matter of the context is idolatry and not sexual distortions, then this verse is really one of only a couple that make any sense here. The fact of the matter is that sacrificing children is equated with sexual immorality.

Hartley comments on its connection:

> To a modern reader the law in v 21 appears out of place in the second set of laws . . . There are several indicators, though, that it was formulated for this location. The opening phrase מִזַּרְעֲךָ, "any of your seed," ties directly to לְזֶרַע, "for seed," in v 20aβ. The prohibition לֹא תִתֵּן, "do not give," resounds the prohibitions

---

33. Cf. the Jewish idea found in Sirach 23:23d–25: "[23d]She has committed adultery and brought forth children by another man. [24]She herself will be brought before the assembly, and her punishment will extend to her children. [25]Her children will not take root, and her branches will not bear fruit."

found in vv 20a and 23. The strong wording, "profane the name of your God," expresses that this activity is even more polluting than the other offenses in this set and accords with the strong declaratory formulae of this set. Furthermore, the grounding of the law with the self-introduction formula "I am Yahweh" increases the weight of this prohibition as well as establishing a tie with the first series of laws (v 6) and the parenetic framework (cf. v 2). Thus the speaker composed this law carefully to fit this context. The close tie between sexual offenses and sacrifices to Molek is further attested by the placing of laws against offerings to Molek just prior to a series of laws against sexual offenses in chap. 20. Israel thus made an ideological connection between sexual offenses and certain pagan rites.[34]

However, if we see that the context has to do with the right use of the sexual act, then we see that having a child only to sacrifice him or her instead of raising him or her for God in the community is also condemned as sexual immorality. This is the case because the sexual act has not been used as a means to have godly children, but as a means to produce children simply to sacrifice them for a greater chance of prosperity. In fact, the command includes a prohibition against associating the name of Israel's God with the act of *halal*, "a sexually corrupting act." Hence, to sacrifice a child to Molech is a sexually corrupting act.

Here, as in other places in the Bible, we also realize that the intended result of the sexual union is not simply to have a baby but to bring up that child to the Lord. Inherent within the biblical concept of childbearing then is also childrearing. As Augustine explains its purpose, the sexual act is not only for bringing children into the world, but also for "the receiving of them lovingly, the nourishing of them humanely, the educating of them religiously."[35] Accordingly, then, to set the primary purpose of the sexual act upon any other foundation than the one which God has laid down is truly an act of sexual rebellion and immorality.

In v. 22, God commands: "You are not to lie with a male as one lies with a female; it is an abomination."

Some scholars will argue here that the text is referring to a ritual prostitution instead of a general prohibition against homosexuality.

34. Hartley, *Leviticus*, 288.
35. Augustine, *On Genesis According to the Letter*, 9.7.

However, a comparative *min*[36] is used in order to qualify what is meant by the phrase "lie with a male." This means that the "lying with a male" is equivalent to the "lying with a woman."

Some argue that this passage refers only to homosexual sacred prostitution, which is conjoined to idolatry. If the general practice was considered morally acceptable, however, one could expect the statement "You are not to lie with a male prostitute (with some argument attempting to make *zākār* "male" mean "male cult prostitute" instead of its regular meaning distinguishing male and female from one another) as one lies with a man ('*îš* instead of '*iššā[h]*); or one might at least see the word *zākār* (interpreted as "male cult prostitute) in contrast to *neqēbā(h)* (also interpreted as "female cult prostitute").

Of course, even if this were attempted, none of the words suggested (*zākār*, "male;" *neqēbā(h)*, "female;" '*îš* "man;" or '*iššā[h]*, "woman") are the words the Hebrew Bible uses to describe a cult prostitute. The words used to describe a male and female cult prostitute are *qādēš* and *q*e*dēšā(h)*. The argument, therefore, that this text is speaking of cultic prostitution fails from the analysis of lexicography alone.

Furthermore, the comparison is not made between one kind of male and another kind of male because the prohibition is meant to be against all males engaging in a sexual act that should be exclusively practiced by a man and a woman. The contrasted word '*iššā(h)*, "woman," is used instead of the normal *neqēbā(h)*, "female," in order to show the intimacy of the word "to lie." The word '*iššā(h)* is the more common word that refers to a man's wife, and thus, the reference is to the type of sexual relationship a man has with his wife.

Finally, according to the overall context, if sexual immorality is a sexual act that is not open to God's creation of a child through the natural means given to the man and woman in order that God might have godly offspring to Himself, then all forms of homosexuality (ritual or otherwise) would fall under this condemnation.

The pronouncement that it is an "abomination" is an interesting one, since all of the acts listed are cited as such. The word *tô'ēbā(h)* connotes something that has been polluted, distorted, or of a lesser standard than is appropriate. Here, as in the rest of this section of Scripture, God communicates to us that these are examples of sexual distortions, pollutions

36. *IBHS* 11.2.11e.3.

of the sexual act. None of them provide God the opportunity to create a child for His community by using the right act of sex with which He originally instructed the man and woman to use. The goal of the abominable sexual act is pleasure or intimacy absent of procreation. Accordingly, they are all summarized as "abominations."

Finally, in v. 23 the example of bestiality comes into play: "Also you shall not have intercourse with any animal to be defiled with it, nor shall any woman stand before an animal to mate with it; it is a perversion."

Here we have two prohibitions in one. The man is not to have sex with an animal, which would obviously not bring forth human offspring for the covenant community; neither is the woman to let an animal have sex with her, since this also cannot be used naturally by God to create human children.[37]

This prohibition harks back to the Garden of Eden, where the man needs a helper in order to fulfill the mandate given to Him by God to "be fruitful and multiply and fill up the earth." The animals are all brought to him, but none of them has the possibility of being his helper in this way (i.e., not one could be used by God to make a human child). Animals are all rejected as a suitable helper in procreation due to this fact. The sexual act with these animals, although repulsive to us as well, is primarily prohibited because of the impossibility of God producing a human child through the natural processes He created.[38] The woman is then created because of this very thing. Instead of the man remaining a single unit, which God says is not good, the woman is able to be his helper to increase his number through family. Hence, bestiality is condemned here precisely because it ignores the purpose of sex that this passage teaches us can be accomplished only through the man-wife union, the procreation of covenant children.

We, therefore, see that each element condemned in Leviticus 18 is done so precisely because it threatens the procreation of covenant chil-

37. The prohibitions are directed toward the one in power (i.e., the one who is making the decision to initiate the sexual act).

38. Although the sexual sins mentioned in Leviticus 18 are repulsive to most people, an argument from that standpoint alone cannot support the claim that they are morally wrong. Obviously people are able to overcome this feeling toward these sins, since various people practice them in certain instances around the world. The duty of the Christian is to make a valid biblical argument that supports the claim being made. An argument from feeling does nothing but distort the issues at hand.

dren within the family.[39] God then sums up, creating an *inclusio* for the entire unit, by an expanded reiteration, where Israel is warned not to use the sexual act for the same purposes the Canaanites had—lest they be rejected from being God's people, and cast out along with them. We are left with these words:

> [24]'Do not defile yourselves by any of these things; for by all these the nations which I am casting out before you have become defiled. [25]'For the land has become defiled, therefore I have brought its punishment upon it, so the land has spewed out its inhabitants. [26]'But as for you, you are to keep My statutes and My judgments and shall not do any of these abominations, [neither] the native, nor the alien who sojourns among you [27](for the men of the land who have been before you have done all these abominations, and the land has become defiled); [28]so that the land will not spew you out, should you defile it, as it has spewed out the nation which has been before you. [29]'For whoever does any of these abominations, those persons who do [so] shall be cut off from among their people. [30]'Thus you are to keep My charge, that you do not practice any of the abominable customs which have been practiced before you, so as not to defile yourselves with them; I am the Lord your God.' (vv. 24–30)

The severity of punishment displays the severity of the crime being committed; and these crimes carry such a severe punishment that one can only conclude that they are vehemently hated by God like no other. The explanation for such an outcry against these is evident when one considers that they obstruct the very purpose for which God made the human couple (i.e., to have covenant children, who represent His majesty, fill up the earth).

A major question for the modern evangelical is whether his or her sexual practices reflect those of the people of God or those of the Canaanites. Do their sexual practices fulfill or frustrate the primary task God gives to the human couple to fulfill?

---

39. Dearmen, "Marriage in the Old Testament," 58–59.

5

The New Testament

WE COME THEN TO the New Testament teaching, which assumes the Old Testament. If we understand the term *porneia*[1] "sexual immorality" to include all the expressions of Leviticus 18, then we see that the New Testament also condemns these practices along with any implications they have upon further non-procreative practices not explicitly mentioned, such as pedophilia, sex with inanimate objects, masturbation, and the use of birth control.

THE TERM *PORNEIA* IN THE NEW TESTAMENT

It is common now among modern Christians to define the term *sexual immorality* as "sex outside of marriage," or on a more popular level "sex before marriage," based on the Old Testament concept, which classified a woman who had sex outside of a marriage commitment to a man as a prostitute or an adulteress. However, even in the Hebrew Bible, if a woman who had sex before marriage because she had been taken forcefully by a man married that individual with whom she had sex, it was not considered sexual immorality. Instead, it was considered a theft on the part of the individual with whom she had sex, whereby he had to give restitution to the father for having taken his daughter without paying the bride price (Exod 22:16). If her father did not want her to marry, he simply took

---

1. The word *porneia* is the New Testament's adoption of the LXX translation of the words z*enûth*, "prostitution," and z*enûnîm*, "acts of prostitution," as well as the verb *zānā(h)* by the Greek *ekporneuō*, which by the time of the Koine Greek of the New Testament, the *ek* preposition was dropped (with the exception of Jude 1:7, where archaic uses are displayed from earlier pseudepigraphical readings) and just *porneuō* is used. The New Testament also adopts the terms *pornē* and *pornos*. The term, by the time of the Second Temple Period had expanded from referring to mere prostitution and encompassed more broadly the sin expressed in the various sexual acts described in Leviticus 18.

back his daughter and kept the bride price for himself (v. 17). This was still considered a shameful thing because he treated her like a prostitute (cf. Gen 34:31), but it is not considered sexual immorality in the New Testament sense. Therefore, "sexual immorality" is not sex before, or outside of, marriage in the sense that many use the term today.

A woman was also permitted to be a prostitute as long as she was not a daughter of a priest, a cult prostitute, or sought to marry a man.[2] God, however, makes numerous statements in the Hebrew Bible of His displeasure of the occupation, and by the time of the New Testament, will prohibit it completely.[3] Yet, "sexual immorality" as we see it in the New Testament is also extended to the act of prostitution as something contrary to the raising of covenant children. If "sexual immorality," in the likeness of Leviticus 18, were equivalent to prostitution in the Bible, it would never have been tolerated at all. Whereas prostitution (like polygamy) was once tolerated in the Hebrew Bible, due to the extended moral requirements in the New Testament, those who practice this egregious act will not enter the kingdom of God.

All of this to say that "sexual immorality" as we think of it today has never been what the Old Testament means by the term, and its meaning shifts even further from our understanding by the time of the Second Temple Period.

In the New Testament, the term *zānā(h)*, "sexual immorality," is translated by the Greek word *porneia*, "sexual immorality." Although adultery, as we will see, can be considered sexual immorality at certain points in biblical history, the term is much broader and has its emphasis not on the ownership of the married partner, as the narrow term of adul-

2 The Lord makes a major exception, of course, to this rule with the Prophet Hosea in order to make a huge point by portraying Israel's unfaithful conduct as harlotry.

3. The prostitute became an adulterous only when she attempted to marry someone else; and the penalty for such was death (Deut 22:20–21). Although the word used here for what she has done (*liznôth* from the verb *zānā[h]*, "to act as a prostitute") is often associated today with what we call "sexual immorality" as modern Christians think of it (i.e., sex before marriage), it is rather associated more with adultery (i.e., sex with a man while committed to another) in the OT. The difference between the two in Old Testament times is that one is a matter of ownership (i.e., adultery) and one of frustrating the sexual goal of creating a covenant child (i.e., sexual immorality). One may have been a prostitute and not have been killed for it (even though God clearly does not like it), as long as she neither had, nor sought in the future, a husband. At the point that she did so, her prostitution became adultery and she was to be executed for it according to biblical law (Deut 22:21).

tery carries with it, but on the actual intended use of the sexual act itself. All adultery, and later in the Second Temple Period all prostitution, can be deemed sexual immorality;[4] but not all sexual immorality expresses itself in adultery or prostitution. In fact, by the time of the Second Temple Period, as evidenced both in Second Temple literature as well as in the New Testament, the term came to be used primarily in reference to the distorted use of the sexual act as displayed in Leviticus 18. As Friedrich Hauk and Siegfried Shulz conclude: "Later Judaism shows us how the use of πορνεία ["sexual immorality"] etc. gradually broadened as compared with the original use."[5]

We see the term's development in texts such as the *Damascus Document* at Qumran. This text describes three traps that are set up by the devil. The first mentioned is *hazzenût*, which one might be tempted to translate as "prostitution," yet the act is described in a lengthy description mimicking the statements against incest in Leviticus 18.[6]

The Greek word used by the New Testament, *porneia*, in the *Testament of Reuben*, is used to describe Reuben's incest with his father's concubine.[7]

In the *Testament of Benjamin*, the homosexual behavior of Sodom is called *porneia*;[8] and it is considered to be sodomy in the *Sibylline Oracles*, where it is contrasted with rearing one's own offspring instead of killing them.[9]

The verbal form of the word *porneuo* in Jude, a book renowned for furthering themes found within Second Temple Judaism, describes angels having sex with human women (v. 6), the homosexuality of Sodom and Gomorrah (v. 7), and most likely masturbation or *coitus interruptus* (v. 8).

4. This is the case due to the fact that prostitution was counter productive to the creation of covenant children, both because the family unit was broken and defiled and because contraception and abortion were associated with prostitution by the time of the New Testament.

5. *TDNT* 6:587.

6. For a fuller treatment of this text and its application to the New Testament divorce prohibitions, see Fitzmeyer, *To Advance the Gospel*, 79–111.

7. 1:6; 4:8; also see the *Testament of Judah* 13:3, where his sexual immorality describes his taking of a foreign woman (thus raising a non-covenant child) and engaging in a sexual act with Tamar, a woman given to his son (thus a Second Temple insinuation of incest).

8. 9:1; cf. also *Jubilees* 16:5; 20:5.

9. III. 764; IV. 33–36.

In Matthew 15:19, we see that the word has expanded from its Old Testament usage when Matthew distinguishes between *porneia*, "sexual distortion," and *moicheia*, "adultery."

In the Book of Acts, 15:20–29, the Jerusalem Council concludes that Gentiles need to abstain from *porneia*, along with two other practices at which they may not have taken offense as the Jews had. This shows us that the concept of *porneia*, "sexual distortion," is distinguished from mere adultery (which would include sex before marriage), since the Gentiles all had laws that addressed the latter but relatively few concerning the former.

In 1 Corinthians 5:1, Paul refers to the incestuous relationship of a man and his father's wife as *porneia*. We are told here that not even the Gentiles practice this kind of sexual immorality (i.e., incest between a son and his father's wife). Of course, this also tells us that the Gentiles partake in a large variety of other kinds of *porneia*. Hence, the prohibition handed down by the Jerusalem Council is well fitting to the Gentile situation.

Finally, in First Timothy, we have sexual immorality mentioned yet again.

> [8]But we know that the Law is good, if one uses it lawfully, [9]realizing the fact that law is not made for a righteous person, but for those who are lawless and rebellious, for the ungodly and sinners, for the unholy and profane, for those who kill their fathers or mothers, for murderers [10]and immoral men and homosexuals and kidnappers and liars and perjurers, and whatever else is contrary to sound teaching. (1:8-10)

For the most part, the list of sins in the passage is constructed in doublets; and the word for sexual immorality (*pornos*) is parallel to *arsenokoitēs*, "homosexuality."

[A] lawless // [A′] rebellious
[B] ungodly // [B′] sinners
[C] unholy // [C′] profane
[D] killers of father and mother // [D′] murderers
[E] sexually immoral (*pornos*) // [E′] homosexuals
[F] kidnappers/criminals // [F′] liars // [F`] perjurers

The word *pornos*, "a sexually immoral man," may be used here to describe a male who practices what would be the type of sex that would be practiced in the male-to-male sex act described by *arsenokoitēs*, "homosexual."[10]

The word for "homosexuals" here, and elsewhere in the Pauline corpus,[11] is made up of the words for "male" and "the ejaculation of semen."[12] Paul uses the latter word (i.e., *koitē*) generically to describe the emission of semen.[13] In the LXX, the word is used in contexts when describing the incest of Reuben, the sacrifice of a child to Molech, the sexual activity between two males, etc. The point is, of course, that the emphasis of this Pauline word for "homosexuality" is on the sexual misuse of semen in a male-to-male relationship. In other words, what is wrong with this particular act of homosexuality is the waste of the semen, and we would further the argument that it is a waste primarily because semen is divinely ordained for procreative purposes, which are shunned through the homosexual act.

The identification of the term in Second Temple Judaism with Leviticus 18 does not mean that the word in the secular Greek world became associated with that passage, and there are uses in the New Testament that evidence the Greek idea of a *pornē* (a different word, but still a cognate to *porneia*) in its classical sense of "prostitute," which also fits the occasional Old Testament use of *zānā(h)*.[14] However, it is clear that the word within Second Temple Judaism had come to refer to the sexual offenses of Leviticus 18. It is, therefore, the condemnation of that

10. The fact that the word for homosexual here describes the male offender in the homosexual act gives further credence to the idea that the condemnation of the act is in the waste of semen. The male offender in the heterosexual immoral acts described by *pornos*, therefore, in parallel with the former word, receives the same condemnation.

11. cf. the use of *koitē* in Pauline texts, such as Romans 9:10; 13:13

12. In general, the term literally means "bed," but Paul's specific use has to do with the use of semen in the sexual act.

13. Hence, when Paul creates this word from the LXX version of Leviticus 18:22, his interpretation of that passage emphasizes *coitus* event within the act of homosexuality.

14. It is difficult to know if Paul adopts the Second Temple Jewish use or the secular Greek use in 1 Corinthians 6:15–20. It is possible that prostitution had been sub-categorized as a form of sexual immorality in the sense in which we have spoken of it here, but it may also be that Paul is using the secular designation, and not classifying it in the same way, since his audience is primarily a Greek one here. Chances are that the practice is now seen as contrary to the family unit and its intended purposes to raise up the godly offspring of Genesis 1:28, read through passages like Malachi 2:13–16 and Mark 10:6–9. The condemnation may also stem from the later practice of prostitution being associated with contraceptive practices in Greco-Roman culture.

porneia in the New Testament that gives precedent to the claim that Jesus and the apostles condemned any sexual act that did not provide a natural opportunity through which God would create a covenant child.

ROMANS 1:18–32

The first chapter of the Epistle to the Romans has had a long history of scrutiny from all sorts of scholars but has largely been framed around the homosexual question. Indeed, the text is relevant to that issue, but it is also relevant to our current issue as well. In order to see just how it is relevant, we will briefly exegete and exposit some of the passage.

> [18]For the wrath of God is revealed from heaven against all un-godliness and unrighteousness of men who suppress the truth in unrighteousness . . . [23]and exchanged the glory of the incorruptible God for an image in the form of corruptible man and of birds and four-footed animals and crawling creatures.

Here we are told two things:

1. That the wrath of God is not *going to be* revealed (as though it were talking about the eschatological judgment of the lake of fire) but that it *is being* revealed already. This wrath then is something visible that we can see right now.

2. That this wrath has come upon men for suppressing the truth of God's true nature, which is "holy other" rather than "this worldly."

By "holy other" we mean to say that God's righteousness is not of this world's spirit and culture. It does not follow that pattern of worldly thinking that is produced from human culture but instead is often countercultural. We could say then that God is the holy judge who will evaluate men with holiness, or, to put it more specifically, God does not accept impure acts because of His holy nature. Whereas our culture often defines its goodness descriptively (i.e., bases its ideals on the best of what is practiced already in society), God defines goodness descriptively of Himself, and therefore, prescriptively of human society. In other words, since God is the ideal, the standard of morality is based on His nature and deeds rather than on the ever-swinging pendulum of human culture.

Because God's nature does not cause people to think well of themselves, and indeed causes fallen humans to view themselves as evil instead of good, man's rebellious tendency is to change God rather than himself.

God then is brought down a bit to man's level and made a little corruptible (i.e., more inclined to pass over what we do), so that the wicked can feel good in that they are bonded with a common nature with God.

The god we craft is much more accommodating and manageable. He requires from us only what we wish to give him and nothing more. We thus pull God down to our level in an effort to feel better about what we do. This suppression of the truth (i.e., that God is holy other and requires us to have different practices than that of our culture) brings about only anger from Him, and results in our subsequent slavery to those very things for which we originally sought to enslave the truth.

> [24]Therefore God gave them over in the lusts of their hearts to impurity, so that their bodies would be dishonored among them. [25]For they exchanged the truth of God for a lie, and worshiped and served the creature rather than the Creator, who is blessed forever. Amen.

These two verses parallel the preceding section (v. 18 // v. 24), where God's wrath is expressed by His handing over the minds of individuals to their impure pleasures in order that they would do what is not honored by God with their bodies.

Likewise, vv. 19–23 are parallel to v. 25, showing the reason why God gave them over (i.e., they did not acknowledge His holy otherness but sought to make Him think like them). We then are told again in vv. 26–27 what God does as a result of their distorting His nature.

> [26]For this reason God gave them over to degrading passions; for their women exchanged the natural function for that which is unnatural, [27]and in the same way also the men abandoned the natural function of the woman and burned in their desire toward one another, men with men committing indecent acts and receiving in their own persons the due penalty of their error.

The phrase *pathē atimias,* "degrading passions," is often in contrast to something that is made to fulfill a special purpose for God. Twice Paul uses the imagery of pottery (Rom 9:21; 2 Tim 2:20) to contrast those who God chooses to fulfill the purpose for which He made them (i.e., to worship Him) versus those He designates as *atimia,* "dishonorable," (because they do not use their lives to worship Him).

In 2 Timothy 2:21, Paul describes how one might throw off his or her dishonorable status and become useful for God's purposes: "Therefore, if anyone cleanses himself from these [things], he will be a vessel for honor, sanctified, useful to the Master, prepared for every good work."

The idea is that what is honorable is what is set apart for God for His use and purposes. The passions/urges in Romans 1, therefore, are not used in a way that is set apart for God's intended purposes but in a dishonorable way to worship the self.

The statement that *their* women exchanged the natural function for that which is unnatural may be a fascinating one for those who think the Bible does not address our subject specifically. First we must note that these women may be married. The statement is that "their (in the masculine gender) women" exchanged the natural for the unnatural.[15] If this is true, then this verse would not be talking about lesbianism, but a use of the sexual act between a man and a woman that is not used for God's purposes and therefore "unnatural."[16] The contrast between what is natural and unnatural clearly refers to what is according to God's purposes in the created order as opposed to the uses for the sexual act He did not intend.[17]

15. Note that v. 26 states that "God gave *them* [masculine] over to degrading passions." The statement may indicate that the men have been given over to unproductive sexual acts, both because their women exchange the natural function of the sexual act for non-procreative acts with them and because they engage in homosexual activity which is also non-procreative. See Miller ("The Practices of Romans," 10), who states: "Thus the similarity in function described in Romans 1:26 refers to non-coital sexual activities which are engaged by heterosexual women similar to the sexual activities of homosexual males. So females, described first, exchange natural function for unnatural, but an exchange of partners is not indicated." Fredrickson ("Natural and Unnatural Use," 201) also states that "Paul is not alluding to lesbianism in 1:26. . . . Rather the reference is to inordinate desire within marriage." These men state this in hopes to fortify their case that homosexuality is not condemned by these verses. Ironically, however, they have only shown that the heterosexual distortions in v. 26 set up a kind of merism with v. 27, which would subsequently condemn any and all non-procreative sexual acts, including all forms of homosexuality. This becomes all the more likely when one realizes that anal intercourse, both with male and female, was a common contraceptive practice utilized by the culture in an effort to limit one's heirs.

16. Homosexual behavior is clearly mentioned in v. 27b and c. The two sins mentioned here would not be lesbianism and homosexuality, therefore, but men who use certain unnatural functions of their female partners (perhaps a reference to anal or oral sex) in v. 27a, and still other men engaging in homosexual behavior in v. 27b and c. Hence, a merism is created for the condemnation to encompass all unproductive sexual acts.

17. See Moo, *The Epistle to the Romans*, 115: "In keeping with the biblical and Jewish worldview, the heterosexual desires observed normally in nature are traced to God's creative intent. Sexual sins that are 'against nature' are also, then, against God, and it is this

Hence, the reason for mentioning the woman first is that it encompasses all forms of sexual immorality by contrasting the two:

(1) That when a man has unlawful sex with a woman it is not in a procreative way; and

(2) a man who has sexual relations with another man also cannot produce offspring. Instead, this act destroys his own line; it is the killing of himself.

This interpretation is not conclusive, but it is interesting to note its possibilities. However, it is also possible that "their women" refers only to Gentiles in the context as well. I would argue, of course, that it is plausible that the "their," in the phrase "their women," refers to Gentile husbands, and thus, the above interpretation would be accurate.[18]

However, whether the woman using a non-procreative sexual act in marriage is *explicitly* condemned here or not, the passage would still *implicitly* condemn the use of contraception.

The word *chrēsis,* "function" or "use," tells us that there is a natural use of the sexual act that is not being fulfilled in the act of homosexuality. If advocates of birth control are correct, and the sexual act can be used either for the primary purpose of pleasure or intimacy apart from the opportunity for procreation to occur, then Paul's words here are false. Why? Because the homosexual sex act can fulfill both the functions of pleasure and intimacy. However, if Paul's words are correct and the homosexual act does not fulfill God's intended purpose/use of the sexual act as set down in creation, then we only have one element that cannot be fulfilled through the homosexual sex act: procreation.

---

close association that makes it probable that Paul's appeal to 'nature' in this verse includes appeal to God's created order." Also cf. the references under meaning III in BDAG 1070; meaning III in LSJ 1964–65 and in Thayer 660. Jewett (*Romans,* 175) seems unaware of the distinction between the Stoic view of *physis,* which is according to *lex naturalis* and the biblical arguments, which argue from *physis* stemming from *ordo creatus naturalis.* Cf. 1 Corinthians 11, where Paul distinguishes the argument from *ordo creatus naturalis* (vv. 7–9) and the Stoic argument from *lex naturalis* (vv. 14–15). This error causes him to imagine that Paul is saying nothing about procreation in the sexual act.

18. In v. 26, God is said to have given *autous* (masculine) "them" over to degrading passions, and then speaks of *thēleiai autōn* (masculine) "their females" exchanging the natural function for the unnatural. Again, it is possible that *autous* refers to both Gentile men and women generically, but it is far more likely from a grammatical standpoint that *autōn* refers back to *autous* and speaks therefore of the Gentile men. If this is true, then the depravity to which the men are given over includes heterosexual non-procreative sexual acts as well as homosexual acts, which are also unproductive.

It is clear either way that Paul is condemning the sexual act in Romans 1:26–27 because it cannot fulfill the creation mandate "to be fruitful and multiply and fill up the earth" (Gen 1:27). It is also clear that Paul is making direct allusions both to Genesis 1:27–28 and Leviticus 18,[19] which may also allude to the Genesis passage in its use of the term "male" instead of "man." Paul purposely uses the words *thēlus*, "female," instead of *gunē*, "woman," and *arsēn*, "male," instead of *anēr*, "man," because these are the words used for the man and woman in the LXX translation of Genesis 1:27.[20]

This is also made clear by the fact that Paul states that the Gentiles know the ordinance of God. This is a fascinating statement since the Gentiles would not have known the Levitical law. Paul, however, as a Second Temple Jew of the day, links Genesis 1–11 as ordinances given to the entire world, not just to Israel. This is why he also argues from "nature" (i.e., what God has instituted at creation for all mankind to obey). Furthermore, since this mandate is given to the entire world, he seems to be saying that the ordinances in Leviticus 18 are ordinances that even the Gentiles know within themselves. Hence, Paul's argument stems from Genesis 1–11 generically and Genesis 1:27–28 specifically. Paul is therefore saying that the wrath of God that is revealed is a judgment that enslaves a society's practice of the sexual act to be non-procreative. In other words, God is reversing the creation of man and his community by giving them over to engage in non-covenant, non-productive sex acts.

It is for this reason that Luther called the practice of contraception "sodomy," since at the root of each sexual distortion lays the same basic, non-procreative sin. Calvin's comments, therefore, that Onan's act was that of murder of humanity, stems from the understanding that to engage in contraception is to engage in the reversal of humanity's creation upon the earth.

POTION MAKERS IN THE NEW TESTAMENT

The condemnation of contraception may also exist in a use of a New Testament word that is often passed over or misunderstood by the mod-

19. This seems clear if not merely from Romans 1: 32, where he states that they know the ordinance of God and that their actions are worthy of death, which is the penalty of God's ordinance in Leviticus 18.

20. LXX Genesis 1:27: "And God made man, according to God's image, male (*arsen*) and female (*thēlu*) He made them."

ern reader. The word often translated as "sorcery" in the New Testament denotes to the reader that the Bible is condemning either a fortune teller or some sort of Walt Disney version of a witch. However, the Greek words used are *pharmakeia*, "potion making,"[21] or *pharmakos*, "potion maker"[22] (Gal 5:20; Rev 9:21; 18:23; 21:8; 22:15), and they refer to the production of herbal medicines, or to put it in modern terms, "drugs."[23]

Ancient society's use for the potion maker/sorcerer often encompassed the control of fertility, either to enhance or to hinder it. One would not go to a secular pharmacist, as we perceive that today, to get contraceptive drugs; instead an individual would go to the *pharmakos*, "potion maker." This potion maker was also one who knew spells and incantations to affect fertility, and amulets and drugs were often used in conjunction with them.

The negative disposition of the New Testament toward these potions seems to indicate that these are contraceptives,[24] since medicine in general as well as fertility drugs would not have been condemned.[25] The only reason for such a condemnation of *pharmakeia* would be both the drugs'

---

21. MM, 664; LSJ, 1917; Thayer, 649.

22. See MM, 664; LSJ, 1917; *NIDNTT* 2:558; and meaning I in BDAG, 1050.

23. The *pharmak-* family of cognates is derived from the word *pharmakon*, "drug."

24. The prohibition against idolatry in the New Testament covers the occultic use of other spirits and gods in these rituals, and the spiritual nature of medicine is used even by Christians. Hence, it is not the spiritual nature of the potions that are emphasized here, but the drugs themselves.

25. The Christian understanding concerning medicines that heal are the same as seen in Sirach 38:1–15: "Honor physicians for their services, for the Lord created them; ²for their gift of healing comes from the Most High, and they are rewarded by the king. ³The skill of physicians makes them distinguished, and in the presence of the great they are admired. ⁴The Lord created medicines [*pharmaka*] out of the earth, and the sensible will not despise them. ⁵Was not water made sweet with a tree in order that its power might be known? ⁶And he gave skill to human beings that he might be glorified in his marvelous works. ⁷By them the physician heals and takes away pain; ⁸the pharmacist makes a mixture from them. God's works will never be finished; and from him health spreads over all the earth. ⁹My child, when you are ill, do not delay, but pray to the Lord, and he will heal you. ¹⁰Give up your faults and direct your hands rightly, and cleanse your heart from all sin. ¹¹Offer a sweet-smelling sacrifice and a memorial portion of choice flour, and pour oil on your offering, as much as you can afford. ¹²Then give the physician his place, for the Lord created him; do not let him leave you, for you need him. ¹³There may come a time when recovery lies in the hands of physicians, ¹⁴for they too pray to the Lord that he grant them success in diagnosis and in healing, for the sake of preserving life. ¹⁵He who sins against his Maker, will be defiant toward the physician."

hindrance of conception and/or many of their abortifacient qualities if one had already conceived.[26]

The practice's ties to sexually immoral acts in the Bible also give credence to its use. Perhaps the most striking example of this is found in the Apocalypse. The book uses the imagery of sexual immorality throughout its argument as an example of theological and moral corruption in society as well as within the church. Hence, purity of relationship with Christ, who is called the Church's "first love" and "bridegroom," is portrayed as a marriage relationship, and the Church's devotion to Christ is described as virginity (14:4). Likewise, committing acts of sexual immorality (2:16, 21–22; 3:4; 14:8; 17:2; 18:3; 19:2) is imagery employed to convey the doctrinal and ethical unfaithfulness of the apostate church. In fact, the false church is described as the city of Babylon, which is called "a harlot" in line with God's designation for unfaithful Israel in the Old Testament prophetic books.

An interesting contribution to the argument exists within the Apocalypse's condemnations of "Babylon the Great." Each time a condemnation is pronounced against the city, it is said that all the nations partake of her *porneia,* "sexual immorality" (14:8; 17:2; 18:3; 19:2). However in 18:23, the author switches from *porneia,* "sexual immorality," to *pharmakeia,* "the use of drugs/potions." In 21:8 and 22:15, the condemnations of "sexual immorality" and "the use of potions" appear together in alternating order as though the thought of one led to the thought of the other in the author's mind.[27] The fact that the two are so closely related that they can be interchanged as the author sees fit tells us that the drugs mentioned have something to do with sexual immorality, or to put it plainly, are being used in a sexually immoral way.

G. K. Beale notes this very thing when he states that fornication and sorcery are equated in the Apocalypse precisely because the Old

---

26. Cf. the *Testament of Reuben*, where the wife of Pharaoh sought to entice Joseph to sexual immorality and summoned the "magicians" to bring him "potions" (4:9). The argument that these potions were used as sexual enticements alone fails to note that most contraceptive drugs had dual purposes, one of which was their use as aphrodisiacs. In fact, it may have been the contraceptive promise to relieve one's sexual partner of the anxiety of having a child through the act that made the sexual act more enticing.

27. It is also interesting to note that murder and idolatry, the two other sins attributed to the use of contraception by the Fathers, appear around these two concepts in each instance as well.

Testament imagery it uses equates them.[28] He also notes Nahum 3:1–4, which states that Nineveh is full of murder due to her sexual immorality and "sorcery."[29] Hence, it is likely that the author has in mind contraceptive drugs used in the sexual act.

Noonan comments concerning the close relationship between the sexual act and the use of these potions:

> The close association between magic and contraceptives should be remarked. The herb potions were "rational" methods of achieving control of fertility in the sense that there could be a causal relation between the properties of the herbs and the consequences for the female reproductive system. But the herbs were the special resources of the magician. The homeopathic basis for a number of potions—the sterile willow causes sterility, sterile iron causes fertility—is one of the oldest forms of magic.[30]

These factors strongly suggest that *pharmakeia* in the New Testament negatively refers to distorted sexual practices in which drugs are taken to either prevent conception or terminate a child already conceived.

1 TIMOTHY

Finally, we see in the New Testament a confirmation that the woman's path to redemption includes childbearing.[31] 1 Timothy 2:15 says: "But [women] will be saved through the bearing of children if they continue in faith and love and sanctity with self-restraint."

Although the idea of raising children in godliness is implied, the emphasis of the word used here is on giving birth. Perhaps this is the case due to the fact that in Ephesian culture, as we have seen in larger Greco-Roman culture, women were encouraged, both by their husbands and each other, to have only a single male heir, and to practice various methods of birth control thereafter. Paul counters this by stating that it is through the act of childbearing that a woman is saved (i.e., sanctified and restored to that intended prelapsarian, godly role that was divinely

28. Beale, *The Book of Revelation*, 922–23.

29. Ibid., 923. See the other verses he quotes that equate sexual immorality with "sorcery." Ibid., 922–23.

30. Noonan, *Contraception*, 33.

31. If one remembers the woman's purpose in creation according to Genesis 2, and the subsequent curse of that purpose in Genesis 3, then Paul's argument for her restoration here becomes very poignant.

instituted for the woman), implying that one ought therefore to do so without hindrance. Of course, Paul does not say that this is the only factor through which she is saved, but that one of the primary elements of a woman's salvation is her restoration to motherhood. Through it she becomes what the woman was to be before the Fall—not only a mother of the living, but a godly mother who raises her children in the presence of God. Her glorification of God, therefore, comes through her practice of childbearing (i.e., obedience to the original command given by God in Gen 1:28 that counteracts her disobedience in 3:6).

In 5:9–10, Paul states that only a widow who has brought up children is to be considered eligible for the assistance provided by the Church.

> ⁹A widow is to be put on the list only if she is not less than sixty years old, [having been] the wife of one man, ¹⁰having a reputation for good works (i.e., if she has brought up children, if she has shown hospitality to strangers, if she has washed the saints' feet, if she has assisted those in distress); if she has devoted herself to every good work.

Note that the types of godliness in which she partakes are of the highest deeds in Scripture. The elements of godly character, "sandwiched" with an *inclusio* in between "having a reputation for good works" and "devoted to every good work," are described as such. Whereas being sixty years old is a neutral element, and being the wife of one man is an abstention from the evil of adultery, the other elements mentioned are actually the *doing* of good works. Hence, the good works mentioned are bringing up children, showing hospitality to strangers, serving other Christians, and helping the needy. All of these elements have to do with the giving and preservation of life, which is what good works primarily are in the Bible. Paul here places the highest of importance on childbearing as a good work, which here serves as a major indication of a woman's genuine relationship with God.

Paul then tells us that only if her works prove her claim is she to be supported financially by the Church. We see then that Paul places the procreative sexual act as of primary importance to one's claim of godliness. A once-married woman who did not have children, and was able to do so, was considered suspect of the crime of contraception. Hence, these passages serve as an indication that the Apostle Paul condemned such a practice. If nothing else, these two passages at least argue against its exclusive use; but I would also reaffirm that the New Testament's teaching concerning morality is not based on situation but is instead absolute. If this is true, then Paul's condemnation of a woman's refusal to have children in general would also condemn a woman's refusal to have a child specifically. In other words, the standard of godliness is the bearing of children, and anything that falls short of that (whether a specific instance or the specific instances that together make up a general lifestyle) is to abstain from the doing of good. Hence, Paul's statements here would uniformly condemn the use of contraception for any reason.

The argument from the Bible is much stronger than I would suspect some to have previously believed. This perception stems not from exegetical study of the Scripture but from a selected reading, and occasionally a misunderstood translation of the text. It is clear from all of these factors, however, that the Bible condemns the use of contraception among God's people.

The point, of course, is that the New Testament is not silent on the issue of contraception for five reasons: (1) The New Testament teaching on morality implicitly assumes the Old Testament teaching against unproductive sexual acts rather than contradicting it;[32] (2) often when the New Testament uses the words for "sexual immorality" it is negatively addressing our subject explicitly; (3) the passage in Romans 1–2 condemns the practice either directly or by implication; (4) there is most likely a condemnation of the practice within the condemnation of using certain drugs closely associated with the sexual act; and (5) the New Testament reaffirms the positive Old Testament teaching that the primary use of the sexual act is for procreation by stating that those who have a genuine relationship with God practice it.[33]

---

32. Matthew 5:17–19: [17]"Do not think that I came to abolish the Law or the Prophets; I did not come to abolish but to fulfill. [18]"For truly I say to you, until heaven and earth pass away, not the smallest letter or stroke shall pass from the Law until all is accomplished. [19]"Whoever then annuls one of the least of these commandments, and teaches others [to do] the same, shall be called least in the kingdom of heaven; but whoever keeps and teaches [them], he shall be called great in the kingdom of heaven."

33. Cf. the New Testament emphasis on giving what is needed to survive to those who are in need of it, i.e., the giving of the life one has to another who needs it so that they themselves may live (Matt 25:31–46; Jam 1:27; 2:14–16; 1 John 3:15–18).

Part Three

The Systematic Argument

Every man's life is a plan of God

—Horace Bushnell

6

The Argument against Contraception
from Systematics

THE BIGGEST PROBLEM IN the debate over the use of contraception is that two Christians who discuss the issue are often arguing from two different worldviews. Although many think that both are "Christian" in nature, nothing could be further from the truth. We have consistently maintained that there is but one view for the Christian when it comes to the use of contraception, not many. One view is gained from a Christian worldview and one from what can only be described as a naturalistic worldview. For instance, the typical person in favor of the use of contraception will argue similarly to the following:

1. I believe God decides to give us every child that we have.

2. I believe we have a responsibility to decide for ourselves how many children we have.

These two propositions seem contradictory in nature, but the meanings behind them clarify what the person is saying:

1. I believe God gives us a generic ability to have children at creation and/or then blesses our choices whether to have them thereafter.

2. I therefore believe it is the responsibility of each person to decide for him or herself how many children they will have.

Note the change that has taken place in the clarification between the two former statements and the latter. The first set of propositions is redefined by the second. The first set conveys the idea that God decides to give an individual every child that he or she has but then states that it is the responsibility of the individual to decide how many children to have. The second set of propositions, however, states that God is really a passive agent in conception. He either gives children only *in the sense that*

He gives the *ability* but then has no creative interaction thereafter; or He is passive until the individual decides to have a child, and He then will intercede and accommodate the wishes of the person.

However, both of these assume a non-Christian view of God's interaction in conception. The first assumption is purely philosophic naturalism in the form of an altered form of deism. In this view, God simply sets up the world and its functions, but has no direct interaction except to sustain the abilities of his creation. He is, therefore, only an indirect cause of events that take place in the world, but not the direct cause. He may manipulate things from a distance and direct natural courses, but he is not within those natural courses himself. Likewise, he creates only the function to have children, but not the children themselves—not directly anyway.

THE PLAGUE OF NATURALISM

It is this philosophy of naturalism that pervades the modern evangelical's thinking of the natural world and hinders him or her from believing in a supernatural agent who uses the natural world as a means. Naturalism carries with it an assumption that "whatever is *in* nature is caused *by* nature."[1] Geisler sums up a typical naturalist way of thinking about the world as follows:

1. Science qua science must assume that all events are naturally explainable.

2. But if all events are scientifically explainable then no events are supernatural or miraculous.

3. Therefore, science as science eliminates the supernatural.[2]

The first premise is that all events are explainable. What is explainable, to the modern evangelical, is that natural biological processes (which may have been created originally by God and even may be sustained by Him currently) produce children. Since it is explainable, per the second premise, it is not supernatural. Since it is explainable, and therefore not supernatural, the natural human biological processes create children on their own. They can do so without God making any decision about it, since He has already decided to give the ability. He does not need to per-

1. Geisler, *Christian Apologetics*, 270.
2. Ibid., 271.

sonally produce a child through the biological means because the biological processes are able to accomplish it on their own.

Since this is the case, one can decide if he or she will let the biological processes take their natural course or interrupt their natural course, since the individual would only be making a decision as whether to allow or hinder his or her mere bodily functions from creating a child. Ironically, however, if he or she does allow the conception of a child to take place, then he or she will often attribute the creation of that child to God as well. If, however, he or she chooses to hinder it, then apart from an ability granted, God has nothing to do with the creation of a child.

Another idea is that perhaps God decides to give a child to a person only after the person decides to have one. This idea is contradictory, but the person seldom notices it. If God decides to give a child only after the wishes of the individual, then what would be the need of any sort of contraception? Usually, however, both of these views are used in conjunction with one another. We choose to use contraception as a way of saying no to God (either to His initial provision of our ability to procreate or to His normal activity of giving children unless we say no to Him). In other words, unless we tell God, by using contraception, that we don't want Him to make children through us, He will give them to us.

Of course, neither one of these views is compatible with a Christian worldview. Both of them assume God is passive in the conception of life. Once that presupposition is removed, and an individual comes to the belief that God is active in the decision, then the argument advocating the use of contraception falls apart.

Furthermore, the idea that God is mindlessly giving children to people unless they wisely stop Him from doing so is so far from the biblical view of God and mankind that we will not display the legions of evidence to the contrary here. I will only mention that the argument that one who does not use birth control will automatically have lots of children can be, although not necessarily if understood correctly, just as naturalistic as the one that claims that the biological processes alone give us children.

The key here is the assumption of naturalism, which is then applied to the God of the Bible. A syncretism takes place between the two worldviews: a supernatural God functioning within a philosophically naturalistic framework. The problem with this is that supernaturalism, which is what one sees in the Bible, and naturalism, which is the worldview created by certain views of God's absence in the world, found within such streams of thought as atheism and agnosticism, are diametrically opposed to one another.

Naturalism largely stems from three views of God: atheism, agnosticism, and deism, none of which are biblical views of God. In these views, God is either absent from the everyday processes of the world and life or His interaction with it is generalized to simply that of a cosmic maintenance man. He either doesn't exist, is not known to exist, and therefore cannot be factored into our reasoning, or He exists but leaves the details of nature unrevealed. The human plight is simply to discover them for oneself and use the power of nature as one sees fit. In other words, regardless of where the natural processes of the world came from, God is not to be factored into how we think of them.

Now, no biblically informed Christian would intentionally believe such a thing. Unfortunately, however unintentional it may be, the Christian born and raised in a society that assumes the worldview of naturalism within its bioethical rationale adopts just such a view of life. But it is not adopted alone. It is then combined with Christianity to create a hybrid view of God and His workings in the world. This syncretism sees God interacting in the world He initially empowered, but only on the level of the miraculous. For the modern evangelical, everyday events are naturally occurring events and have no need of any supernatural explanation. God intercedes only miraculously, in a world that would largely go on to function without Him, in order to accomplish His goals for certain things; but He is not the source of all of these natural events. When He is not interacting miraculously in the world, He is simply sustaining the universe's abilities (like a power source). So God is much closer and more personal than the naturalistic view would have Him be (a result of Christian influence) but further away than the Bible indicates (a result of the person's naturalistic influences).

Hence, as stated before, the argument in favor of the use of contraception, being rooted in the idea of God's absence from the conception event, stems not from Christianity, but from atheism/agnosticism/deism/philosophic naturalism. Hence, the arguments used to support the use of contraception among Christians are not Christian arguments at all.

Many Christians have noted this problem in other areas of their lives and sought to counter their naturalistic tendencies by reconciling those various aspects of their lives to a Christian worldview. Unfortunately, however, when it comes to the issue of contraception (because the mod-

The Argument against Contraception from Systematics

ern Church's view concerning the purpose of the sexual act is identical to the culture's), the average churchgoer's view of the sexual act remains corrupted.

The view of the Church has always been a supernatural one. By the term "supernatural," of course, I do not mean that the conception of an individual is a result of God bypassing any natural biological function. Such a radical dichotomy exists only for those who divorce the supernatural and natural worlds as contradictory to one another rather than seeing them as complementary. Instead, the term "supernatural" used here means that God is the primary source of the conception event, and the natural function of the biological process is the means through which He brings about that decision.

As an example to this, we know that the baby is formed by natural processes within the body, and yet the Scripture tells us that it is God who forms our inward parts and forms us in the womb. It is not that either God forms us *or* natural processes do. It is that God uses the biological process, which He created through the male and female sexual act to make a human being, to create a human in the conception event.

FEARFULLY AND WONDERFULLY MADE

The most common presupposition, hailing from a naturalistic worldview, can be seen in the following sentiment: God sustains the ability given to humans to make a child and that is the extent to which He is involved in the process. His interaction with creation at that point is no different than Him giving humans the ability to eat or sleep. The human has the choice to eat food or to take a nap—all within his or her responsible steward-ship of each. The choice is therefore a human one, even though God in His providence sustains our abilities to do so. This is more of an indirect interaction, where God sustains the ability, but does not interact directly with the biological process in order to cause it to conceive a child.

Unfortunately, for those who make this argument, this is not the picture we have received in the Bible. What we have in Scripture is God *directly* interacting with the biological process. This direct interaction is one of creation. It is not the same as an endowed ability that is simply in-directly sustained by God, but is a direct act on God's part—a conscience decision and intention to create a child through the sexual act.

The Bible states over and over again that conception is not a purely natural event, but that God is the one who chooses to give, or to hold back, a woman's fertility. He is the one who chooses to open the womb (Gen 25:21; 29:31; 30:22; Ps 113:9; Lk 1:7, 13) or causes a woman to be barren (Gen 20:17–18; 25:21; 30:2; 1 Sam 1:5–6; Hos 9:14).[3]

In Psalm 139:13–16, we find the biblical view of conception. David speaks to the Lord in acknowledgement of how he came to exist.

> [13]For You formed my inward parts;
> You wove me in my mother's womb.
> [14]I will give thanks to You, for I am fearfully and wonderfully made;
> Your works are beyond comprehension, and my soul knows it very well. [15]My frame was not hidden from You, when I was made in secret, skillfully wrought in the depths of the earth;
> [16]Your eyes have seen my unformed substance; and the days that were ordained [for me] were all written in Your book, when as yet there was not one of them.

The word in v. 13 that is often translated as "formed" is actually the Hebrew word *qānā(h)* we saw in Genesis 4:1. As we discussed before, this word is often used in archaic texts to refer to creation through a sexual act. In Ugaritic literature, it is the word used for the creation of mankind *via* the sexual act between the patriarchal god 'Ilu and the goddess 'Aṯirtu (or El and Asherah). The word here then tells us that it is God who creates[4] the very inward parts of a human being through the sexual act at conception. The term *kilyā(h)* literally means "kidneys," but in poetic texts, like this one, may refer instead to the inward part of the person, the seat of

---

3. In Job 15:34, the phrase, "the company of the polluted man is sterile" may refer either to the fact that those who are godless use contraceptive methods, as the secular nations of Job's day in fact do, or that God causes them to be sterile because they are polluted. The word *ḥāneph* is used in contexts where the violations are against the covenant in either taking a life or sexual immorality, which would make it an interesting study for our present subject. However, nothing would definitively lead to one interpretation *versus* the other. Either option, however, would contribute to our argument from different angles.

4. To state again, by "creation" I do not mean that God creates something completely absent from, or different from, the physical (and perhaps even spiritual) materials that belong to the parents but that He makes a child from them. The argument against the use of contraception then has nothing to do with the *creationist/traducionist* debate, unless that traducionism would argue that God is not personally and directly involved, in which case it is atheistic in theory or practice.

moral thought.[5] In other words, God creates personhood in the very act of conception.

The second phrase, "You wove me in my mother's womb," uses the word *sākak*, "to weave together," which has its closest parallel in Job 10:11. The idea is that of something unformed being knit together. In fact, v. 16 talks about God's knowledge of the Psalmist's *gōlem*, "unformed substance." Although some lexicons translate the word as "embryo," the word appears only once in the Hebrew Bible, and the cognate information, the context, and the parallel in Job 10, which speaks of the pre-embryonic stage at conception, would indicate that the word refers to a pre-embryonic person who has yet to be put together.[6]

The Hebrew word for "secret" in v. 15b speaks of the womb of the Psalmist's mother, where God puts his substance together. The synonymous parallelism in v. 15c describes the "making" in 15b as "weaving together" and the "secret" place as the "depths of the earth," an ancient image often used to describe the womb.

Job 10:8–11 is very similar to the passage in Psalm 139.

> [8]Your hands fashioned and put me all together, and would You destroy me?
> [9]Remember now, that You have made me from clay;
> and would You turn me into dust again?
> [10]Did You not pour me out like milk
> and curdle me like cheese;
> [11]Clothe me with skin and flesh,
> and knit me together with bones and sinews?

Here we have a very vivid description of the making of a human being from the unformed substance at conception to the putting together of the embryo. Job tells us that God is involved in every step of the process. He is not some distant deity who originally endowed us with a procreative ability and now steps back to watch us create children on our own. He is the God who creates life, all life, at all times.

He actively chooses to create through the sexual act. Hence, the text uses imagery of the emission of semen as something that is poured out like milk. He actively chooses to make a human from the man and the woman. The text, therefore, also uses imagery of the semen mixing to-

---

5. See *NIDOTTE* 2:656, where our very verse is said to refer to God as "the Creator of this moral/ethical center."

6. The translation in *HALOTSE* (1:194) as a "formless mass" seems closest.

gether with the fluid/egg of the woman as congealed like cheese (i.e., from a liquid substance to a solid). He actively chooses to put a human together from the unformed substance. Hence, the text speaks about the human being given skin, flesh, bones, and sinews.

If God's decision to make a child is a necessary part of conception, and without that divine decision a child would not be made, is the use of contraception to undermine that decision not a human act seeking to prevent God from making a child?

What else can be concluded but that God is intimately involved in the sexual act in order to create a future human person? When we seek to counter that divine action, therefore, we are not combating mere natural, biological processes that function on their own, but God Himself.[7] The arguments then that naively assume the presuppositions of philosophic naturalism are clearly unbiblical and thus should be discarded.

ALL MY GOOD PURPOSE

Job 23:13 tells us that God does whatever He wants. This is a fascinating statement in that it displays that God never acts against His will. He always does what He wishes to do. The creation of children is no exception. We have already seen that God's participation is essential to the creation of a human being, and apart from Him no human can be made. Now we turn to the following syllogism in order to see this argument more clearly.

Premise One: God chooses to make every child.

Premise Two: No child is made apart from His choice.

Premise Three: He never does anything against His moral will.

Premise Four: Creating the child is His moral will, since He is the One doing it.

Conclusion: Therefore, the person using contraceptive methods, so that the child is not created, is going against God's moral will.

---

7. Cf. also Job 31:15: "Did not He who made me in the womb make him, and the same one fashion us in the womb?"

Psalm 22:9: "Yet You are He who brought me forth from the womb; You made me trust [when] upon my mother's breasts."

Ecclesiastes 11:5: "Just as you do not know the path of the wind and how bones [are formed] in the womb of the pregnant woman, so you do not know the activity of God who makes all things."

Let's look at the above premises more closely:

Premise One: God chooses to make every child.

There are two biblical ideas at work in this single statement. The first is that God is the one who actually makes each and every child. The Bible never presents children as solely the product of two humans but indicates that God is intimately involved in the process. Without His making a child one cannot be made through the sexual act.

The second is that the child, regardless of being wanted by the human parents, is wanted by God. Being perfect, He never makes a mistake, and He always does what He wishes. Therefore, He chooses to make every child.

Premise Two: No child is made apart from His choice

If only God can make a child, and the biological processes apart from Him are incapable of doing so, then this leads to only one conclusion: God choosing to create is *the* key element in the creation of a child. In fact, when all of the natural processes are non-functional, He shows us that occasionally He will still create a child, although this is not the norm. The point is that if God is the key factor in the creation of a child, then no child can be made without Him choosing to do so.

Premise Three: He never does anything against His moral will

If Scripture teaches us anything, it is that God does not do anything He does not want to do. As discussed before, Job states that He does whatever He wishes. Psalm 115:3 contrasts Him with man-made gods who are often directed by the choices of men, and instead, states, "Our God is in the heavens, He does whatever He pleases." Psalm 135:6, in showing that He is above all other gods, states that "whatever the Lord pleases, He does." No one forces His hand, nor does He make any mistakes. He has told us in the Scripture that the making of a child through the sexual act is His moral will, and thus, one who uses the sexual act appropriately is in accord with the will of God. One who does not is moving contrary to His will.

Therefore, God is not bound by anything beyond Himself. If He chooses to make a child, He wants to do it. It is His will.

Premise Four: Making the child is His moral will

Hence, since God is seeking to make a child through the sexual act, and He never does anything against His will, it is His will to make the child. By "God's will" I mean to say His moral will, not His decretive will. God's moral will is for a person to obey all of His commands, but God's decretive will is His plan, knowing that a person will not obey all of His commands. For instance, it may be God's moral will that no one is ever murdered, but since people will murder and be murdered, His decretive will plans for those murders and the consequences that take place from them. One cannot, therefore, argue that whatever happens is what God wanted morally to happen, but instead that it is that which God planned for in a world filled with the wicked decisions of humans. When I say that God wills for every child to come into existence, then, I am referring to His moral will, not His decretive one. Likewise, a person will be held accountable on judgment day for whether he or she followed God's moral will, not His decretive.

Conclusion: Therefore, the person using contraception so that the child is not made is going against God's moral will.

The conclusion is that the person who uses contraception is not simply limiting a biological function, nor simply being responsible with his or her body, but is directly attacking an act of God. He or she is going against God's hand in the act of conception and, hence, is going against His will. All such acts, as the Church has always concluded, therefore, are acts of rebellion. God wants to make a child through the sexual act, and the person wants to prevent Him from doing so.

BEFORE YOU WERE FORMED I KNEW YOU

We also see God's knowledge of future persons in Psalm 139:16. The Psalmist states not only that God formed him in the womb but that his entire life was mapped out by God before he ever came into existence. Similar to this is Jeremiah 1:5, where God states that he knew an individual (Jeremiah in this case) before He had formed him in the womb. In Hebrews 7:9–10, Levi, who lived about two hundred years after Abraham fathered Isaac, is said to have existed already in his "loins." The term translated as "loins" here refers to the genitals as the place in which semen is stored. As Millard Erickson initially observes, "Taken at face value, this comment would argue for the humanity not only of an unborn fetus, but even of persons who have not yet been conceived."[8] This shows that, although we cannot see the future person to be made, and therefore may feel indifferent toward that person, God does see and know the person he has not yet made.

In God's perspective, then, the person is alive before coming into existence. With this in view, it would seem odd that destroying the person, whether at conception or thereafter, would be considered murder by the Almighty in the latter but not in the former. If there is the intention of a person to wipe out another person known by God, there would seem to be little difference between the act of contraception, abortion, or the murder of a post-natal human being (i.e., infanticide). The question with which the modern evangelical must come to terms is this: Is contraception murder if it intentionally wipes out the existence of a human being?

YE WILL BE LIKE GOD

Another theological argument is that God has reserved the making and taking of life as His right. One who seeks to take control of these (i.e., the bringing about of a human being or the destruction of one) is really seeking to become God, since it is the usurping of His power.

In 1 Samuel 2:6, Hannah gives thanks in a prayer to God for opening her womb, she proclaims: "The Lord kills and makes alive; He brings down to Sheol and raises up."

In Deuteronomy 32:39, God declares that He alone is God and therefore He alone is to control life and death:

> Understand now that I, I am He, and there is no god besides Me; it
> is I Myself who puts to death and gives life. I have wounded and it
> is I who heal, and there is no one who can deliver from My hand.

We find in these passages the intent of God to reserve both the giving and the taking of life as His domain. We may partake in both within the boundaries He has set for us, but no one is to seek control of them apart from those boundaries.[9]

8. Erickson, *Christian Theology*, 554. Although Erickson goes on to argue that the text is a better argument for traducianism, I would not see these as mutually exclusive options.

9. For instance, we participate in God's giving of life through the sexual act, or the taking of life through war or in the punishment of a crime. However, as one ought not to

It is interesting to note that in Genesis 2 and 3, the man and woman are naked and unashamed (an idea expressing the fearlessness of the sexual act). When sin (i.e., the attempt to become like God) enters in, however, they are ashamed of their nakedness (an idea expressing fear of the sexual act). The text may, therefore, be a subtle hint that when humans attempt to play God, they have a distorted and fearful view of the sexual act's purpose to bring forth children, which causes them to engage in sex in a shameful, non-multiplying way. It is no mere coincidence that the first Fall (i.e., that of Adam and Eve), which combines the elements of the deification of the self and sexual distortion, expresses itself again in the second Fall (i.e., that of Ham and his father Noah) through sexual distortion, and in the third Fall (i.e., that of Babel) through self-deification.[10] The act of playing God seems to be intimately connected to a distorted view of the sexual act and its purpose.[11]

Ultimately, therefore, if the decision to make a child is God's decision, then mankind has become a god in that he now chooses whether or not a child is made. He will now choose whether future persons will be allowed to exist.

Does this mean that humans can thwart God's decision by using birth control? God surely knows that a couple will use it and thwart the conception. Does that mean, as some charge, that we are downplaying God's sovereignty? "Surely," they say, "God brings about what He wants. Therefore, there is no need to worry about whether one uses contraception or not, since whatever the Lord wants will come about."

However, this fails to note that God has allowed for us to sin within His sovereign rule. One could make the exact argument for those who have an abortion. Can man thwart God? Obviously God was giving a

---

take life beyond those boundaries, he or she should also abstain from seeking to control the giving of life, specifically by preventing it. The irony is that the contraceptive act may be seen as a desire to control both life and death, and therefore it is the ultimate form of self-worship and blasphemy, where one raises oneself to the position of God.

10. It is, of course, not that these are literally second and third lapsarian events, but instead are meant to reflect that the postlapsarian age continues even though the flood had "cleansed" the earth.

11. Note that, in each case, the humans involved either attempt to *see* something with their own eyes, or God confounds their wisdom (as in the case of Babel) in order that they may not understand and become like Him. The point here is that the seeking after deity is the quest to see and make decisions based on one's own understanding, rather than to trust in God.

child. If He really wanted you to have it, it would have survived the abortion. Any evil can be justified this way. Such reasoning falls apart as soon as the individual realizes the absurdity of the argument being made.

Could God miraculously override a contraceptive attempt? Of course, just as He could miraculously override an abortion, or someone shooting you between the eyes. But if He has let sin occur, He usually lets it run its course; and the negative effects from sin lay waste to our becoming like Christ. They are devastating to the lives of others. They are acts of defiance against God's lordship and fully deserve the due penalty for such evil.

CONTRACEPTION AND THE WORSHIP OF THE SELF

Often, one of the components of the pro-contraceptive lifestyle is that it is practiced not for the glory and goals of God but to fulfill the individual's goals, whether they be secular or religious in their intentions. The one who decides, and also provides the basis for what is decided, does so because that person has only herself or himself in mind. God is not Lord of the person's thoughts and decisions. God is often given control over what cannot be controlled by the individual (like eternal destination), and the individual is therefore under the illusion that God is Lord because he or she trusts this aspect of life to Him.

However, this is the equivalent of giving authority to the weather, since a person cannot control it anyway. If an invention were made whereby the individual could control it, one would cease to hand that authority over to it. Hence, it is not a voluntary submission to the control of another but a forced submission. When the submission is no longer forced, the individual proves true allegiance by claiming that control for oneself. It is in this act that an individual is able to discern that he or she may have never come into a submissive relationship to God at all. One may give God authority over oneself at death (i.e., eternal destination) because the individual cannot control that, but in the area of contraception, where the person can control the outcome of the sexual act, he or she does not relinquish control to God. This is what we call the worship of the self. It is an act that seeks to retain control for the self that should be relinquished to God. True worship is in submission to the will of another. In fact, the biblical words for worship literally mean "to bow down to." If one does not yield to God in the area of the sexual act, then any claim that of being submission to God as Lord is false. In fact, the Lord tells us that many who claim to be Christians will come to Him on judgment day with evangelism, miraculous feats, and great displays of divine authority under their belts; but the Lord will declare to them, "I never knew you; depart from me, you who practice lawlessness" (Matt 7:23). The word for "lawlessness" is *anomia*, which essentially means in this context that the person is not ruled by the Lord, but instead by the self. There never was a servant-to-lord relationship with Christ; hence, He never knew that person in a salvific way.

We can, therefore, see that true Christianity exists when Christ is Lord of the person in all things, and false Christianity thrives in giving over only what the person cannot control already. When this is applied to the sexual act, one can easily see that the lordship of Christ is scarcely to be seen within the modern evangelical conscience. One thinks only of what he or she wants because he or she is the only god who needs to be pleased. God does not need to be obeyed in controllable circumstances because He is not the true Lord of the individual. In fact, God Himself is often used by the individual as a means to please the self, rather than sacrificing the self to please God. The hostility, of course, that arises when this issue is presented to the self-ruled individual, can be almost solely attributed to the fact that two claimants to the throne are at odds. When the Lord finally comes to take His place over the individual, that person wants nothing of it. Although this does not prove that this is the case in the area of contraception, the reaction one has when confronted with the argument may, in fact, uncover a hidden self-worship and, therefore, be of service to anyone who wishes to relinquish control to the Lord.

PART FOUR

The Practical Argument

*The Christian home is the Master's workshop, where the processes
of character molding are silently, lovingly, faithfully
and successfully carried on.*

—RICHARD M. MILNES

7

Practical Arguments against Contraception

IT SHOULD BE NOTED that practical and pragmatic arguments are not the same. In practical arguments, the thing argued for or against is related to everyday life. These arguments are largely applications, but are still biblical and theological applications nonetheless. In pragmatic arguments, however, the thing argued for or against is largely conveyed in what is perceived as convenient or temporarily beneficial to the situation. They are descriptive (i.e., arguing from what occurs in life and culture) instead of prescriptive (i.e., arguing for what should occur in life and culture). As such, this section is concerned with practical, not pragmatic arguments (as the latter are completely unbiblical).

AN INHERITANCE OF YHWH

In Psalm 127:3–5, we are told that children are the inheritance of the Lord.

> ³Behold, children are the Lord's inheritance,
> The fruit of the womb is a reward.
> ⁴Like arrows in the hand of a warrior,
> so are the children of one's youth.
> ⁵How blessed is the man whose quiver is full of them;
> They will not be ashamed when they speak with their enemies in
> the gate.

Here it is evident that children are presented as a positive blessing given by God to His people as a reward for their service to Him. The term *naḥᵃlat YHWH* in 1 Samuel 26:19 refers to the people of YHWH's community who worship the true God as opposed to false gods. In 2 Samuel 20:19, it also refers to the people of God.[1] The "inheritance of the Lord"

1. See also 21:3; Jeremiah 10:16; 51:19.

is referring to God's giving of covenant children to his people as a reward for their service to Him. The inheritance itself is a portion, a possession, of the one who gives it. In this case, that One is God Himself. Covenant children, therefore, are God's possessions, who are given to His people as both rewards to worship Him as well as means through which to worship Him. These children are one of the ways the covenant community survives and has further influence in the world. The *śākār*, "reward," is a payment, a wage, for being God's people. The bearing and rearing of these children in the Lord will counter an opponent's argument at the judgment that the man did not further the covenant community's existence (and thus was not a *geber* "nobleman" for God's purposes) because he did not raise children to the Lord.

Likewise, children are given to Christians by God to further the community in both number and influence in the world. Having and raising them is an essential part of being a member of God's community. Although Christians can fulfill this by preaching the gospel and making spiritual children through discipleship of non-biological children, one would be hard pressed to argue that this means that a Christian couple could forego the responsibility of having biological children to raise in the Lord.

First of all, who among God's faithful people would give up the opportunity to have individuals who not only give them a few minutes of their time to be discipled by them but their entire young lives (at a time in their lives when they are most receptive)? Discipleship among Christians ought to start first in the home, and that discipleship should be unlimited both in quality and quantity. No one would argue that it would be morally acceptable to desire to disciple only a couple of people instead of many. The desire to partake in the inheritance of the Lord, that is, to raise His children to be worshippers of Him, is the desire of every true Christian couple, since it is God's desired purpose for His family.

Therefore, to have and raise covenant children is to seek the perpetuation and influence of the covenant community in the world without limitation. The desire for every believer ought to be the perseverance of the community's vitality and its greater influence and light in this dark place. In no other way can this be accomplished to a greater degree than with a believer's children, who have a greater capacity to learn, a more open mind to do so, and the largest amount of time to give to the task of being discipled. To shun one's discipleship responsibility in this area is to reject the inheritance, the reward, and the defense against claims of disingenuous membership to God's community (see 1 Tim 5:9–10); and ultimately it is to reject a large application of the Lord's commandment given in the Great Commission (Mark 16:15).

MALACHI AND THE GREAT COMMISSION

Behind the Malachi text, as well as all of the texts that prohibit the marrying of a religiously foreign wife,[2] may be the principle of the sexual act's purpose in having and raising covenant children. The text of Malachi 2:11–16 reads as follows:

> [11]"Judah has dealt treacherously, and an abomination has been committed in Israel and in Jerusalem; for Judah has profaned the sanctuary of the Lord which He loves and has married the daughter of a foreign god. [12]"[As] for the man who does this, may the Lord cut off from the tents of Jacob [everyone] who awakes and answers, or who presents an offering to the Lord of hosts. [13]"This is another thing you do: you cover the altar of the Lord with tears, with weeping and with groaning, because He no longer regards the offering or accepts [it with] favor from your hand. [14]"Yet you say, 'For what reason?' Because the Lord has been a witness between you and the wife of your youth, against whom you have dealt treacherously, though she is your companion and your wife by covenant. [15]Did He not make [them] one? (And the life giving spirit belongs to Him.) And why did He make the one [flesh]? Because He was seeking the covenant children. Therefore, guard your life-giving spirits; and do not deal treacherously with the wife of your youth. [16]"For I hate divorce," says the Lord, the God of Israel, "and him who covers his garment with wrong," says the Lord of hosts. "So take heed to your spirit, so that you do not deal treacherously."

There are a few reasons why I would argue that this text combines the condemnation stemming from the purpose of God through the sexual act with the condemnation of marrying "the daughter of a foreign god" (v. 11). First it must be noted that the entire passage is focused not simply on a cultic purity but on a sexual one. The sexual overtones of the passage, and hence the sexual error being made here, are overwhelming.[3]

2. Exodus 34:15–16; Deuteronomy 7:3; Joshua 23:12; Ezra 9:2; Nehemiah 10:30; 2 Corinthians 6:14—7:1; 1 Timothy 5:11–12.

3. Glazier-McDonald, *Malachi: The Divine Messenger* (193–206) concurs. Contra

The statement in v. 10 is that Israel has one Father who "created" Israel as a familial-centered, covenant community. The act of marrying a foreign woman is unfaithfulness to that community, which exists to bring up children to the Lord. Instead, the religious education of the children that comes about through that unholy union is compromised. At this point, not many theologians would disagree that the act of marrying/ having sexual relations with an unbeliever is treachery in that it breaks the contract, not only between the man and wife, but between God and community; but the text also indicates that this sin is a form of sexual immorality in that it uses the sexual act not for God's purpose of creating covenant children but for the autonomous, selfish purposes of the individual.

In v. 11, the act is condemned as a *tôʿēbā(h)*, "abomination," or "distortion." The reader will remember that this word is the chosen designation for the judgments against the non-procreative/non-covenantal sexual acts in Leviticus 18. The word in the Hebrew Bible speaks of something that is of an inferior class to something else, a distorted or unacceptable thing. It is possible that what is considered *tôʿēbā(h)* here is simply the marrying of foreign wives, but coupled with the other statements, the passage becomes more clear.

In vv. 10–11, the word *ḥālal* "pollute" is used to describe Israel's actions. The word appears in contexts condemning the immoral sexual acts of incest (Gen 49:4) and the sacrificing of children (Lev 18:21; 20:3). The word, in general, speaks of the polluting of something holy. Once again, this can be seen as polluting the community alone, but it is the final two elements of the passage that show us otherwise.

In v. 12, the judgment is that the Lord is to cut off the man who practices this from the tents of Jacob.[4] This same judgment is applied to the person who practices a non-procreative act in Leviticus 18 (see v. 29). It is not only the man, who is cut off, however, but the woman and her

---

Peterson, (*Zecheriah 9–14 and Malachi*, 205–6), however, I reject the notion that the marriage relationship here is primarily metaphorical for YHWH's relationship with Israel. This pericope simply does not read that way when compared to other metaphorical representations of YHWH as Israel's husband, and makes much more sense in the context of covenant faithfulness to YHWH through faithfulness to produce covenant children through the marital relationship.

4. This also harks back to the event at Baal-Peor, where the Israelites defiled themselves by having sexual relations with pagan women (Numbers 25).

children as well.[5] This physical death is preceded by a spiritual one in which God no longer gives a hearing to the prayers of the guilty individuals (Mal. 2:13).

Finally, v. 15 states:

> Did He not make [them] one?[6] (And the life-giving spirit[7] belongs to Him.) And why did He make the one [flesh]? Because He was seeking covenant children.[8] Therefore, guard your life-giving spirits; and do not deal treacherously with the wife of your youth.

This passage indicates, through the use of the creation account, that the male and female were made one flesh in order to raise up offspring for God. The divorce of the covenant wife in order to marry pagan women for the purpose of sexual pleasure, rather than for covenant children, is condemned by God. In fact, He uses the strong statement that He "hates divorce" in v. 16; and this, doubtless, refers to divorce among His covenant people. This act of marital unfaithfulness, specifically here the trading of covenant women for non-covenant women, perpetrated by the Israelite men, distorts the purpose for the sexual act by not seeking *covenant* children through it; and along with it, has the potential to destroy the covenant community itself.

Therefore, the act of divorce, and especially the act of marrying an unbeliever, is the act of destroying the purpose of marriage, sex, and community among God's people. This is true because the primary reason for marriage is to come together in the sexual act so that God can create a person, who in turn can be discipled by the covenant parents. The application to contraception is made with ease in that the contraceptive act does not allow a covenant child to be conceived through the sexual act in the first place. It would seem odd to conclude that God is horribly angry

---

5. Mitchell et al., *A Critical and Exegetical Commentary,* 50.

6. Glazier-McDonald sees the "one" not being able to create as a contrast to God who creates children, and concludes that "it implies that the man who commits (עשׂה) the sin of intermarriage will be unable to create (עשׂה), i.e., to have children" (106).

7. Glazier-McDonald calls this the "vital principle" that makes man a soul (Ibid. 107). See her alternate interpretation of the text's meaning (Ibid. 106–9). My issue with her approach is more in the conclusion. It is not that YHWH will not allow the man to procreate *any* children, but according to my reading, the text would indicate that *covenant* children are in jeopardy of not being created due to the pagan influence of the mother.

8. *zera* ʾᵉlōhîm, literally "seed of God," where it is parallel to šᵉār rûaḥ "remnant of the creative spirit," and indicates that the seed/remnant are covenant children, which God desires to be created. Hence, I have translated the phrase, "covenant children."

with those who threaten the raising of a covenant child through intermarriage with pagans, but has no problem with His people not allowing those covenant children to live in the first place. If the goal of the sexual union is to raise up godly offspring, then to hinder the sexual union's purpose is to hinder a godly offspring from being born and raised as such. The couple, therefore, who decides to hinder the sexual act, has essentially committed a worse crime than the person who marries an unbeliever, since the child born in a religiously mixed marriage may still become a covenant child; but a child that is never conceived has no possibility of doing so.

All of this is to say that the reason God wants his people to marry (i.e., why He made the sexes and the sexual act itself) is that He seeks covenant children through it. The Great Commission in Matthew 28:19–21 ought to, therefore, include, not only foreign families but our own. This does not mean only that we ought to disciple our own children, but that we ought to have them in order to be discipled in the first place. The people who seek something different in the sexual act, to the exclusion of what God seeks through it, commit a sin so severe that God will, indeed, cut them off from His people.

PRO-LIFE?

Of all the claims of the historic Church concerning the morality of this issue, the most absurd and offensive to us is that the use of contraception is a form of murder. Such a statement seems too extreme for our culture, not because the culture has thought through the issue and concluded that contraception is not murder but because the practice is so widely accepted and normative to us that such a revelation is more than our presumptions can take. Murderers are those evil people who go out and take the lives of others. We are good people, and any suggestion that we, as good people, are anything close to murderers is to be dismissed immediately without a second thought. Indeed, without argument, our assumptions would all conclude with Norman Geisler that "whatever one can say for or against birth control, it is not murder."[9] But it is precisely where we have the greatest amount of assumption without argumentation that we should have the greatest amount of caution. Assumptions of innocence have played a large role in a long history of atrocities. Evangelicals do not need to perpetuate another example of this by assuming what they

9. Geisler, *Christian Ethics*, 184.

have yet failed to prove. In fact, the Bible presents us all as murderers, not simply because we all go out and take a life that exists, but because we all have participated in the apathy toward the life of another person at one time or another. But it is precisely the move away from love of self and apathy toward others that distinguishes the true disciples of Christ from the false ones (John 13:35).

A fundamental Christian moral, therefore, is often missed in this debate, and can be traced back to the Book of Genesis. In contrast to the line of Cain (i.e., the murderers), the line of Seth (which represent the people of God in general) are life givers. In fact, from the beginning, this element is what has distinguished the community/children of God from the community/children of the adversary (1 John 3:10–12). Christianity, being in the line of those who walk with God, therefore, produces life not death. We are the advocates of life in a world that exerts itself over the lives of others (even to the extent of blotting out those lives for selfish and distorted reasons). Whereas the world that does not walk with God is a part of the culture of death attributed to the serpent's seed, Christianity, as God's covenant community, is a part of the creation, procreation, and preservation of life that characterizes the godly seed of the woman.

This is why the New Testament expands the sin of murder to any act that withholds what another person needs in order to live (vv. 14–18). The Apostle John then goes on to tell us that "no murderer has eternal life abiding in him" (v. 15). John concludes this based on the argument that if a person truly has life in him or herself, that person will become a "life-giver" to others. We, therefore, see that to be a Christian is not simply to refrain from explicit acts of what one would normally consider "murder," but to continually be involved in giving what is needed to another person so that they might live. In other words, as our lives have been saved, so now we also save the lives of others. We do this by giving clothing, food, drink, medicine to those who need it to survive; we do this by providing food and shelter in hospitality to people who are in need of it in order to survive their journey; we do so, most importantly, by preaching the gospel we have been given in order to save lives eternally; we do so by becoming advocates for the unborn, who are threatened by the culture of death; and we also do so by using our sexual acts as instruments of life, rather than death. In fact, withholding life in the last act must be seen as the ultimate form of murder, precisely because it withholds life at the very beginning. All other forms seek to withhold life that has already come into existence from a person who needs it, but the last act does not even allow life to be given in the first place. We thus understand why Christians ought to refrain from participation in any form of contraception from this standpoint alone.

Christianity is not individualistic, and consequently does not allow for the self to exert itself to the expulsion of another's life. We are the "sacrificers" of self, the bringers of life, the priests of covenant growth and discipleship, the practitioners of faith without fear, the lovers of people, especially of children. Christ Himself stated that the children should not be hindered from coming to Him, and that those who harm them will be harshly judged. Yet, the modern evangelical Church has become the line of Cain, the exalters of self, the hinderers of life, the destroyers of covenant growth and discipleship, the fearful, the haters of others, specifically of the children who would exist at the cost of their future plans. Arguments in favor of contraception should be pulled through the grid of scrutiny, where the Christian asks whether this act favors the life and love of another. When arguments are made against life and absent of love for the child who could be, it inherently must be seen as altogether unchristian.

PART FIVE

Opposing Arguments

Understanding is the reward of faith. Therefore seek
not to understand in order that you might believe,
but believe in order that you might understand.

—AUGUSTINE, ON THE GOSPEL OF JOHN

8

Modern Evangelicals Argue
the Strength of Their Case

BEFORE WE GET STARTED, I wanted to comment on the type of argumentation presented by the opposition. The type of argumentation, hoping to establish a moral equivalence to the "procreationist" viewpoint, presented by modern evangelicals is purely from the negative. In other words, there are no positive arguments offered by the opposition. Their case consists primarily of explaining away the positive case. They attempt to explain away verses (either by reinterpreting them or limiting their application to their original setting); they attempt to explain away theological arguments (either by undermining them with experiential arguments or fallacious reasoning); and they attempt to dismiss the historic arguments (by seeking cultural reasons for historic Christian beliefs rather than biblical reasons for them); but there is no positive evidence offered whereby one might go to Scripture and see God's favor upon a contraceptive practice performed. There is no historic argument given for why Christians in the past have seen contraception in a good light. None of this evidence is offered because none of this evidence exists. The opposing position is substantiated by an argument from silence, which then proceeds in its attempt to knock down the numerous positive arguments against contraception in an effort to place it on equal footing. It is the hope of this book to show that the experiential arguments, presented by the opposition, that attempt to dismiss the positive presentation made against contraceptive practices, neither "knock down" the positive case, nor are they, in qualitative terms, "equal."

As a further observation, the pro-birth control argument is riddled with logical fallacies. In fact, I have yet to observe a single valid argument given, from a Christian perspective, in favor of the practice. Instead, the arguments presented fall prey to fallacious reasoning in that they consist of straw men, begging the question, false dichotomies, *ad hominem* attacks, and genetic fallacies. One has to wonder that if the position is so solid, why it is that it must be primarily supported with arguments from silence and fallacious reasoning.

POISONING THE WELL

As a further precursor to this discussion, I wanted to comment on the common practice of poisoning the well. The discussion of whether contraception is morally permissible is a serious issue, and the tendency for advocates of contraception to characterize our position as "the Roman Catholic view" is dishonest and amounts to numerous logical fallacies, *ad hominem* being the first which comes to mind. Some even attempt not only to make an improper association of the historic position with Roman Catholicism, but even attempt to connect the idea to Mormonism! As I have already stated, the RCC position is not the historic Christian one, and the Mormon argument against contraception (i.e., that it should not be practiced because spirit children need to come to earth in order to progress into godhood) is the furthest thing from the historic orthodox Christian argument.[1]

I have also read many books that downplay the collective voice of all Christians (from the Fathers to the Reformers to the Puritans to even the modern Church) by stating things like "some Christians were for it and some were not," or "there was no official view of contraception in the church"[2] in an effort to convey the idea that there really is no Christian view of the subject.

---

1. Note that the Mormon position has also changed with the times. "It is the privilege of married couples who are able to bear children to provide mortal bodies for the spirit children of God, whom they are then responsible to nurture and rear. The decision as to how many children to have and when to have them is extremely intimate and private and should be left between the couple and the Lord. Church members should not judge one another in this matter. Married couples also should understand that sexual relations within marriage are divinely approved not only for the purpose of procreation, but also as a means of expressing love and strengthening emotional and spiritual bonds between husband and wife" (LDS Church, *Church Handbook of Instructions,* 186–87).

2. This statement, which stems from a lack of information regarding the historical record, can be seen in certain works like Paris, *Birth Control for Christians* (20): "Throughout Christian history women have regulated their fertility with the help of midwives and herbalists, and while Christian leaders sometimes condemned and sometimes

Such attempts are meant to give the reader of these works a disposition against the procreative arguments being made, and to give the person a false impression that the arguments can simply be dismissed without any thoughtful consideration. It is clear, however, that these authors are largely oblivious to the historical data. They should not be charged with attempting to be purposefully deceitful (although there does seem to be an attempt to use what is perceived to be true as a part of an argument from the genetic fallacy). Either way, it would be my hope that this old lawyer's trick would not hinder the investigation of the truth among those who would seek it for the glory of God.

IS GENESIS 1:28 A BLESSING OR A COMMAND?

Not much discussion has been given to this text thus far primarily because this verse is illuminated not only by the rest of literary argument being made by the author of Genesis but also by the entirety of the biblical evidence that indicates that God sees the primary use of the sexual act as procreative and condemns those who do not use it as such. However, a few brief comments may help the reader understand this disputed text a little better.

The common argument presented against the interpretation that this text is a command is that it is really *only* a blessing.[3] The advocates of this argument make the claim that a blessing is more of a privilege given to people, not a requirement that God has set for mankind. The imperative is interpreted, as it often appears in the Hebrew Bible, as a wish: *May you be fruitful and multiply and fill up the earth.* J. Walton argues for this view in his commentary on Genesis.

---

affirmed these practices, for a long time no official or widely enforced church policies were in place." Note also that the only arguments concerning the morality of the practice presented by this author were those that were given by the 1930 Lambeth Conference and the National Council of Churches, which supported the use of contraception based on arguments from situational ethics.

3. Such is the interpretation of Raymond Van Leeuwen ("Breeding Stock or Lords of Creation," 37) who states that "only one comment is essential, because it is utterly decisive: Genesis 1:28 is not a commandment, but a blessing . . . The text says, 'God blessed them, and God said to them, "Be fruitful and multiply." This, of course, is a false dichotomy. One must ask the question as to whether it is only a blessing, or if it is also a command. Leeuwen's either/or assumption pits the two against each other, as though God's commandments that benefit us are not also blessings.

> First of all, granting a blessing (as in 1:28–30) must be recognized as delineating a privilege, not an obligation. In the ancient world, the ability to reproduce was seen as a gift from God. No one in that world would have considered foregoing the opportunity. It would be inappropriate, then, to consider this as a command that couples must have children.[4]

Walton's argument, that the reader should take the blessing as a privilege instead of a command, is set on the foundation that no one in the ancient world would need this command, since no one in that world would have shunned the opportunity to procreate. This, as we have already seen, is completely false. The entire ancient world, in which Israel resided, not only would forego the opportunity but made the habit of doing so. Israel alone is distinguished from these other civilizations due to this distinctive command given to it. Apart from this teaching within Scripture, Israel would have been like the other nations in this respect. This argument, then, is the equivalent of saying that no one in the ancient world would have committed homosexual acts and therefore there is no need to command Israel to do otherwise. This sole premise, which has led to Walton's conclusion, is erroneous.[5]

Apart from the fact that Genesis is countering the *Atra-ḥasīs* myth, which argues that people ought to engage in non-productive sexual acts in order to reduce population growth, the literary context of Genesis also shows us that Genesis 1:28 should be taken as a command.

Furthermore, if the text meant only to display God's permission, not His command, one would then have to wonder why He blesses with children those with whom He finds favor, why He destroys Sodom and Gomorrah and kills Onan for practicing non-procreative sexual acts, and why He repeats the phrase to Noah.

Furthermore, are we to suppose from this argument that if Adam and Eve, or Noah and his wife, wanted to remain childless, or limit their children, that decision on their part would have been morally acceptable to God? If one argues, however, that it would not be morally acceptable

---

4. Walton, *Genesis: The NIV*, 134.

5. Walton also makes the mistake in taking the blessing as a gift of the power of fertility or ability to reproduce, which is not the purpose of the blessing. See Mitchell, *The Meaning of BRK*, 62.

for the direct recipients of the statement to limit their children, then the phrase really can't be taken as permissive, but as a command.[6]

Nanette Stahl sees that the blurring of lines between law and blessing is part of the balanced nature of the creation, where God transfers some of His creative responsibility to humans.[7] Although Stahl's analysis includes an assumption of naturalism, which I have addressed previously, her comments concerning the command are interesting to note. She states:

> God's enunciation of this mandate can be seen as a speech act of blessing, וַיְבָרֶךְ אֹתָם ('and he blessed them'), but the articulated semantic content is that of command. . . . The deity grants humanity the privilege of populating the world and ruling it, but in the form of a charge: human beings are the *agents* for enacting God's blessing; they are accountable to God in fulfilling this obligation.[8]

Furthermore, imperatives[9] in the Hebrew Bible are an expression of desire, or a request, only when an inferior is speaking to a superior. When a superior speaks to an inferior, they are always commands.[10] For instance, in Genesis 28:1, Isaac blesses Jacob ("he blessed him"), which is described as commanding him ("and he commanded him"),[11] as he tells him in Decalogue fashion, "You shall not take a wife from the daughters of Canaan." Whether the commands are expressed in wishes or not is irrelevant in these contexts since, in the ancient world, a superior expects an inferior to serve/fulfill his wishes. Hence, all wishes (i.e., sentences translated as "May you . . .") in these superior-to-inferior contexts take

6. See also Thielicke's argument (*Theological Ethics*, 202 n. 3) against Karl Barth's claim (*Church Dogmatics* III. 4, 268) that the command has ceased to be unconditional now that Christianity has come, as a confusion between a law and a command of creation, which, in Thielicke's view, reflects Barth's unbiblical position concerning the nature of man.

7. Stahl, *Law and Liminality*, 31.

8. Ibid.

9. "The terms imperative and jussive refer etymologically to absolute expressions of will (Latin *impero* 'to command,' *jubeo* 'to order'). . . . Through the volitional forms a speaker aims to impose his or her will on some other person (or, in figurative language, thing). The force with which that will is exerted depends on various factors, including the speaker's social standing *via-à-vis* the addressee, the social context of the discourse, and the meaning of the verb" (*IBHS* 34. 1c).

10. See the discussion concerning volitional uses of the non-perfective, which are often used in conjunction with imperatives, in Ibid. 31. 5a.

11. This probably should be taken as a hendiadys "blessing, he commanded him . . ." Hence, the command is in the form of a blessing.

upon the force of commands.[12] Therefore, the imperatives in Genesis 1:28 should be categorically received as imperatival commands.

Thirdly, when a person gives a blessing in the Bible, he or she is expressing his or her desire that something be done. When a human makes the blessing, it is often meant as a request made to God to fulfill it. When God blesses something, it is His desire that either He or humans accomplish it. In Genesis 2:3, God again blesses something (i.e., the Sabbath), but then makes it according to His blessing.[13] He blesses and responds to that blessing by fulfilling it.[14] Therefore, the blessing is the desire of a person that something be fulfilled. It is in the very concept of the blessing that the concept of wanting that desire to take place exists. For a human, the blessing/desire that X takes place may not be something that another human needs to fulfill; but for God, the blessing is something He expects to be fulfilled by His subjects. Therefore, the pro-contraceptive position is essentially asking, Is God telling us to procreate or only expressing that He wants us to procreate? Our answer, of course, is, "What's the difference?" As we have seen, there isn't one. God wants something to be done, and it is nothing but the oddest biblical interpretation that would argue that what God wants us to do does not need to be done.

MAY I BE EXCUSED?

A few of the more popular arguments, also offered by theologians, attempt to legitimize the use of contraception by appealing to circumstance. This is called situational ethics because what moral choices a person makes depends upon the particular circumstance in which he or she finds him or herself. The idea is essentially that the individual must become the decision maker in allowing a particular moral principle to be applied to any given situation. The argument from the *imago Dei*, which we will

12. Cf. also Genesis 35:9–12 for the blessing in the form of commands, one concerning Jacob's name and one concerning procreation.

13. See Matthew Henry's comments on Genesis 1:26–28.

14. "Because the formula is a blessing, it expresses God's approval and desire that they [i.e., the humans He made] reproduce. The formula is an illocutionary utterance equivalent in meaning to God saying: 'I hereby declare my desire for you to reproduce and so fill the earth" (Mitchell, *The Meaning of BRK*, 62). God has already bestowed the biological functions of the man and woman within them at creation. The blessing conveys that He wants them to use them appropriately. Hence, in this case, the blessing conveys the idea that God wants the man and woman to participate in the sexual act without hindering its productivity.

examine later, is made to provide a foundation for situational ethics, since divine-like wisdom would be needed in determining whether moral X can be applied to situation Y. Situational ethics has at its roots the concepts of relativism and pragmatism, which seek to find the answers to the question, What works?, but fails to address anthropological questions concerning the fallen nature of humanity that would indicate that humans are not capable of assessing morality correctly without the aid of an absolute principle that must be applied regardless of the situation. It also assumes a very generic relative principle (like an abstract concept of love) as the only binding norm that can be subjectively applied at the discretion of the fallen human. This, however, assumes the inadequacy of the specific laws given in Scripture that are meant to convey God's intended application of the principle of love. Situational ethics essentially is antinomian in disguise because, while accepting the idea that an absolute norm exists, it denies any external interpretation of that norm as authoritative. Hence, when the situation arises, the individual does what he or she thinks is morally acceptable rather than what is expressed to be morally acceptable through the divine revelation of the Bible.[15] The refutation of situationalism comes by way of understanding Biblical anthropology (Jer 17:5–10) and the need for an external authority in the application of ethical principles (Ps 19:89–112), without which the community deteriorates into chaos where "each man does what is right according to his own opinion" (Jud 21:25).

The Economic Argument

One of the more popular arguments is that a person may simply be incapable of affording children. This "economic argument" states that people should not have children if they cannot afford them. If they cannot afford them, but seek to be married and have sexual relations with their spouses, they ought to be allowed to use contraception.

Of course, this is also an argument used by abortion advocates, since if contraception fails, this line of reasoning would indicate that abortion should be an option. The argument also implies that poor people shouldn't have children. Apart from the offensiveness of such a way of thinking, this argument assumes that people make children and that God has nothing

---

15. See Norman Geisler's discussion (*Christian Ethics*, 43–78) of both situationalism as well as the expression it often takes in the form of utilitarianism.

to do with it. If it is God who decides to give people children, including poor people, who is anyone else to say otherwise? The problem, however, is that advocates of contraception are philosophic naturalists on this issue, through and through. If people make children, then they should limit them, since they decide whether they can afford these little pets; but if God makes them, then He decides whether He will give the couple the task of raising children with difficulties (financial or otherwise).

I once had a friend who said she thought it was immoral for anyone to bring a child into an evil or impoverished situation. I thought, "Does that mean God is immoral? Does He not bring every child into the world, and many into evil situations at that?" Of course, she had not even thought of that, since the naturalism she had adopted when it came to the issue of conception prevented her from seeing what she was actually saying about God. The common assumption, which we dealt with in the systematic argument, is that God has given men and women the ability to have children. He does not decide to actually make children personally. (For a refutation of that concept, the reader is directed to Chapter 6.)

Another aspect of the economic argument is the reasoning that children should be limited if a couple wants to live a certain lifestyle that would not be possible with the expense of too many children. For obvious biblical reasons this argument is overwhelmingly condemned even by the theologians who advocate that contraception is acceptable. The primary reason many of them condemn it is that this way of thinking is blatant materialism, where indulgence takes precedence over morality and obligation to God. The sin committed here is that of idolatry, where the individual worships the self, instead of God, by using for indulgence the money God has granted to him or her for His own purposes. If God wishes the couple to have covenant children given to them through the sexual act as He sees fit, then the couple who uses a contraceptive method in an effort to thwart God's will is serving mammon instead of God. There can be no such thing as two Lords in an individual's life (Matt 6:24), and Christ has certainly indicated that He will not share His rule with the self (Matt 16:24; Mk 8:34; Lk 9:23).

Such superficiality has always deceived people into thinking that riches have to do with money and comfort. Joseph Hall[16] (ad 1574–1656)

16. Hall was the Bishop of Norwich, who was both appointed Dean of Worcester and sent as a representative to the Synod of Dort by James I. Later, the revenues from his see were sequestered by Parliament, which threw him into great suffering and poverty. See

once related an experience, which strikes at the heart of this type of thought.

> I remember a great man coming into my house, at Waltham, and seeing all my children standing in the order of their age and stature, said, "These are they that make rich men poor." But he straight received this answer, "Nay, my lord, these are they that make a poor man rich; for there is not one of these whom we would part with for all your wealth."[17]

I would pray that any parent, whether of current or future children, would gladly stand with Mr. Hall against the murderous self, which would trade the children of Christ for a mere earthly and illusory thirty pieces of silver, along with the false security and temporal comfort it may bring.

It's a Fall World After All

A species of this situational ethics argument is that, since we live in a fallen world, what God desires of us cannot always be fulfilled. This argument is offered by Helmut Thielicke in his *Theological Ethics*.[18] The argument is essentially that even though God commands us to fulfill the creation mandate, and this mandate is binding upon all humans for all time, God makes concessions for us to use contraception in certain circumstances because of our fallen situation.[19] He uses as an example the divorce certificate God allowed the Israelites to use due to the "hardness of heart" (Matt 19:8; Mk 10:5), even though divorce is outside of the created order and not according to God's will.[20] I refer to this as "postlapsarian" ethics.[21]

The honesty of Thielicke's work is refreshing, but in the end, his attempt to undermine the very thing he admits is unconvincing. This type of argument allows any evil, of any sort or degree, to be justified as appropriate in certain situations. One could argue that the divine order is that a pregnancy should go to full term, but in our fallen world, God makes concessions for us to use abortion to terminate that pregnancy. Other

---

Horn, "Joseph Hall," 447.

17. As quoted in Spurgeon, *The Treasury of David*, comment on Psalm 127.

18. Thielicke, *Theological Ethics*, 202–15.

19. Of course, Thielicke's situations include almost any reason a person would use for contraception in today's society.

20. Ibid., 203.

21. This view is also espoused by Patricia Goodson, *Ethics of Contraception*, 34–49.

examples of homosexuality (which in fact, some evangelicals justify by this very argument[22]), idolatry, murder, telling lies, committing adultery, etc. could be used, since anything and everything can be justified by looking first to our present situation and arguing backward to what is permissible.

Instead, the point Jesus is making with the certificate of divorce, to which Thielicke seems to be oblivious, is that God permitted Israel, before Christ's advent, to practice what was not complete and orderly in His eyes, but now that the Lord has come, that concession is no longer in effect. Hence, Peter argues against the heretics who use this argument to justify their disobedience by stating that, through Christ, God's "divine power has granted to us everything pertaining to life and godliness . . . that you may become partakers of the divine nature, having escaped the corruption that is in the world by lust" (2 Pet 1:3–4). Hence, any excuse that stems from the limitations of the sinful nature is to be rendered invalid due to the advent of Christ joining us to God and His unlimited power to live out the life of godliness to which He has called us.

Furthermore, those practices that God permits in the Old Testament (e.g polygamy, divorce, etc.) do not contradict the purpose of creation (i.e., to have children and fill up the earth) but the means to that purpose (i.e., the *two* becoming one flesh). The temporary concession upon the *means* in Old Testament situations cannot be confused with the strict obligation God sets for His people to observe the *purpose*. Thielicke has failed to make the appropriate distinction, and as such, his argument falls prey to a chaotic consequence to biblical ethics, in which anything can be justified. It is clear that concession is never made for sexual immorality because the *purpose* of creation is at stake (i.e., the filling up of the earth with covenant children through the sexual act). When God does see the *purpose* of creation threatened with divorce or polygamy (specifically in the marrying of foreign wives) He categorically rejects their employment. Thielicke's argument is of no avail, then; and using the fallen world as the "fall guy" for excusing a person's sins is to argue from the descriptive (i.e., what is) to the prescriptive (i.e., what should be)—something Christianity, as a responsible and consistent system, has never done.

22. See Seow, "Textual Orientation," 17–34.

Ready or Not, Here They Come

A large issue brought up by more popular works is that people simply may not be ready to have children. Children can be overwhelming and a huge responsibility to newly married couples. However, this argument is an interesting one in that it shows how far the modern concept of marriage has strayed from the biblical concept. In the Bible, the entire point of marriage is the sexual act (Song of Solomon) that brings about covenant children (Mal 2:15)—thus creating a family devoted to God (Psalm 127). If a person is ready to get married, then that person should be ready to have children as well; but far too often marriage is simply a path of self-fulfillment. God's purposes are not always considered. Due to this self-centered view of marriage, the individuals no longer understand that marriage is for procreation (i.e., the raising of all of the covenant children God may choose to give to a couple). If an individual claims to worship God, and that individual wishes to get married, then he or she also ought to seek to worship God, instead of self, when choosing to get married. Therefore, the decision to get married is the decision to have children. Marriage for any other reason, to the exclusion of the primary purpose for marriage, is selfishly unbiblical.

Furthermore, not very many couples feel they are ready for children. It is common to be afraid of the responsibility that comes with children. However, true freedom and joy comes from the fact that God is the one who decides whether a couple is ready, and we know this because only He can give the couple a child. If that couple has committed their lives to trusting and serving God, then there is no reason for them to believe that He will give them children to ruin them. This is where the claim of faith becomes truly faithful. Certainly, God is the wisest of all judges and is able to see what the human couple cannot. He is the only perfect predictor of how things will turn out, so trusting Him is not an act of irresponsibility. In fact, it would be irresponsible to trust the deceptions of the wicked self instead of Him.[23] We are people of faith, and that faith requires us to walk into areas that frighten us, knowing that God will work according to His good pleasure in us as we do His will.

23. The Bible continually warns people that they should not trust their own way of thinking, but to trust in God's wisdom instead (Prov 3:5–7; 16:25; Jer 17:9–10; Ps 9:10; 20:7).

A Further Note concerning These Arguments

The interesting thing about so many of these arguments is that they are not arguments at all. They are excuses. They are excuses telling us why one might use contraception, but not why it is historically, biblically, theologically, or practically acceptable in the sight of God. They create situations, much like the arguments in favor of abortion, that beg the question of morality (i.e., Is contraception morally permissible?); and then play off of the sympathies of society. For instance, stealing is wrong, but if a thief can convince a jury that he was hungry and his children were starving, they will have sympathy and excuse the crime. A well-attested practice is that of trial lawyers when they seek to convince the jury that a murderer is mentally ill. This illness is meant to lend sympathy to the murderer, so that the jury sees him as the victim of his situation. If the lawyers are successful at this, the jurors will often excuse the criminal from his crime.

This practice is not simply an American courtroom phenomenon. In fact, it stems from how the common modern person argues ethics. Ethics are situational. What is wrong in one instance may not be wrong in another. If one commits a crime, the crime is wrong, but is excusable if the criminal's circumstances are seen as causing the crime.[24]

We encounter that same line of argumentation when we hear arguments in favor of abortion and contraception. Too often the cases of rape and incest are used as shaming tools to embarrass a pro-life advocate by the implication that he or she has no sympathy for victims of horrible crimes. Of course, this is simply a continuation of the "guilty with a good excuse" trajectory of reasoning. Because an individual may have endured a horrible crime against her does not mean that she has the right to commit another crime upon another individual (even if that individual is genetically linked to her assailant). For instance, no one would argue that because a man is attacked by another man in the street, he then should be excused when he goes to that man's house and attacks his children.

Situational ethics then plays on emotion, and I dare say, the emotion is anger in the case of abortion (and most likely in certain cases of contraception as well). It seeks to stir up a hornet's nest so that people are blinded from rationally evaluating the morality of an act. In other cases, it seeks

24. One might in fact conclude that this is mankind's oldest excuse, since the man blames his sin on the woman and the woman on the serpent in the Garden of Eden. Blaming something or someone else for a criminal's actions is as convincing to God as the original couple's argument was.

to stir up sympathy to the degree that the criminal is seen as the victim of circumstances, and as such, should be allowed to practice the crime.

This tactic, however, convinces only those who have already drunk the Kool-Aid and keep coming back for more. It is powerless to reveal what is right and wrong with any given act; and in fact, it is powerless to help anyone realize the need for condemnation of any act (regardless of how atrocious that act may be).

Of course, the victims of crime do not argue this way, as they have, through the overwhelming pain of that crime, understood evil in the sense that the Bible portrays it (i.e., that God does not care what excuse an individual has for committing a crime; He cares only whether that person is punished according to the statutes He set in place). Biblical law has no trial for the criminal to explain why he did such and such an act. It only has trials to discover whether someone committed the crime. If a person is guilty, the excuse for why he committed the crime (although it is natural for humans, in the act of self preservation, to try to escape punishment this way) is irrelevant in the eyes of God. If there is a motive, there is a crime. It does not matter what situation(s) caused the motive.[25]

All this to say that if this is how God thinks about situational ethics, then the Christian will want to be like minded and cease to argue in such a way.

SINGLENESS PROVES RELATIVITY?

Some argue that the command to procreate is not absolute since Jesus, Paul, etc. never obeyed it.[26] It is, therefore, up to the individual to decide if he or she wants to obey it in his or her given circumstance. There is, of course, a fundamental misunderstanding with this statement. The command in Genesis 1 is not given to single individuals, as were the Lord Jesus Christ and the Apostle Paul. It is given to couples. Note that "He

25. Note Proverbs 6:27–31: "Can a man take fire into his bosom and his clothes not be burned? Or can a man walk on hot coals and his feet not be scorched? So is the one who goes into his neighbor's wife; whoever touches her will not go unpunished. Men do not despise a thief if he steals to satisfy himself when he is hungry; but when he is found, he must repay sevenfold; he must give all the substance of his house." Regardless of a person's reasons for committing a crime, or the sympathy one might have for his circumstances, his crime has caused irrevocable damage and must be punished.

26. See for example, Davis, *Evangelical Ethics*, 40: "The general mandate to be fruitful and multiply (Gen. 1:28) does admit of some exceptions, as the cases of Jeremiah, Paul, and Jesus attest."

blessed *them*" once He had made them male and female. It is the male and female coupled together who are commanded to be fruitful and multiply, fill the earth and subdue it. Single individuals have different roles to play in God's plan (although it still involves parenthood and begetting of children through a spiritual avenue instead of both the physical and spiritual). This argument fails to recognize the intended audience for the command, commits the straw-man fallacy, and is, therefore, irrelevant to our discussion.

WHAT THE BIBLE DOESN'T SAY COULD KILL YOU

Another common objection, which displays the assumption that the rejection of contraception does not stem from the Bible, is argued by J. Jordan below.

> Jesus repeatedly denounced the Pharisees for their additions to the Law of God. Thus, we must be extremely careful about what laws we lay down for people. Does the Bible clearly state that contraception is sinful, or that people are obligated to have as many children as possible? If the Bible does not say these things, we need to fear God and be frightened of adding to His Word.[27]

This, of course, is not an accurate statement. First, the problem with the Pharisees is that they *do not* obey the Scripture and therefore set up ritual practices and offerings to give to God in order to replace obedience. Notice that Jesus tells them that they "do away with the Word of God" for the sake of their human-made, cultural ideas (Mark 7:13). The rebuke of the Sermon on the Mount is that the righteousness of the Pharisees does not take into account the spirit of the law and what it implies, and the Pharisees instead attempt to get away with only what they technically have to obey when the Scripture is explicit (ironically what Jordan and his ilk are arguing). The Pharisaic problem, therefore, is that they do not extend the moral applications of the Scripture (which represent Christ's lordship over one's life) into those areas in which they want to remain disobedient (and thus attempt to bribe God with religious service as a way to avoid judgment and maintain the estimation that they are "good people"). This, however, has nothing to do with our subject here; and ironically, Jordan has taken what could be considered the more Pharisaic position here by

27. Jordan, "The Bible and Family Planning," 4.

implying that only what is made explicit in Scripture is to be appropriated to the Christian.

Furthermore, the charge that Christians who condemn contraception do not fear God could also be applied to Jordan by his own argument. Does Jordan fear God when he condemns pedophilia or abortion? Is he adding to God's Word because it does not explicitly and clearly condemn these practices? I would argue that pedophilia, abortion, and contraception are condemned by the Bible's view of the primary purpose of the sexual act (i.e., none of them has procreation as their main purpose in the sexual act). Hence, I am able to give a precise reason for the evil of these sins, whereas Jordan would be hard pressed to argue against the former two and maintain his words here against the latter at the same time.

In fact, Jordan's "a moral must be stated explicitly" argument itself is not explicit in the Bible, and yet he uses it to condemn the positions of others. Is he not adding to the Bible then? He instead is using an application of his popular, and erroneous, view of Pharisaic legalism in order to argue an absolute against other positions. His argument, therefore, is self defeating.

Finally, Jordan would actually condemn the Lord Jesus when He expanded the explicit commands (e.g "honor your father and mother," "thou shalt not murder," "thou shalt not commit adultery," etc.) to their fullest moral applications, and subsequently condemned the Pharisees for not practicing those moral applications. Modern evangelicals, like Jordan, might want to tread a little more softly when their hermeneutics attack the hermeneutics of the One who actually gave us the Bible in the first place.

A similar argument to this is one presented by John MacArthur. He argues:

> To begin with, we know God looks approvingly on the bearing of children. That is evident from Titus 2:3–5 and Paul's exhortation to young widows in 1 Timothy 5:14. Psalm 127:3–5 says children are gifts from God and the man who has many of them is blessed. A large family involves increased responsibility, but children raised in a godly way will influence the world for good and for God's glory.[28]

Up to this point, we would agree, but he continues:

---

28. MacArthur, "What Does the Bible Teach about Birth Control?" Also cf. this material collected in MacArthur et al., *Right Thinking in a World Gone Wrong*, 87–88.

> Nevertheless, nothing in Scripture prohibits married couples from practicing birth control, either for a limited time to delay childbearing, or permanently when they have borne children and determine that their family is complete. In our viewpoint, birth control is biblically permissible. At the same time, couples should not practice birth control if it violates their consciences (Romans 14:23)—not because birth control is inherently sinful, but because it is always wrong to violate the conscience. The answer to a wrongly informed conscience is not to violate it, but rather to correct and rightly inform one's conscience with biblical truth.[29]

Note, however, that MacArthur has allowed a person to simply insert any non-explicit idea into his argument—thus showing it to be no argument at all.

> Nevertheless, nothing in Scripture prohibits married couples from practicing *abortion*, either for a limited time to delay childbearing, or permanently when they have bore children and determine that their family is complete. In our viewpoint, *abortion* is biblically permissible. At the same time, couples should not practice *abortion* if it violates their consciences (Romans 14:23)—not because *abortion* is inherently sinful, but because it is always wrong to violate the conscience. The answer to a wrongly informed conscience is not to violate it, but rather to correct and rightly inform one's conscience with biblical truth.[30]

Setting aside the abuse of Romans 14 and 15 until later, it follows that MacArthur and others would then, of course, say that Scripture does teach against abortion because it is murder. This assertion, however, is an extended moral application to the law against murder, not an explicit statement of any given biblical passage, as abortion as the sin of murder is never mentioned in Scripture. However, as J. Carl Laney argued, abortion did not need to be explicitly condemned due its implicit condemnation through the moral extension of existing biblical concepts:

> Why was abortion an unthinkable act for the ancient Israelites? First, children were recognized as a gift or heritage from the Lord (Gen 33:5; Pss. 113:9 ; 127:3). Second, God was seen to be the One who opens the womb and allows conception (Gen 29:33; 30:22 ; 1 Sam 1:19–20). Third, childlessness was thought to be a curse, for the husband's family name could not be carried on (Deut 25:6;

29. MacArthur, "What Does the Bible Teach about Birth Control?"
30. Ibid.

Ruth 4:5). Barrenness meant the extinction of the family name (cf.
Jer 11:19). Induced abortion was so abhorrent to the Israelite mind
that it was not necessary to have a specific prohibition to deal with
it in the Law. Sufficient was the command, "You shall not murder"
(Exod 20:13).[31]

The same can be said in the case of contraception. At this point,
it should dawn on the individual arguing such that Scripture need not
explicitly mention a horrible sin in order for it to be a horrible sin, drawn
as an implication and application from what Scripture does say. The question, then, is not whether Scripture explicitly prohibits contraception, but
whether it prohibits (a) uses of the sexual act that do not intend to bring
about a covenant child, (b) the unauthorized taking away of a life, (c) the
usurping of God's role in giving and taking life, (d) the view of conception
that does not give glory/credit to God for the act, (e) an act of faithlessness and shunning of God's revealed decisions, (f) a rebellion against the
use of family to help fulfill obedience to the Great Commission. In other
words, the questions one must ask are whether the use of contraception is
murder, sexual immorality, idolatry, and is contrary to Christian discipleship and faithfulness—i.e., the very questions I have put forth here.

MacArthur et al. all fail to make this connection with their arguments. Instead, they seem to be making up the rules as they go. If one is
talking about something seen as evil, then Scripture need not be explicit
on the subject in order for us to condemn its practice. If one is talking
about something seen as morally acceptable, then Scripture must be explicit on the subject in order for us to condemn it. In this scenario, the
individual's personal opinion becomes the standard by which a moral is
evaluated; and Scripture is being used only as an authoritative platform
that the individual can wield in order to give credence to that opinion.
This, of course, is a subtle way of denying the authority of the Scripture
when it comes to issues the individual does not like.

Furthermore, I'm not quite sure how Scripture would be more explicit on the subject, since the ancients had no term for contraception
as we do. Nor is it convincing that Scripture would explicitly have to
prohibit something that it explicitly and continuously condemns through
its advocacy of the opposite position—namely, that God's people are to
engage in sexual acts that provide an avenue of procreation. The argu-

31. Laney, "The Abortion Epidemic," 346.

ment that the explicit, procreative command does not also include within it the condemnation of the rejection of that command is like saying that the command to receive Jesus Christ does not then tell us that God would condemn our rejection of Christ. This is not to mention the fact that, as we have seen, the rejection of the command is condemned in Scripture over and over again when it speaks of sexual immorality.

John Frame[32] also argues that there must be scripturally acceptable, alternate purposes of the sexual act because, if it were not acceptable, there would be prohibitions against sex after menopause in Scripture. Frame, of course, would not argue that the dozens of sexual sins not explicitly prohibited in the Bible are morally acceptable by this sentiment. However, his argument does just that. The Scripture does not need to explicitly condemn something that it assumes to be wrong in its teaching of the contrary.

Furthermore, it is not the position of Scripture that those who are of old age, and past child-bearing according to human understanding, should then cease from participating in the sexual act, as God will occasionally decide to use those natural means to create a child (e.g Abraham and Sarah). Hence, no one has argued this way. The prohibitions in Scripture are against humans purposely engaging in a sexual act that prevents it from becoming God's natural means to create. If the man and woman participate in the sexual act as instructed, and something else hinders the procreative process, it is for God either to decide whether He will choose to override that hindrance. The argument here is that a human with moral responsibility ought not to hinder what God has set in place to use for His purposes.

The Feinbergs also state if *coitus interruptus* were prohibited, it would appear in Leviticus 20:10–21 as well.[33] This argument, as the one above, fails to note the host of damnable sexual sins not listed in Leviticus 20:10–21 or elsewhere in the Bible. This is because the Bible is not an exhaustive rule book, but a teacher of the mindset of God. It teaches us the purpose of the sexual act and gives some examples of distorted uses, but it is not going to list every sexual sin possible to man. The mind of God teaches us to apply them in areas the Scripture does not mention. This is the difference between those who live by the letter of the law, seeking to

---

32. Frame, *Pastoral and Social Ethics*, 5.
33. Feinberg and Feinberg, *Ethics for a Brave New World*, 177.

permit themselves in areas the Scripture does not explicitly condemn, and those who live by the spirit, seeking to please God in all areas, explicitly or implicitly mentioned in the letter of the text (e.g, Matthew 5). The people of God ought to use caution when using arguments from the letter that are opposed to the spirit; or to put it in modern terms, one ought to seek not only what is explicitly communicated in Scripture but also its fullest moral application to all aspects of life.

THE GIFT THAT KEEPS ON GIVING

John Piper's ministry throws their hat into the ring with a few common arguments that provide for us an opportunity for discussion. Their first argument stems from a disagreement with those who advocate that, since children are a gift from the Lord, it is wrong to reject them. Piper's ministry (referred to as PM from here on)[34] argues:

> It is very important to delight in the reality that "children are a gift of the Lord." But some people go further and argue from this that since children are gifts from God, it is wrong to take steps to regulate the timing and number of children one has.
>
> In response, it can be pointed out that the Scriptures also say that a wife is a gift from the Lord (Proverbs 18:22), but that doesn't mean that it is wrong to stay single (1 Corinthians 7:8). Just because something is a gift from the Lord does not mean that it is wrong to be a steward of when or whether you will come into possession of it. It is wrong to reason that since A is good and a gift from the Lord, then we must pursue as much of A as possible. God has made this a world in which tradeoffs have to be made and we cannot do everything to the fullest extent. For kingdom purposes, it might be wise not to get married. And for kingdom purposes, it might be wise to regulate the size of one's family and to regulate when the new additions to the family will likely arrive. As Wayne Grudem has said, "it is okay to place less emphasis on some good activities in order to focus on other good activities."[35]

There are a few assumptions at work here. The first is that of the philosophic naturalism that pervades PM's view of nature, which we will discuss below.

34. I will assume that Piper agrees with his ministry's statement, and perhaps they have even gotten their arguments from him, since it is a part of his ministry. Therefore, I will occasionally refer to these arguments as though Piper himself had stated them.

35. Desiring God staff, "Does the Bible permit birth control?"

The second is that children are "a gift." The Bible actually doesn't say that children are a gift. The phrase used in Psalm 127:3 is that children are a *naḥᵃlat YHWH*, "a divinely ordained inheritance, belonging to Yahweh," or more concisely a "covenant inheritance."[36] They are "wages/payments of the fertility of the womb." Although this may seem arbitrary at first, this distinction makes all the difference in the world to the argument being made. Having covenant children is part of the duty and privilege of God's people; and each child is a covenant inheritance from God, so that a rejection of a single one (whether God seeks to give one or fifteen) is an act of rebellion against God's covenant and a reversal of creation.

The blessing of the man whose quiver is full of children comes from the context in which the couple in the community of God partakes of His ordained "inheritance," which in the Hebrew Bible is a part of redemptive participation of God's people. The inheritance is not like a gift that can be rejected (although Piper has still failed to make the case that even a gift God wants a person to have should be rejected). The believing couple is given children in order to give them back to God as His representative images filling up the earth and reflecting His sovereignty. It is part of the covenant duty of every married couple within the community of God.[37] Compare also Malachi 2:15, where it states: "But did He not make one [flesh]? The remaining [people] of the Spirit of creation belong to Him. And why (did He make) the one [flesh]? Because He seeks godly offspring.[38]

36. See the translation in *DCH* (5:659) as "inalienable hereditary property," and the connection between the term and the eternal relationship between God and His covenant people as reflected in the development of land and people in *TLOT* 2:733 and *NIDOTTE* 3:77.

37. Note the comment by Levenson (*Creation and the Persistence of Evil*, 141): "For all the language of choice that characterizes covenant texts, the Hebrew Bible never regards the choice to decline covenant as legitimate. The fact that a choice is given does not make the alternative good or even acceptable, as a proponent of a purely contractual ethic might wish. In fact, the wrong choice results in nothing short of death."

38. Or "divine offspring," i.e., covenant children (in contrast to the "daughter of a foreign god" in v. 11). Admittedly, the Hebrew here is extremely difficult, and every translation will vary according to words supplied. However, it seems clear from the context that the subject is the purpose of the two-flesh union. Malachi gives an argument for why monogamy, kept within God's community, needs to be upheld—i.e., that God made the union to produce covenant children for Himself and the two become one flesh in that way. Therefore, divorce is hated by God (v. 16) because it works against God's purpose in the couple raising covenant children. Hence, the Israelites should not defile that relationship.

This idea is clearly seen in Exodus 13, where the firstborn offspring from every womb in the community of God belongs to God. The dedication of the firstborn conveys the idea that *all* of the fruit of the womb, every child (present or future) within the community, is God's. Either way, the question becomes, "Can someone ever reject the *naḥᵃlat YHWH* and still consider him or herself part of the believing community, free from any charge of rebellion?" In fact, the pronounced sentence, which God decrees should be carried out in the cases of sexual immorality, has this idea at its base. The person who rejects this duty is to be "cut off" from God's people (Lev 18:29).

Therefore, PM's argument fails on the fact that they compare gifts, which supposedly are optional, that God has bestowed upon His true people. PM's argument, then, is a false analogy.

Furthermore, even the example PM gives to prove their point about a "gift" of God, which one can take or leave, is false. Proverbs 18:22 says nothing about a wife being a *gift* from the Lord. It only says that "he who has found a wife has found a good thing and will obtain favor from YHWH." There is no mention of a gift, and the favor is undoubtedly due to the fact that a man who seeks a wife seeks to have children. The favor bestowed upon the individual in the biblical context, then, is because the man is seeking to fulfill the creation mandate to be fruitful and multiply, which would have been an immediate connection made in the ancient Israelite mind. This passage, either way, is irrelevant to PM's argument.

THE PROMISE OF PEOPLE INCLUDES THE PROMISE OF LAND TO SUPPORT THEM

The next argument given comes from the idea that a "blessing" can be limited by us, since the land, which we are told to have dominion over, should not be continuously cultivated when we don't need it. Piper's argument is as follows:

> When I was teaching a summer course at a seminary in Africa, a student of mine made a perceptive observation along these same lines. He noted first of all that in the creation account the command to multiply is given together with the command to subdue the earth: "And God blessed them; and God said to them, 'Be fruitful and multiply, and fill the earth, and subdue it; and rule over the fish of the sea and over the birds of the sky, and over every living thing that moves on the earth (Genesis 1:28)." He then asked how

a farmer (he lived in a largely agrarian society) knows how much land he should cultivate. The answer, of course, is that a farmer seeks to cultivate what he believes he can reasonably handle. He doesn't take this command to mean that he needs to make his farm be as large as is naturally possible. Likewise, then, it is right for a couple to seek to have the number of children that they believe they can reasonably nurture in light of the other callings they may also have on their lives.[39]

This argument fails to recognize three very important elements.

The first, which we have already discussed, is that the blessing in Psalm 127 is connected to the *naḥᵃlat YHWH* and should therefore be limited only by God.

The second is that people cannot have as many children as naturally possible because God is the one who gives children. Therefore, people can have only as many children as God chooses to make through them. Piper's argument then stems from a naturalistic view of the biological process, which is seen as creating children on its own and thus can produce "as many as possible."

The third is that the blessing of land is always coupled in Genesis with the blessing of offspring because Genesis is countering the ancient Near Eastern idea, which most likely produced the argument found within *Atra-ḥasīs*, that overpopulation leads to a lack of resources/land. The land, therefore, is cultivated through the filling, not apart from it. Hence, the Genesis author combines filling with cultivating. An example of this is found in the English phrase "divide and conquer." The dividing is the means to conquering. They are not two different commands, and therefore, one would not seek to perform one apart from the other.

This also explains why God in the book of Genesis is so opposed to people overpopulating cities when He commands that they spread out and fill up the earth. God seeks to comfort His people, so as He gives children they are to partake of the resources that will support them. In other words, the procreative command and the dominion command are one. The dominion command is to let us know that we may cultivate as much land as we need for the offspring God produces through us. It is God's desire that people fill up the earth. The command to fill the earth is, as J. Walton concludes, "a result of the lack of any limitation on the

39. Desiring God staff, "Does the Bible permit birth control?"

privilege."[40] In other words, because God commands people to be fruitful and multiply, He also lets them know that there is no limit to this command by telling them to fill up the earth in doing it.

Piper, therefore, has misunderstood the command, which is progressive in its delineation. One must be fruitful in order to multiply; one must multiply in order to fill up the earth; one must fill up the earth in order to subdue it. In other words, someone can't just go take extra land, as it seems this student was wondering, and think that he or she is fulfilling the command here. One must be fruitful, and by doing so, fulfill the other three subsequent commands. God wishes his people, then, to subdue the earth by having children, not apart from it. Therefore, the limits of the amount of land one takes will be limited by the amount of children one is given. Thus, it is God who expands and limits the filling and subjugation of the land. Piper is mistaken.

Therefore, Grudem's argument, quoted by Piper, that "We aren't required to maximize the amount of children we have any more than we are required to subdue the earth all the time—plant, grow, harvest, etc." is a misunderstanding of why this command is given with the other. If one understands the polemical argument of Genesis together with the unity of the four elements of the command, he or she will cease to argue this way.

IT'S REALLY ALL ABOUT STEWARDSHIP

PM continues their argument with the "stewardship within the sovereignty of God" fallacy. I say it is a fallacy in this case because it begs the question. For instance, PM argues as follows:

> Sometimes people also reason that if you really want to "trust God" to determine the size of your family, then you should not use birth control. The assumption seems to be that if you "just let things happen naturally," then God is more at work than if you seek to regulate things and be a steward of when they happen. But

40. Walton, *Genesis: The NIV*, 135. I disagree with Walton that the "filling" command is not a part of the procreative command (it is clear in Genesis that it is); and we also differ in that I see the blessing as an indisputable command; but I quote him here because it conveys the fact that the command to "fill up the earth" is connected to the procreative command in that it tells us there is no limitation to it. Apparently, God does not believe the overpopulation arguments made by those who would limit children for this reason. It may, in fact, be the case that the imperative is meant to be an imperative of purpose, which would then cause us to translate the passage as: "Be fruitful and multiply, so that you fill up the earth." See Williams, *Hebrew Syntax*, 35.

surely this is wrong! God is just as much in control of whether you have children when you use birth control as when you don't. The hands of the almighty are not tied by birth control! A couple will have children precisely at the time God wants, whether they use birth control or not. Either way, then, God is ultimately in control of the size of one's family.[41]

This of course begs the question on two accounts:

(1) PM assumes that the conception of children is a natural event in the same vein as getting a haircut. Procreation is an ability God gives us and may sustain, but it is not the result of God willingly creating a child through the sexual act. Otherwise, if PM does believe that God is purposefully going to create a child through the sexual act, then they are essentially arguing that to go against God's will in the creative act is morally permissible, since God will accomplish His goal even when you oppose Him.

(2) Their argument, since they assume that the conception event is natural, is that if God wants a child created, He will, in His sovereignty, choose to override our contraceptive methods, and if not, He has, in His sovereignty, chosen to use our contraception to avoid conception (see the sovereignty argument above). Of course, this then assumes the naturalism of the event, since PM would then have God moving against Himself in the creative act of conception.

Of course, if PM's assumptions were to turn in a more biblical direction, they would have to conclude that God is making a willful decision to create a child through the sexual act and would not be using our rebellious decision to go against Himself. They would also have to conclude that, if something is morally unacceptable, we are not being good stewards by doing said evil deed simply because God is not tied by our evil actions. If God wishes to do A and humans wish to do B, then God in His sovereignty may override B and do A, or He may choose to let B stand. The point is that B is not A. What God wishes morally (A) is not done by the person who does B. It is the moral responsibility of a person to do A if God morally wishes for him or her to do A. If a person does B, regardless of what God decides to do with it at that point, that person will be judged for not doing A.

41. Desiring God staff, "Does the Bible permit birth control?"

Furthermore, let me apply PM's line of reasoning to a moral evil and let us see if it is an effective argument to discover what is morally right and wrong.

Let's suppose that a person is at home with his family and a man breaks in and threatens to kill two of his children because the killer thinks that his family's size is too large. He could then use PM's line of reasoning as follows: "God is just as much in control of whether I choose to kill your children as when I choose not to kill them. The hands of the almighty are not tied by my murdering your children! A couple's children will die precisely at the time God wants, whether they are shot by me or not. Either way, then, God is ultimately in control of the size of your family. Therefore, I can shoot away. My act is morally acceptable."

Of course, this is absolutely ridiculous, and Piper, being the trained theologian that he is, would never argue this way on any other moral subject. But this is precisely the problem. The erroneous assumptions surrounding this issue have really damaged the consistency of the Christian worldview when even the best trained theologians engage it. PM, and those who argue likewise, are really the victims of a philosophic naturalism that has never been removed by the modern evangelical from this subject. Hence, the modern evangelical is plagued with logical fallacies and self contradictions when he or she seeks to reconcile the practice of contraception with the Christian worldview. As we have seen, the naturalistic assumption is unbiblical, and to prove it as such is to prove the arguments for contraception also to be unbiblical.

Furthermore, stewardship has to do with how one manages another's possessions. What is ironic about this argument, then, is that true stewardship of children can only come when one has and raises them in the Lord. It has nothing to do with how many the Master gives to the servant. That is for the Master to decide. Therefore, anyone arguing that rejection of God's possessions is an act of stewardship has misunderstood what the responsibility of such really is. In the Parable of the Talents, the master (i.e., God) gives his money to each servant in order that they might increase it for him. Of course, the evil servant does not increase it and is eternally condemned; but imagine if one of the servants had rejected how much the master wanted to give to him in the first place. Are we to really believe, as the advocates of contraception argue, that rejecting the predetermined amount of possessions the Master gives us, when He commands His servants to take and increase His possessions, is an act of good stewardship? Stewardship, therefore, can only take place when a servant has something over which he can exercise that stewardship in the first place, and our stewardship over children in the Bible is that we are to have them and raise them in the Lord. We are never told, explicitly or implicitly, that our stewardship is in the number of children the Master chooses to give us any more than it was the stewardship of the servants in the Parable of the Talents to determine how much money their master gave them.

Instead, Piper once again is arguing from a naturalistic mindset that believes the stewardship is over the natural biological, reproductive machine over which we now have complete control. We must, therefore, use the machine responsibly by producing a limited number of products/children that we determine to be appropriate to our individual situations. There is no need to reiterate here the unbiblical worldview driving this sentiment. Ultimately, God is the Master of the machine, deciding how many children His servants should have, and we are but the servants who should be eager and grateful for the amount the Master has predetermined for us (no matter how large or small that amount may be).

PERMISSION GRANTED FROM THE *IMAGO DEI*

J. Davis argues primarily from the image of God in man, and states that "just as God himself created the human race and recreated a fallen humanity according to a conscious plan, so it would follow that mankind, as God's vice regent on earth, should imitate God by exercising his procreative gifts according to a conscious plan. God did not create by a blind act of passion and will; neither should those made in his image."[42]

Bound up in this assertion is first and foremost the naturalistic idea that people create children on their own. Davis would surely not suggest that if God wanted to create a child, the humans should first decide if that decision is a correct one. Instead, he assumes the conception event to be a natural one, which must be then controlled by the people involved. This, as we have seen already, is not the Christian stance on the conception event.

Secondly, Davis has fundamentally misunderstood the passage in Genesis 1:26–28 by stating that the image of God implies that humans

---

42. Davis, *Evangelical Ethics*, 41.

have the responsibility to decide if having children in a given situation is appropriate toward God's goals as they are revealed in Scripture.[43]

What Davis seems to have missed is that the image of God refers to mankind's representation of God's rule over the earth and is connected to the command for humans therefore to rule over the earth as God's representatives. Davis may not have a problem with this observation at this point. However, the ruling over the earth in v. 28 is accomplished by the means of procreation in the first place. In other words, God tells the man and woman to "be fruitful and multiply, fill up the earth, subdue and rule over it" as a delineation of how the ruling is to take place: i.e., through procreation.

If this is true, then a person cannot make the argument that he or she should use the image of God to thwart procreation in some circumstances, because the command to take hold of the position of God's image in the world is only fulfilled through the very obedience to the procreative command. Saying then that the image should be used to thwart procreation in some circumstances is like saying that a human should use his or her humanity to decide when it's appropriate to become fully human; but is this not the purpose for which humanity is given? To be fulfilled? B is given in order to fulfill A. Therefore, A should not be used to nullify B. If B is nullified by A in order that A might be fulfilled, then, ironically, neither can A be fulfilled.

Davis's misunderstanding of the image and how it relates to the command, therefore, has led to a treatment of the image as a philosophical similarity with God, where humans become like God in making decisions about whether or not a command (in this case the procreative command) will be obeyed in every circumstance or not. But is this not the very interpretation the serpent gives to the image in Chapter 3 of Genesis? It is acceptable to disobey the command given precisely because the man and woman will be fulfilling their role in being "like God." The teaching of 1:26–28, however, is that mankind is set as God's image, a representative of His rule over the whole earth, accomplished through the filling up of the earth with covenant children who rule over it.[44] The

43. Ibid.

44. The phrases "in our image" and "like our likeness" in v. 26, as well as "in His image" and "in the image of God" in v. 27, are extremely important for this discussion, since humanity is *contained within* and *similar to* God's image, not God Himself. Man is not "like God" as the serpent implies to Eve, but instead is "like/as His image," which is a

man and the woman are made "in His *image*" and "like His *likeness*," not "like Him." The text does not teach, therefore, that the man and woman are "like God" in that they can make creative decisions that belong only to the Creator Himself. Davis has confused the terms and in doing so has argued the serpent's case for him.

WHOSE NATURE IS IT ANYWAY?

Another misconception is that the argument from nature refers to blind natural forces that must be left uncontrolled by humans. Davis seems to have this misunderstanding when he states that "man's calling is not simply to let 'nature take its course,' but to consciously redirect nature to the fulfillment of the divine plan."[45]

Piper's ministry continues its argument by displaying a fundamental misunderstanding of the argument from nature. They state:

> The "trust God, therefore don't use birth control" thinking is based upon the incorrect assumption that what happens "naturally" reflects "God's best" for our lives, but that what happens through human means does not. Why should we conclude that the way to let *God* decide the size of our family is to get out of the way and just let nature take its course? We certainly don't think that way in other areas of life. We don't reason, for example, that we should never get haircuts so that "God can decide" the length of our hair.[46]

First, PM clearly does not understand the procreative view because of their view that the conception event is merely a natural event. They also do not seem to understand the historic Christian argument from nature, which does not view nature as set up by God and then only governed by Him from a distance, but instead sees nature as that which is set up by, governed by, *and* intimately contingent upon God's decisions. For instance, when God sets up the roles between the man and woman at creation, the Church would argue that this is therefore the "nature" of the relationship between man and woman. They would state that we know from "nature" that man and woman are in a protector-protected role. The argument is not saying that we should have these roles because natural

---

symbol for God's rule over the given area in which the image resides. Hence, filling up the earth with covenant children is necessary to display God's rule over the whole earth.

45. Davis, *Evangelical Ethics*, 41.

46. Desiring God staff, "Does the Bible permit birth control?"

things that occur in the world tell us that it should exist this way. There seems to be confusion here on PM's part.

The argument from nature is that God has set up the reproductive system of humans in order to create children through it by means of the sexual act. He has conveyed this purpose at the creation of the sexes, as it is related in Scripture. Thus, (1) no argument is made that there are no human means in the sexual act and everything just happens; and (2) obviously, if God is making a willful decision to create a child for us it is "God's best" for our lives. Only PM's obliviousness to this fact causes them to treat the conception event like that of the mere human decision to get a haircut. (3) Because PM sees the conception event as natural in an atheistic sense, they fail to note that one might grow one's hair without the direct intervention of God, but one cannot make a human child without Him. (4) We are never commanded to grow our hair long, told that our hair is made for the primary purpose of growing long, told that our long hair is a part of our inheritance in YHWH , told that cutting our hair is an abomination; intentionally wiping out the future existence of a living personal being by cutting our hair, etc.

Furthermore, what does PM mean by "naturally" versus "through human means"? I know of no one who argues that conception naturally happens apart from human means. This of course could be a misspeak, but their analogy depends upon it. Hair grows if an individual does *nothing*. Children are created if humans and God do *something*. How are they related? If humans do something and then nothing, PM might have an analogy; but the fact is that humans make a decision to do something in the sexual act, and our responsibility as Christians is to discover whether that "something" is morally acceptable. The argument set forth by PM, therefore, creates a straw-man fallacy as it has nothing to do with what is argued by the opposition.

An Analysis of PM's Method of Argumentation

To sit back for a moment and view PM's form of argumentation, we see in it a few fallacies common to those seeking to justify the practice of contraception. The most prominent among them is that of *analogy*. Analogy, of course, is not an argument. It is an explanation, an illustration. It exists only to clarify a point, but it does not make a point itself. For instance, if I say that a farmer puts a seed in the field always hoping that the seed will grow and bear fruit, so also should man plant his seed always hoping the same, Piper will not then grant me the victory of the argument with my great analogy because, in fact, I haven't made an argument at all. Likewise, to compare having children with having land, getting haircuts, etc. does little for PM's case beyond attempting a rhetorical affect upon the reader. Instead, what it has done is to show us that PM views the conception event as being as natural an event as getting a haircut or choosing to own land. The attempt to use analogy as argumentation, unfortunately, just doesn't prove that it is. What it also indicates is that PM is without a real argument, and hence, they have resorted to mere analogy. As stated before, this just does not help their case.

Another fallacy committed by PM, and common to modern theologians, is that of question begging. The advocates of contraception assume that the conception event is a purely natural phenomenon, where a man and a woman choose to have children or not, and God simply chooses to sustain their ability to do so. This, of course, cannot be substantiated biblically, as we have seen, and perhaps that is why begging the question is such a powerful ally to advocates of contraception: because it is better to beg the question than to discuss it and lose all that ground.

However, I do not believe that such a fallacy is willful on PM's part, nor anyone else's. The problem is that the assumption of naturalism in our culture, especially when it comes to this issue, is so strong that one fails to realize the contradiction in seeing conception as God's creative choice and doing when a baby is allowed to exist as opposed to the sole creation of humans when one is prevented from existing. No Christian, of course, would argue that his or her current children are merely products of biological processes; and yet, when deciding whether to have future children, the couple automatically thinks of the process, that takes place in order to have them, as a purely biological one.

Finally, there is a bit of the straw-man fallacy (i.e., the fallacy that sets up and then refutes a weaker argument that the opposition is not presenting in order to give the appearance that the opposition has been refuted) used in PM's arguments, partially perhaps, because PM has never encountered the real positions, or perhaps has failed to understand what they have encountered.

IF IT'S SQUARE, IT CAN'T BE YELLOW

Some advocates will propose that, because Scripture presents the sexual act as something in which we should have pleasure, this somehow proves that any given sexual act can be used *solely* for the purpose of sexual pleasure absent the opportunity of God using it to create a child. This, however, is a false dichotomy where the person is arguing that *either* sex can be used for procreation *or* it can provide pleasure as a secondary purpose and benefit.

For instance, let's take the article by Greg Parsons, "Guidelines for Understanding and Utilizing the Song of Songs," which appeared in *Bibliotheca Sacra*, as one example. Parsons's argument repeats the common line that "the message of the Song gives a wholesome view of sex not merely for procreation (no children are mentioned in the book) but for pleasure (a divinely endorsed celebration)."[47]

Here we see the argument that, because the book does not explicitly restate the view that we have seen in the rest of the Bible (i.e., that the sexual act is to be used primarily for the purpose of procreation), then this must mean that the sexual act can be used for pleasure apart from the opportunity of procreation. In other words, what the text says excludes what the text does not say. If the text says B, and does not mention A, then A is not a part of B. Of course, this is a false dichotomy; and unless Parsons can demonstrate that to see sex as pleasurable excludes the view that the end goal of that pleasurable sex is the creation of a human child, he has failed to make a sound argument.

Contrast this fallacy with the correct analysis (that although A is not mentioned it may in fact be assumed and/or complementary to B) when Parsons answers the very type of false *either/or* fallacy he previously made concerning procreation, in a feminist claim that the text is egalitarian and counters complementarian/patriarchal ideas.[48] In order to answer this feminist argument, Parsons correctly tells us, "The book does not

---

47. *BibSac* 156 (1999), 422; identical arguments are made by Hess, *Song of Songs*, 35; Hubbard, *Ecclesiastes, Song of Solomon*, 268, and Kinlaw, *Song of Solomon, Expositor's*, 1207.

48. Parsons, *Guidelines for Understanding*, 422: "Feminists have argued (as part of the process of 'depatriarchalizing' the Bible) that the Song of Songs endorses the liberation of women, since there is no hint of male dominance, female subordination, or stereotyping of either sex."

advocate a change in traditional differentiation of sexual roles nor does it imply that differentiation is wrong."[49]

In other words, since the text does not explicitly counter a previously established biblical principle, it is incorrect to interpret what should be seen as complementary to that principle as a counter argument to it.

If we now apply this correct assessment to Parsons' argument concerning procreation, we then see that the statement that sex is "not merely for procreation" since "no children are mentioned in the book" is false.[50]

---

49. Ibid.

50. This claim is also false due to the fact that there are indications within the Song that the couple, who is seeking to engage in the sexual act, is doing so to create a family: "our bed flourishes [i.e., produces]; the beams of our household are cedars, our rafters are cypresses," seems to indicate that the couple desires to produce a large and strong family through the sexual act. This is confirmed by the groom, who associates her with the *ᶜalāmôth*, which are women who are eligible to get pregnant, since they are not already. See John Walton ("עֲלוּמִים" in *NIDOTTE* 3:415–17), who concludes that this term is connected to childbearing.

Regardless, however, the Song has never been a text used by the people of God to discover the morality of a sexual act. It simply says nothing as to what is moral. It is descriptive with no prescription. Instead, it is an ancient Near Eastern love poem (similar to those found in Egypt) expressing the sexual desire of an engaged couple on the one hand, and provides an illustration for God's desire for us and our desire for God on the other hand. It, therefore, says nothing to the morality of the sexual act, its primary purpose, etc. This is why Jesus, the Apostles, the Fathers, the Reformers, the Puritans, etc. do not use it as a text to discuss sexually moral issues. Instead, the two texts from which the New Testament's teaching concerning morality is derived are the book of Genesis as it is understood through the Holiness Code in the book of Leviticus. For the rest of the post-apostolic Church, following the Lord and the Apostles, sexual morality is based on these same texts as they are understood through New Testament texts, such as Romans 1:18–32. To argue one's case using the Song (or Wisdom literature in general) is not just a confusion of genre, but also an example of heterodoxy *par excellence*, since it is to reject the line of reasoning that Jesus and the Apostles take in order to substantiate their arguments. Although all of it is Scripture, some Scriptures are used as controlling passages, which in turn are used as the standard to which other passages must be harmonized. To come against this line of reasoning is much like Arius' rejection of the historic Church's use of passages that speak of the divinity of Christ as controlling in order to use those that speak of His humanity as controlling. Instead, of arguing that Christ is divine and those passages which refer to His humanity as being in harmony with that, Arius argued that Christ was essentially a created being, and harmonized the passages which referred to His divinity to mean that He only reflected God, not that He was God Himself. Controlling passages mean everything in discovering the truth, and it is up to the Lord and the Apostles to determine what passages on any given subject are to function as such; and it is incumbent upon the teachers they left behind to follow that same pattern of argumentation. To fail to do so is to reject the guidance of the Lord both directly and through the Holy Spirit upon His Church through the ages.

Sex in fact is for the purpose of procreation *and* it is a greatly intimate and pleasurable thing as one seeks to fulfill that goal. Parsons, then, provides the basis for rejecting his own argument.

The Scripture never gives an indication that the act of using sex for pleasure is in contrast to it being used as procreative. This would be like arguing the following:

(1) The Bible says that we are to worship God with the purpose of pleasing Him.

(2) However, the Bible also says that we should have pleasure in worshipping Him.

(3) Therefore, sometimes we can worship God to please Him and sometimes we can worship God to please ourselves absent of pleasing Him.

This, of course, is absurd. Our enjoyment of worshipping God comes through our primary purpose of pleasing Him in our worship. The two are not opposed to one another, but instead one is an outflow of the other. Without the primary use of worship (i.e., pleasing God), however, using worship to please ourselves (a secondary benefit), would be a grievous sin (something for which the Pharisees were truly rebuked). Likewise, the sexual act's primary purpose is to bring covenant children into existence and we are to have pleasure in that act; but the act without its primary purpose is nothing but self worship and sin.

Now, to be clear, I am not saying that Parsons is being dishonest. Far from it! Instead my contention is that a different set of standards for arguing one's case in the advocacy of use of contraception is common practice. I believe that the adoption of such bad reasoning displays the weakness of the contraception advocate's position. In essence, such bad reasoning is adopted to justify a deeply held belief and staple behavior, not to come to the truth of the issue.

We further see this false dichotomy displayed in the statement by the Feinbergs that there is no "evidence that objects geared to perform a particular end may not also serve other ends just as well and 'naturally."[51]

But the argument against the use of contraception is not that the sexual act cannot perform other ends, but that the primary end should

---

51. Feinberg and Feinberg, *Ethics for a Brave New World*, 174.

not be thwarted. This false dichotomy, therefore, has caused the Feinbergs to make a straw-man fallacy as well.

We encounter this line of reasoning again in Bruce Waltke's argument that sex has manifold purposes. He notes four purposes of the sexual act that he maintains would argue against the idea that procreation is its only purpose.[52] The four purposes are:

(1)   company for the lonely,[53]

(2)   unity,

(3)   pleasure, and

(4)   procreation.

It is argued that if the sexual act has other purposes, then it does not need to be open to the procreative purpose every time it is performed.[54]

If, however, one steps back and looks at the passages cited by Waltke, which supposedly support his alternate views of sexual purpose, his argument falls apart.[55]

For the purpose of "company" he cites two passages: Genesis 2:18 and Psalm 68:6. In Genesis 2:18, as we have already seen, the passage is concerned with procreation, not companionship. Context is instrumental to understanding such things, and unfortunately it seems to have been ignored here.

The second passage cited is Psalm 68:6 and has nothing to do with the sexual act. God is speaking of the Israelite slaves as those who are in a solitary place and therefore "solitary" and without a home.[56] The Psalm, speaking of Egypt, has application to the Babylonian exiles as well. The land is the home that God will give to them, and they will thus no longer be scattered as single units but gathered together as a nation in the land.

52. Waltke, "The Old Testament and Birth Control," 5.

53. Thielicke (*Theological Ethics,* 204–05) not only sees fellowship as a major component of marriage's purpose, but uses it as the controlling factor. If contraception works against fellowship, it can be discarded. The problem is that this entire argument is based on the misinterpretation of Genesis 2:18. If this word is interpreted in its context, then his entire argument fails, as fellowship, although a spiritual benefit of marriage, is nowhere said to be its primary, and therefore controlling, purpose.

54. Interestingly enough, this argument is also used to justify the use of abortion.

55. Garrett, "Christians and Contraception," who makes extensive use of Waltke's article, encourages us to study the verses cited, and so we shall.

56. Dahood, *Psalms II,* 137.

The common translation "home" is also misleading here as it is the word for "dwelling place." Hence, God is talking about bringing his people into the land of Israel. Giving those who are scattered among the nations a place to live is hardly a comment on a purpose for the sexual act.

We see then that Waltke has not given adequate reason for believing that a primary purpose of the sexual act can be companionship. This is not to say that companionship is not *a* purpose of the sexual act, a secondary benefit; but it is to say that companionship cannot be pitted against procreation, which is the *primary* purpose of the sexual act. As far as the Bible is concerned, however, it seems preoccupied with the primary purpose (i.e., procreation) more than with any other secondary benefit of the sexual act; and more often our experience is what tells us of the secondary benefits. Likewise, the importance we place upon the sexual act from our experience ought to take a secondary role to that which is emphasized in the Bible and throughout the history of the Church.

His second purpose stated is that of *unity*. Why exactly unity between two people is best accomplished through the sexual act is not made clear. However, the verse cited (Gen 2:24) only supports the idea that sexual unity is for the purpose of procreation. The male and female relationship is made to be fruitful and multiply in Genesis 1, and in Genesis 2 the female is made to help the man no longer be a single human being and to fill up the earth. Genesis 4:1 then shows us that the purpose of the sexual union is procreation. Therefore, once again, Waltke has not proven his case, but instead has proven ours.

Finally, we have already dealt with the aspect of pleasure in the preceding discussion. None of the three purposes Waltke places on the sexual act undermine the argument that the primary purpose of the sexual act is procreative. Waltke has fallen prey to the popular use of the fallacy of false distinction.

Stanley Grenz, one of the forefathers of the Emerging Church movement, argued for three other purposes besides procreation:

> It can serve as a beautiful statement of the covenant between husband and wife, as the reenactment, reaffirmation, and embodiment of the marriage vow. Or it can function as a celebrative expression of the submission of the partners to each other in all areas of marital life."[57]

57. Grenz, "Family Planning and the People of God," 38.

Of course, one can think of a hundred different expressions the sexual act can make, but this doesn't take the smallest step toward telling us whether it is acceptable to express these through the sexual act contrary to the overarching procreative purpose the Bible presents to us. If one argues that a couple may engage in the sexual act in order to make a statement about how they feel about one another, it is a giant leap to say that they can engage in it *only* to feel good about each other. That is both a completely different and unproven argument. Likewise, if God desires that the covenant and marriage vows of the man and woman include that they will seek God's will in producing a family, then where is Grenz's argument?

Grenz's third stated purpose, that sex can be a celebration of mutual submission, is an odd one as it assumes an exegetical mistake made in interpreting the phrase "one another" in Ephesians 5:21.[58] Leaving Grenz's egalitarian interpretation of the passage for another time, however, the celebration of sex ought to express submission to God's desires before those of another. If the primary purpose of procreation is allowed to proceed in the sexual act, then all other expressions can be discussed as options (including the many applications to sex which are taught by the passage in Ephesians 5), but if one seeks to undermine the primary purpose with a secondary purpose, he or she is not making a valid argument. Therefore, Grenz also falls prey to the fallacy of false distinction.

The Feinbergs adopted this same line of argumentation in their oft quoted book, *Ethics for a Brave New World*[59] and added two more purposes of the sexual act to Waltke's list: (1) to raise up godly seed and (2) to curb lust.

The first does not need to be discussed, since it is the same as the procreative argument. The strange dichotomy made between procreation and raising up godly seed can only be explained as a misunderstanding

58. The Greek word *allēlous* is not always reciprocal, and the context here certainly indicates that it is not to be taken as such. For instance, if everyone is to submit to everyone, then parents are to submit to children. Instead, "one another" here is explained in the delineation of authority (i.e., "this one to that one"): the Church to Christ, wives to husbands, children to parents, servants to masters, etc. (cf. Rev 6:4). Furthermore, from a logical standpoint, if everyone is in submission, then no one is in authority, and hence, no one can be in submission. Thus, the reciprocity argument is self-refuting.

59. Feinberg and Feinberg, *Ethics for a Brave New World*, 175–76. Liederbach ("Contraception," 135) follows the Feinbergs' argument. Note also that he undermines his own argument for contraception when speaking about the sin of Onan.

of the historical argument—as though by procreation the Church only meant making babies apart from raising them in the Lord.

The second is more important and is commonly advocated in popular forms of the pro-contraceptive argument. In 1 Corinthians 7:1–9, the Apostle Paul states that people should get married because of *tas porneias,* "the sexual immoralities." The Apostle uses the plural here to denote that these are types of sexual immorality, not simply a generic form of "lust" as is often argued. The interpretation then hinges on what types of sexual immorality are in mind. I have already argued here that the term "sexual immorality" in the New Testament takes upon itself the idea of non-procreative sexual acts we see in Leviticus 18, and this is especially true of the plural, which denotes types of sexual immorality. If this is true, then the Apostle is stating that Christians ought to get married if they cannot control their sexual desire and it thus leads to non-procreative sex acts outside of the marriage relationship. Sexual desire can then be directed in a procreative way (one that creates family) inside of marriage, and the individuals will be free from sin. If this is the case, then sexual immorality can be curbed only through the sexual act that is procreative, as the very definition of sexual immorality is an intentional non-procreative sexual act.

If modern advocates of contraception are telling us that Paul is saying that marriage controls lust, then they are arguing that Paul is telling us something untrue, as anyone married knows that this is not the case. Instead, if it is being argued that marriage provides a divine direction for sexual desire, then I would be in full agreement with such an interpretation. However, the latter interpretation is the same as I advocated before. The divine direction is procreation and, therefore, consistent with the rest of Scripture. The critic can say that the divine direction is temporal satisfaction of the sexual urge (which I would say may be a secondary purpose here), but this would be begging the question as no other biblical support is given for such a view. The question would then be, Does 1 Corinthians 7:1–9 teach that the sexual act can be performed for the mere purpose of satisfying a temporal, sexual urge absent of the procreative purpose? To say that it does, with no further evidence, is to assume the very position that needs first to be substantiated with biblical evidence, and the evidence to do so just isn't there. Hence, if one insists that this be the case, he or she will only be begging the question. Furthermore, as stated before, the very definition of sexual immorality, which the individual who marries is trying to avoid, prohibits the idea that the primary purpose of the sexual act is to satisfy an urge absent of the eternal purpose of a child of God coming into existence.

All of the alleged "other" purposes of the sexual act are compatible with the procreative purpose, as long as that procreative purpose is seen as the primary purpose. The arguments from false dichotomy then display some of the weaknesses of the pro-contraceptive case.

IT'S THE ECONOMY STUPID!

Some will argue that the practice of birth control is permissible if someone cannot afford children. This, of course, is another argument from situational ethics, where certain circumstances override the obligation to obey a command from God. This type of argumentation does not hold up when it is applied to other things that people believe are genuinely wrong. For instance, one could make the argument that it is morally acceptable to commit murder or robbery based on one's economic need; but the Bible would tell the individual to trust in God (e.g Matt 6:24–34) rather than disobey Him in order to meet that perceived need. This argument begs the question in that it assumes that the practice of birth control is morally acceptable and proceeds to argue from what it has failed to prove: that a person can practice this morally acceptable thing in a given situation (in this case, contingent upon the economic situation).

The Feinbergs alter this argument by pitting two different commands in the Bible against one another. They argue that the command to provide for one's family, in 1 Timothy 5:8, may be in tension with the command to procreate in Genesis 1:28. If this is the case, then the command to procreate may have to be limited in order to obey the command to care for one's family.[60] This is a clever argument, but it makes a major error in using this as an example.

1 Timothy 5:8 states, "But if anyone does not provide for his own, specifically speaking, for those of his household, he has denied the faith and is worse than an unbeliever." At first, this text may seem to support the Feinbergs' argument, but a closer examination of the context indicates that the passage is referring to an individual who has the ability to sup-

---

60. Davis (*Evangelical Ethics*, 40) follows this argument briefly by stating that "this higher spiritual good [which he says Paul teaches in 1 Corinthians 7] could certainly be broadened to include the good of the family as a whole and the welfare of children already born."

port his immediate family but refuses to do so. Hence, in v. 4, relatives are told to provide for widows if they are able to do so. If widows are able to support themselves, that is a better option than burdening the church. It would be a complete contradiction regarding the New Testament teaching, concerning the poor, to say that someone who is not able to support his or her family is being disobedient to God. The Feinbergs have ignored the context and sought to apply this passage to those who may find themselves in a more difficult financial position because of their choice to obey God in the area of reproduction; when, in fact, it simply refers to a person who refuses to support his family when he is able to do so. This is a clear abuse of the text.

Secondly, the Feinbergs, as other pro-birth control advocates often do, fail to apply their reasoning to other ethical issues in order to test their validity. For instance, would the command to support one's family override the commands concerning murder (specifically in the case of abortion or infanticide), stealing, idolatry, etc.? One could list every moral command in the Bible and make the argument the Feinbergs have made in an effort to undermine that moral. It is the surest proof that an argument in favor of a particular practice is false when it potentially undermines every moral practice presented to us in Scripture.

Instead, we are told that God will provide for those who seek His lordship over their lives as a first priority (Matt 6:32–34). In fact, in Psalm 127, the Psalmist tells us the following:

> [1]Unless the Lord builds the house,
> They labor in vain who build it;
> Unless the Lord guards the city,
> The watchman keeps awake in vain.
> [2]It is vain for you to rise up early,
> To retire late,
> To eat the bread of painful labors;
> For He gives to the person He loves [even in his] sleep.
> [3]Behold, children are an inheritance belonging to the Lord,
> The fruit of the womb is a reward.

God would have us focus on raising our children and trust in Him for the means to do so. If we are to believe God, then we are free to obey Him without worrying about the consequence of unmet needs. If we argue that one must break a moral command in order to fulfill another, however, we are not giving a biblical argument. God would have us obey all of His commands, and they are capable of being obeyed, as long as we understand what each one asks of us in context. Essentially, if the Feinbergs' argument were true, 1 Timothy 5:8 would condemn everyone who was poor, since such a person is not able to provide for a family. In fact, it would also argue that the command in Genesis 1:28 is meant only for the well-to-do. Such, of course, is neither the teaching of Scripture as a whole nor the logic of this passage in context.

Instead, the Christian way of thinking about the subject is summed up in the following comments by Adam Clarke.

> *Lo, children are an heritage of the LORD.* That is, to many God gives children in place of temporal good. To many others he gives houses, lands, and thousands of gold and silver, and with them the womb that beareth not; and these are their inheritance. The poor man has from God a number of children, without lands or money; these are his inheritance; and God shows himself their father, feeding and supporting them by a chain of miraculous providences. Where is the poor man who would give up his six children with the prospect of having more [material possessions], for the thousands or millions of him who is the centre of his own existence, and has neither root nor branch but his forlorn solitary self upon the face of the earth? Let the fruitful family, however poor, lay this to heart: *Children are an heritage of the LORD: and the fruit of the womb is his reward.* And he who gave them will feed them; for it is a fact, and the maxim formed on it has never failed, "Wherever God sends mouths, he sends meat." "Murmur not", said an Arab to his friend, "because thy family is large; know that it is for *their sakes* that God feeds *thee*."[61]

IT'S A MATTER OF CONSCIENCE: ROMANS 14 AND 15 AND THE FREEDOM TO USE AMORAL THINGS

Some people will then claim that Christians are free to practice what they want according to Romans 14 and 15. This passage states that the weaker brother is not able to use certain things like wine or meat (in this case, contraception), but the stronger brother can, and should not be judged by the weaker brother. Christians are, therefore, free to practice what they personally think is right for them.

---

61. Clarke. As quoted in Spurgeon, *The Treasury of David*, comment on Psalm 127:3. See also that same work for the numerous Christian commentators who state the same.

First, a brief note concerning the biblical concept of Christian freedom seems appropriate here. The New Testament concept of Christian freedom stems from Isaiah 61:1, where the gospel that is preached is said to bring "freedom to the captives." The word for "freedom" here is *dᵉrôr*, which often refers to the year of Jubilee, or the Sabbath Year. This is the year that slaves are released from bondage. The central idea of freedom here is freedom from bondage, not complete liberty to do whatever one wants. In fact, Paul explicitly commands Christians to use this freedom to do what is pleasing to God. He states: "For you were called to freedom, brethren; only [do] not [turn] your freedom into an opportunity for the flesh, but through love serve one another" (Gal 5:13). Likewise, Peter tells us to "[act] as free men, and do not use your freedom as a covering for evil, but [use it] as bondslaves of God" (1 Pet 2:16). Peter also tells us that one who uses his freedom to indulge in whatever he wishes is not free at all, but is, instead, enslaved (2 Pet 2:19). Hence, Paul tells us that the Holy Spirit sets a person's mind against his fleshly desires, so that he may not do whatever he pleases (Gal 5:17).

In other words, freedom from the bondage of the law, which cannot justify a person, does not mean that a Christian should not see in the law what is pleasing to God and loving to others within His community. In fact, it is the law that tells a person to love God (Deut 6:5; Matt 22:37) and his fellow Christian (Lev 19:18; Matt 22:39). Christ's liberty gives a person freedom from a self-centered quest to achieve salvation through works (i.e., freedom from focusing on and loving the self) so that one can seek to please God through love (i.e., focusing on and loving God). Hence, freedom itself calls us to seek out what is pleasing to God.[62] In application of this, our present question is doing just that.

But what about the objections, which have been raised from Romans 14 and 15, that argue that Christians are free to practice what they wish? Of course, what this text says and what our post-modern Church culture thinks it says are two different things altogether. The idea that this text is speaking about ethical practices is nowhere to be seen within the text. Instead, the Apostle Paul is concerned here with Jewish-Gentile relations within the Church, which were threatened by the ritual customs of each culture.[63] Therefore, the subject is not morals but cultural customs prac-

---

62. See the article in *NIDNTT* 1:715–20.

63. Cranfield, *A Critical and Exegetical Commentary*, 2:696-97; Moo, *The Epistle to the Romans*, 831.

ticed by the two groups. In the case of the Jews, drinking certain kinds of wine and eating certain types of meat were seen as ritually impure. Hence, Paul speaks about the drinking of wine and eating of meat. Likewise, the issue of holy days was the subject of a long dispute between Jews and Greeks, largely based around whether the culture should follow a solar or lunar calendar.[64] In fact, Paul contrasts these ritual customs with what the reign of God over our lives is really about: righteousness (14:17).

When Paul then turns to theology and morals, i.e., the mind and character of Christ, he tells us to be of "one mind" and to praise God with "one mouth" (15:5–6). Thus, Christian unity is in doctrinal thought and moral practice, not in rituals or customs. A stronger Christian is able to use different amoral, cultural customs without associating them with paganism (as would many of the Jewish Christians), whereas the weaker brother could not in good conscience practice rituals they associated with idolatrous festivals. These are amoral, created *things*, not moral or immoral practices. Hence, the practice of rituals and customs (what to eat and drink, what days to observe, etc.) are dependent upon the faith of the individual. Morals, however, are not up for negotiation. Paul is not suggesting that the stronger brother can practice murder, sexual immorality, or idolatry if he has enough faith. The abuse of this text to justify immoral practices among modern evangelicals is astounding; but it is clear that the attempt to do so falls apart once the context is considered.

Therefore, this passage has little to do with our current issue at hand. As we have discussed here, whether one uses contraception is a moral question, not a ritual or customary one. Hence, the contraceptive lifestyle is not a matter of conscience. Any objection raised on the basis of this misunderstanding is, therefore, irrelevant.

A SPOONFUL OF SUGAR

It is further argued that the rejection of contraception is equivalent to the rejection of the use of medicine in general. There are a few assumptions at work here, but we will discuss the most important distinction.

Contraception is to be distinguished from medicine for one major reason: a future human being is not a disease to be countered. Sickness is a post-Fall condition that is not a part of the original design of God

---

64. This dispute stretches back all the way to early Second Temple times, as reflected in such works as Jubilees, 1 Enoch, and 1 Maccabees.

for the human being. When one counters illness, which is a result of living under the curse of death, he or she is countering a fallen condition and seeking to restore the pre-Fall condition as much as one can in the here and now. In other words, one is not countering God's creative act in the pre-lapsarian design when medicine is used to counter illness, but is instead, working with God in order to worship Him and return to that which God desires the human to be in the fullest.

However, the use of contraception is the exact opposite of the above. The person who uses it is working against God and the pre-Fall design God has set in place. Contraception and medicine, therefore, are as different as night and day. One is pro-creation and one is anti-creation. This is also the reason why the Church has historically referred to contraceptive drugs as "poison." The distinction between the use of medicine, which is meant to cure/give life, and contraception, which is meant to destroy/prevent life, is an absurd comparison of opposites.

Furthermore, this is made evident by the fact that God never tells us to abstain from the use of medicine and to remain sick, whereas He does tell us to have children. This idea, however, that children are to be equated with disease, is itself a mental sickness in our culture. A human being is not a cursed disease to be extinguished but is instead a blessing given by God for the good of the Christian couple, the covenant community, and ultimately for God's glory. The argument that contraception is a type of medicine is an indication of how far modern evangelicalism has come from the biblical view of children. Either way, however, if a person wanted to substantiate this argument, he or she would have to establish from the Bible that a child is a disease in the appropriate sense. I for one have never seen such a gymnastic eisegesis as to turn what the Bible considers a blessing into a curse, but our religious culture's ability to turn good into evil and sweet into bitter (Isa 5:20) in an effort to justify itself no longer surprises me; and hence, I fully expect someone to attempt it to his own destruction (2 Pet 3:16).

"NATURAL" FAMILY PLANNING
AND THE ABSURDITY OF SEMANTICS

Finally we come to the concept of natural family planning (NFP from here on out).[65] Many will attempt a distinction between artificial contraception

---

65. NFP is a modern variation of the older, and less effective, rhythm method. The

and natural methods. In the minds of the proponents of NFP, artificial contraception attempts to prevent a life that would normally come to exist through the fertile sexual act. By engaging in the sexual act at times of infertility, the couple is supposedly avoiding the pitfalls of artificial contraception. Since no child would come into existence through the infertile sexual act, the couple imagines that they are safe from the charge of willfully attempting to counter the existence of a child through the sexual act. The couple is said to willfully abstain from sex during fertile times (much for the same various reasons others use artificial contraception) because they precisely do not wish to counter the conception of a child which would be brought about through that sexual act.

One of the major problems, of course, with this view is made apparent as soon as one realizes that he or she is avoiding fertile sexual acts precisely because he or she wishes for a child not to come into existence. The couple is not abstaining for reasons of prayer as in 1 Corinthians 7, but instead because the couple wishes to avoid an unwanted pregnancy (i.e., to plan their family by limiting children through their manipulation of the sexual act). The NFP position is simply a backhanded way of a bringing about the same results that artificial contraception does, but with a much more hypocritical, religious facade. The point is that a child is not wanted, so the couple abstains from the sexual act, *so that* a child cannot come into existence. The motive is the same, and to suggest otherwise is simply to engage in a ridiculous semantic game, which plays by different rules in order to achieve the same result.

The Bible also presents us with an example of this attitude toward the sexual act. In Exodus 1:9–14, the murderous Pharaoh decides that he wants to limit the fruitfulness of God's people by placing them under hard labor. The thought seems to be that if the Israelites are too tired to have sexual relations with their wives, then the conception of large numbers of children can be avoided. Notice that the Pharaoh's (the Satan figure/serpent's seed in Exodus) first move against God's people is to cause them to avoid sexual relations so that they diminish the existence of their future children. In other words, the plan of the adversary to counter God's plan to multiply His people is to make them avoid sexual acts which may be

---

two are distinguished by the fact that the latter is an attempt to avoid conception of a child through the sexual act by observing the lengths of previous cycles, while the former attempts the same by observing signs of the current cycle. The intent, of course, is the same in both methods.

fertile and hence produce children. The Pharaoh understands that avoidance of the sexual act leads to his desired result (i.e., contraception/the non-conception of a human child). Although contraception is not being practiced by a couple who chooses not to engage in the sexual act because they are tired, if the couple avoids the sexual act for the reason the Pharaoh wished God's people to avoid the sexual act, it is at that point that the couple has entered into the contraceptive spirit and has fallen into the sin that the historic Church would consider to be a form of murder.

Furthermore, as we leave the question of whether NFP seeks to wipe out the existence of a future person, we turn to the question of sexual immorality (i.e., engaging in a sexual act that is known to be non-procreative). Even if, through semantics, the NFP advocates can slide past the charge of murder, the willful practice of engaging in unproductive sexual acts by having sex knowingly in times of infertility does not save them from the charge of sexual immorality. In fact, one destroys the argument against homosexuality, or any other type of sexual immorality for that matter, which is not with another partner of the opposite sex, since the participants are engaging in sexual acts which cannot bring about the existence of a child. There is no reason these sexual acts should not be legitimized by the NFP argument. Unfortunately for NFP advocates, however, these acts are condemned in Scripture precisely for the reason that they are infertile sexual acts. Both the Scripture, in telling them to be fruitful and multiply (Gen 1:28) and to engage only in procreative sexual acts (Leviticus 18 with an emphasis on v. 19 for our present subject), and the historic Christian interpretation thereof (see comments in Chapter 2) explicitly condemn the NFP method.

Furthermore, the NFP displays its guilt of the charge concerning idolatry as well. In its very name we are presented with the idea that humans, rather than God, plan their families (i.e., how many children they will have). Not only does NFP fall prey to the naturalistic interpretation of the conception event, but in doing so lifts the couple up as the gods of reproduction by choosing to engage only in unproductive sexual acts in order to prevent the existence of a child that would result from a fertile sexual act.

The NFP, contrary to what its advocates may assume, is worse than the artificial contraceptive position largely because it attempts to commit the same sins but in a guise of false piety. The NFP proponent is no more in submission to God when it comes to his or her family size than is any other advocate of artificial contraception.

Further questions for the NFP argument are: Is it morally acceptable for a couple to abstain from fertile sexual acts when God made couples to do just that thing? If God had revealed to you that you were to have five children, but you attempted to have only three of them by engaging in infertile sexual acts and abstaining from fertile sexual acts, would you consider yourself in sin? Does God not have our families already planned, and are we not attempting to thwart that plan and the existence of those future children by abstaining from the fertile sexual acts that God would used to make those children?

PROCREATION IS PERFECTED IN THE GOSPEL, NOT REPLACED BY IT

It is often argued that the command to be fruitful and multiply is typological and fulfilled spiritually in the Great Commission. Hence, the bearing of children in the Old Testament is fulfilled by preaching the gospel in the New Testament.

There are three major problems with this viewpoint.

1. Having and raising children in the Lord is seen as "the doing of good." It is seen this way because it is "pro-creative," meaning that it works toward God's ends of filling up the earth with covenant children. The New Testament does not, then, tell us to stop perpetuating human life through the other means presented in the Hebrew Bible (i.e., giving and preserving life through conception, hospitality, philanthropy, etc.) simply because human life is ultimately preserved through the gospel; but instead tells us to "take it up a notch" as a witness to that gospel message. Hence, Paul's definition of the "good" that a godly widow ought to have exhibited in her life includes having and bringing up children (1 Tim 5:10).

2. Although the gospel is the means to ultimately fulfill God's ends in preserving human life and reversing chaos, using it to replace other means of preserving human life and reversing chaos, like having children to whom the gospel would be preached and with whom God's ends would be accomplished, is to create a false dichotomy.

3. If contraception is a form of murder, sexual immorality, idolatry, faithlessness, etc., then one is essentially arguing that it is morally

acceptable to do evil as long as one is doing the good of preaching the gospel (see Matt 7:21-23; Rom 3:8).

The fact is that there is no New Testament precedent where good works are replaced with the preaching of the gospel. The two ought to be done in conjunction with one another, and in fact the preaching of the gospel is limited by the intentional limitation of the recipients of that preaching. What is, therefore, inconsistent with the New Testament mandate to preach the gospel is the limiting of children to whom it would be proclaimed. In fact, the actual command requires God's people to make disciples. That command, therefore, requires both the proclamation and demonstration of the teachings of the gospel in both word and deed. The argument, therefore, that seeks to replace a good work with the work of the gospel is to no avail. One cannot leave out the foundation because the walls and roof are considered to be the ultimate purpose of that foundation. The two must go together.

UNDERMINING THE PRINCIPLE BY LIMITING THE APPLICATION TO ITS ORIGINAL CULTURE

A popular argument today is to maintain that large families were desired by agrarian cultures due to their need of field workers to farm the domestic landscape. This argument perceives the condemnation of contraception as stemming from the social culture in which agriculture was the primary means of resources for a family. Hence, large families were valued and contraception was condemned.[66] Bruce Waltke puts forth the argument as follows:

> In contrast to our society a man living in the Old Testament world valued a large family because it provided both economic and national security. Survival demanded growth and expansion. [Richard M.] Fagley says: "Underpopulation, rather than overpopulation was the dominant reality." In addition, men in the ancient society differed from Christians today in that they sought "social immortality"; i.e. preservation of their memory upon earth through their offspring. Christians, on the other hand, see "individual immortality"; i.e., the hope of life after death. In a word, Old Testament saints living in the structure of a rural society were much more favorably disposed toward large families than many Christian couples today living in overcrowded cities. For us, chil-

66. H. Wayne House, "Should Christians Use Birth Control?"

dren tend to be a financial hindrance rather than help. In the light of these changed conditions we must raise the question: "How relevant is the obviously favorable attitude toward large families in the Old Testament for us?"[67]

Waltke fails to observe that Fagley's perception stems largely from later Greco-Roman times when "underpopulation" became an issue precisely because the widespread acceptance and use of contraception, as well as the cultural propaganda used to promote, had accomplished its goal in convincing the culture that it was a socially responsible practice.

What Waltke also fails to note is the massive evidence that we have telling us the exact opposite of his conclusions. People in the Old Testament world did not value large families. They valued a single male heir, and possibly a second son as a backup, in order to pass along the familial inheritance. This is the primary concern of ancient society, not how many people will be available for farming the land.

This is made clear by their widespread use of contraception, the preoccupation with inheritance issues found within ancient law codes, and overpopulation propaganda, like Atra-hasis, which attempted to convince people to use measures "to stop childbearing."

Waltke's speculation at this point has turned against the evidence that suggests otherwise in order to provide what would otherwise be a fallacious argument anyway. Providing the *Sitz im Leben* for a teaching in the Old Testament as a way of dismissing what is taught as simply a cultural phenomenon is a poor hermeneutical practice at best and a genetic fallacy at worst. It does not matter why a person may decide to do A instead of B. It only matters if A is moral or immoral. It may be advantageous to have more children if one is a farmer, but if one is a coppersmith or a potter, working in a small, hot room, such a prospect may not be as desirable. Either way, it is irrelevant whether obedience to a moral command is also beneficial or unbeneficial to those to whom it is given. Obedience to the gospel causes more difficulties in some cultures than others. This has nothing to do with whether the gospel should be applied to an individual's life.

Waltke may want to make the argument that propaganda comes from the palace, and it is the palace's concern that workers and armies are fortified by population growth. Although this sounds possible at first,

---

67. Bruce K. Waltke, "Old Testament Texts," 8.

what is striking is that the literature which is endorsed by the palace is for, rather than against, population control. This may be the case because the concern is not primarily strength of numbers as much as strength through resources. In other words, the concern is not that the land will not be farmed, since there are always people to work it; instead the concern is how many mouths there will be to use up those resources. A lesser amount of workers may mean more work for farmers, but the palace is not concerned with such things. The primary concern stems from the common belief, derived from living in these small strips of land, is that there are too many people already. We have to remember that Israel too is filled with millions of people. We only need, therefore, to look at the current situation to see that "underpopulation" is not that with which most people living in these regions would be concerned. The push back to this is seen in the propagation of birth control, found within the literature of the surrounding nations, in order to cut the number of people using up the available resources down to size.

Therefore, the evidence suggests that the social situation of the Old Testament is one in which contraception would have been seen as a good thing. The amazing element of the Old Testament's rejection of it can only be explained by a divinely inspired, counter cultural influence placed within ancient Israelite culture through the divine revelation with which it was entrusted. Waltke's arguments to establish a genetic fallacy is of no avail at the starting point, but his irresponsible shunning of the historical material in order to replace fact with fiction displays how powerful the negative customs of our culture determine our desires to explain away the facts.[68]

OBSERVATIONS ON THE METHODOLOGY OF THE PRO-CONTRACEPTIVE ARGUMENT

What is perhaps the most lasting impression one gains from the modern evangelical argument is that it denies the trajectory taken by the New Testament and the historical Christian Church to establish sexual ethics in order to take upon itself the methodology of argumentation of the

---

68. It should further be noted that this argument attempts to place the root of the rationale of a scriptural mandate and view of the sexual act in the culture, rather than in God's desires as they were displayed in creation. The placement of the procreative command in Scripture at creation is meant to express God's desires for humanity regardless of later cultural customs which might be instituted in a fallen world.

larger culture. For example, the method taken by the New Testament authors is to establish the purpose of the sexual act based on Genesis 1–2 for the positive teaching that sex is to be primarily procreative. It then bases its negative case on Leviticus 18 in order to establish the fact that sexual immorality describes any act that negates the primary purpose of Genesis 1–2. The historic Church has followed this same trajectory in determining issues of sexual morality. Onan in Genesis 38 occasionally serves as an example of someone who negates Genesis 1–2 by practicing something condemned by the principle established in Leviticus 18.

However, the modern methodology, whether it be for the purposes of justifying the practice of homosexuality, abortion, promiscuity, contraception, etc. is to undermine these passages by reinterpreting them, limiting their application, or diminishing/diluting their absolute claims by setting other Scriptures or Scriptural principles against them.

We are told time and time again that Genesis 1–2 is not a command (either originally or at least in its application to the modern reader). It is argued that the Song of Songs give us a purpose for the sexual act that undermines the idea that Genesis 1:28 is absolute. We are further told that the image of God is best expressed in Wisdom literature, and provides a basis for us to determine for ourselves what constitutes the highest good in any given situation. Thus the authority of the command is limited by exerting one's own authority in determining its application.

The Leviticus passage is likewise limited in its modern application, since it is interpreted to be a cultural expression of holiness, dealing with a specific concern within the culture, rather than expressing examples of an absolute moral claim.

When these same authors attempt to undermine the historic understanding of the Church, they attribute their interpretations of these texts to cultural philosophical influences rather than to profound Spirit-led insights into the biblical text.

The modern evangelical must understand that the issue hinges on not only *what* is being argued, but really on *how* it is being argued.

A good example of the modern method of argumentation in establishing a sexual ethic is seen in a line of reasoning provided by C. L. Seow.[69]

---

69. Seow, "Textual Orientation," 17–34.

Seow begins his argument by stating that, for Jesus, "human needs provided the hermeneutical key to understanding the legal tradition."[70] He refers to this as theology "from below," which essentially means, for Seow, that the love of people, as presented in the gospel, allows us to determine the limits a command may have in its application to a present person's situation. The command must be filtered through the wisdom of the recipient, and judged by him or her for its practical application to his or her given situation.

Seow advances the methodology of his argument by going through the various passages that have been interpreted historically to prohibit certain unproductive sexual acts, and systematically showing how they do not really say what historical interpreters had once thought they said.[71]

After stating, as is common practice, that procreation is considered a good in Scripture, Seow continues to argue against it being applied to every situation. He states:

> Despite the clarity of the Biblical text, we are aware that procreation is not a command that every human being can keep. There are some people who are biologically incapable of bearing children. Elsewhere in the Bible, too, the problem of human infertility is recognized . . . Then, there are others, who for economic and pragmatic reasons, do not obey the imperative to have children . . . Modern social and economic realities may necessitate a reconsideration of the imperative to "be fruitful and multiply."[72]

Seow then moves on to Old Testament wisdom literature, and argues that the authority of wisdom literature is experiential. In other words, it argues from the situation in which humans find themselves, rather than "from above."[73] It is situational (or relative), rather than absolute. Hence, since all of the Scriptures thought to convey a certain morality of the sexual act are reinterpreted, thus indicating that the Bible does not explicitly teach what the historic Church believed it to have explicitly taught, people should discern what is right and wrong from the wisdom of God given to them through experience as well as the general biblical text.

70. Ibid., 20.
71. Ibid., 21–27.
72. Ibid., 27.
73. Ibid., 31.

This argument should sound familiar to anyone who has read thoroughly through this section. It includes an appeal to a rejection of the historic interpretation in favor of a reinterpretation of Scripture so that Scripture seems to say nothing about the subject, the necessity of considering the recipient's situation in determining whether Scripture is applicable, and the pitting of certain Scriptural principles against other Scriptural principles in a way that contradicts (or undermines the absolute application of a traditionally controlling passage) rather than harmonizes the concepts as working together.

The interesting thing about Seow's argument, however, is that it is not an attempt to establish the morality of the use of contraception (something with which Seow assumes his readers already agree). Instead, this line of reasoning has been made to establish the morality of homosexual relationships.

The point I am making here is not that everyone who argues this way will adopt the same ideas about homosexuality that Seow has adopted.[74] Instead, my point is that this line of argumentation, which undermines the foundation of the historic Christian view of the sexual act in order to establish a modern view of the sexual act as normative, has been adopted by modern evangelicals in order to justify the use of contraceptive practices. If Seow's line of reasoning is invalid in the case of the homosexual argument, why is this line of reasoning perfectly valid in the case of contraceptive practices? If the above arguments presented by evangelicals are true, I see no reason to suggest that Seow's application of those arguments to the homosexual issue is false.

However, if one returns to the methodology utilized by the New Testament and historic Christian authors, the evangelical arguments above, as well as Seow's argument, fall apart. This is why displaying the historic Christian argument is of such a value in seeing not only *what* is argued, but *how* it is argued; and why I have placed such an emphasis on the historic witness of the Church as an authoritative guide to help the modern evangelical restore a hermeneutical trajectory that would lead to a historically unified Christian understanding of the sexual act and its primary purpose.

---

74. It does seem clear that, although evangelicals may be able to hold on to the *what* in the homosexual debate for another generation or two, eventually the failure to course correct the *how* of the argument will inevitably lead later generations to agree with Seow's conclusions.

PART SIX

Dialogues: Discussing Contraception with the Teachers of the Christian Church

As iron sharpens iron, so one man sharpens another.

—PROVERBS 27:17

9

Meaningful Conversations with Our Teachers

THE FOLLOWING FICTIONAL DIALOGUES are meant to illumine the reader further in understanding the arguments presented in this book. They are hypothetical conversations that contain arguments found within the historical persons themselves as well as my own understanding of how I believe they would answer various questions put to them if they were to enter our world today. It is my hope that such a format will offer yet another opportunity to provide greater clarity of the arguments given throughout Church history, and display the unified plurality of voices that have contributed to this discussion.

IS CONTRACEPTION MURDER?

While having lunch together, John Chrysostom and John Calvin are discussing the challenges of writing commentaries on the Bible for laymen when a man approaches them with a question on his mind.

Phoneus: Hello, Professors. My name is Ben Phoneus. I was wondering if you might let me discuss a moral question with you.

Chrysostom and Calvin: Sure. What's your question?

Phoneus: I've read commentaries by both of you that suggest that the employment of contraceptive methods is equivalent to murder.

Chrysostom and Calvin: And your question?

Phoneus: How is the use of contraceptive methods murder?

Chrysostom: Well, first of all, it is clear that contraceptive methods are meant to prevent life. The entire point of their use is that a living child is not made through the sexual act. It is logical therefore to say that whatever prevents a life that would exist from existing is, at the very least, equal to whatever takes a life that now exists.

Phoneus: What if a couple uses contraception because they have a good reason for doing so?

Chrysostom: I wonder if you would argue this way on any other moral issue. I find it interesting that I have called it murder, and you're now telling me that if someone has a good reason for committing the immoral act, it may be justifiable.

Phoneus: I'm not sure on that one, but some people do seem to have their reasons for using it.

Chrysostom: Well, I would suspect that anyone who performs an immoral act would have a reason. There are a variety of reasons why someone might use contraception—perhaps for finances, or less emotional stress, freedom from being tied down by a child, etc. The real question is whether having a "good" reason for committing an evil act makes it less evil.

Phoneus: What do you mean?

Chrysostom: If you are my employer, and I am poor and treated poorly by you, do you think that God would find it all right if I murdered you and stole your business because I had good reasons for doing so?

Phoneus: I suppose not.

Chrysostom: I realize that is an extreme example, but such is necessary in our day. As the world turns to justify itself in every act, we are left with but few examples to which everyone agrees to assign as evil.

Phoneus: I agree. I don't mind the extreme analogies.

Chrysostom: My point through all of this, of course, is that one can justify any, and every, evil act by giving sympathetic scenarios that are sure to soften the heart of every fallen judge but in the end do nothing but deceive us further into darkness as we mask our every evil deed with a good reason.

Phoneus: Then the real question, I suppose, is whether the use of contraception is murder. If it is, then there can be no good reason for committing murder in any given situation.

Chrysostom: Yes, this is the heart of our current discussion.

Phoneus: Why do you say it is murder then?

Chrysostom: I call it murder for lack of a better term. I frankly consider it worse than murder.

Phoneus: How is it worse than murder?

Chrysostom: Because at least a murderer has let an individual come into existence before the person's life was snuffed out. With the use of contraceptive methods a person is not even allowed to ever exist. In this way it is not only murder, but more than murder, and I therefore do not know what to call it.

Phoneus: Don't you believe that contraceptive methods are murder because you have the erroneous concept that the sperm itself is a living human? I think it's called the "garden theory."

Chrysostom: No, despite the common claim to the contrary, I never make that argument. I call it murder, even though it is not the killing of a person who is alive already, because it is the extinguishing of the life before it begins.

Calvin: I would further that stance by stating that not only is one individual being destroyed but an entire line of humans is being wiped away through the act of contraception. The act is not only an individual one, therefore, but a crime against humanity.

Phoneus: I see how that would be logical to your point; but does that mean that any time a murder is committed God imputes to the perpetrator the murder of an entire race that would have stemmed from the victim, instead of just a single murder?

Calvin: I think that, since murder is in the intent, it would not necessarily imply that, but I do think in the murder of one person there is the killing of an entire tribe nonetheless.

Phoneus: Is contraception morally acceptable then because the individual does not intend to wipe out the existence of a future child?

Calvin: The problem is that the very act of contraception is always used to counter conception of a future child—hence, purposely wiping out his or her existence. It really doesn't matter if the person thinks of it that way.

Phoneus: Why not?

Calvin: Well, to give an example, a murderer may make himself believe that when he kills a burdensome individual in his life, he is meaning only to prevent that man from being a further burden to him. However, regardless of "the way he is thinking about it," his intention is to murder the man in order to achieve that result. Likewise, people who practice contraception may believe that they are only relieving themselves of the burden of a child, but they are still wiping out the existence of that child in order to be relieved of that burden.

Phoneus: So intent is not always "the way one thinks about a crime," but it is always a part of that crime nonetheless.

Calvin: Exactly. Proverbs 16:2 tells us, *All the practices of a person are clean in his own opinion, but YHWH weighs the intentions.* Notice, then, that the verse divides the way a person thinks about a practice from the true intention of the practice.

Phoneus: But a child will be created if God wants one to be; and if He doesn't, then He will use the wise decision of the couple (i.e, to use contraception) as a means to His sovereign decisions. In other words, those who condemn the use of contraceptive methods really don't understand the sovereignty of God.

Calvin (*staring for a moment at the irony*): This sort of argument is interesting. Essentially what it is saying is that humans can do whatever we wish, and since God is sovereign, God's plans will not be thwarted.

Phoneus: Well, the last part I think is true, but the first part I don't agree with.

Calvin: Why not?

Phoneus: Because humans have a moral responsibility to do what is pleasing to God. I do think, however, that God can use our contraceptive choices as a means to His choices.

Calvin: Oh, I definitely would not disagree with any of that.

Phoneus: Really?

Calvin: Sure. My point is not that God's decretive plan is thwarted in the use of contraception any more than His plan is thwarted by my pulling out a sword and killing you right now. I think that if I were to do such a thing, it would prove that God's plan was for you to die right now. Would you agree?

Phoneus: Yes, but I get you're illustration, so let's not physically demonstrate it.

Calvin (*smiling*): Agreed. My point is that it may be God's set plan in a fallen world that you die right now by my hand, but this has nothing to do with whether I should murder you—i.e, whether it is pleasing to God morally.

Phoneus: Can we use another example? I'm starting to get nervous.

Calvin: No problem. How about this one: it may be God's set plan in a fallen world that unborn babies die at the time their mothers kill them in the act of abortion, but this has nothing to do with whether a mother should kill her unborn child because, as you stated, "Humans have a moral responsibility to do what is pleasing to God." And what is pleasing to God is according to His moral will (i.e, what God desires men to do morally), not his decretive will (what God has decreed and therefore desires to take place in the fallen world in order to accomplish all His good purpose, knowing that men will do evil, and that He has chosen to work through their actions rather than thwarting every single one).

Phoneus: Maybe couples who use contraception are simply figuring out what his secret decree is for them personally.

Calvin: Well, we already know what the moral decree is. They don't need to figure it out. God has revealed in His Word that the sexual act has at its primary purpose the procreation of covenant children.

Phoneus: What if a couple feels, however, that God's will is that they use contraception and that His revealed will is no longer in effect for them personally?

Calvin: How exactly are they discovering God's will apart from the Scripture?

Phoneus: They personally feel through prayer and Bible study, personal conversations with friends and professionals and so on, that this is the way to go.

Calvin: Well, if it's through Bible study, they would discover that God's will is that they use the sexual act as a means for God to create children through them.

Phoneus: OK, well, maybe it's more through prayer and conversations.

Calvin: So they experientially feel that it's now acceptable to come against God's directives in Scripture because they found out His secret will for them personally through alternative means?

Phoneus: Well, I probably wouldn't frame it that way, but sure.

Calvin: Are you familiar with this verse: "The secret things belong to the Lord our God, but the things revealed belong to us and to our sons forever, that we may observe all the words of this law." Do you know from whence this comes?

Phoneus: Isn't it Deuteronomy 29:29?

Calvin: Do you know the context?

Phoneus: Enlighten me.

Calvin: God has now revealed His moral desire for His people and is telling them that if they practice it, He will bless them, but if they do something else, He will curse them.

Phoneus: I see.

Calvin: Why do you think God tells them that His secret will belongs to Him, but what He has revealed belongs to His people forever?

Phoneus: Because the people would probably try to subvert what He revealed to them by thinking they had discovered for themselves His secret will, which would undermine the revealed?

Calvin: I think that is true, and I would further it by saying that God is telling them to be concerned with what He has said and not try to seek another way because it becomes an opportunity for us to deceive ourselves. Proverbs states again and again: "There is a way which seems right to a man, but its end is the way of death."

Phoneus: So you would say that this couple is trying to seek another way than what God has revealed, a human reasoning in which they have been deceived into thinking that they have discovered God's secret plan for them . . .

Calvin: . . . through their mystical means rather than through the Word revealed. Yes. You've understood it well. The claim, then, that a couple now feels that they personally don't need to follow the scriptural mandate because of the authority of their experience in determining God's will, may be a religious claim, but it is not a Christian one.

Another type of this practice to undermine what God has revealed is to reinterpret biblical concepts like love or the image of God in such abstract ways so they can then be used as instruments to "override" specific concepts revealed by God.

Phoneus: Can you give me an example?

Calvin: Sure. It is a common practice for some to reinterpret the biblical concept of love as an abstract feeling or acceptance of a person and his or her actions. This reinterpreted concept of love is then used to undermine a practice that may be condemned in the Bible but accepted by our modern culture. The issue of homosexuality comes to mind, but there are numerous others I could mention. Essentially, this method consists of applying a reinterpreted, generalized principle to undermine the very specific examples that originally complemented the abstract principle. Hence, true love is not acceptance of a person's evil, but a striving against the evil that seeks to consume the mind and heart of the person loved. In the original concept, homosexuality is condemned precisely because the person condemning loves the person consumed by it. In the reinterpreted concept, however, love is seen as contradictory to the condemnation of the practice.

Phoneus: Do you have an example of this being attempted with the contraceptive issue?

Calvin: Sure. The biblical concept concerning the *imago Dei* is lifted out of its procreative context, reinterpreted as something that makes us "like God" in our creative abilities, and therefore concludes that humans have the right to use this status to determine if a child will be brought into existence through the sexual act.

Phoneus: I see. Thank you for the discussion, Professors. We'll have to talk more some time. Goodbye.

Calvin: I would enjoy that. *Adieu.*

Chrysostom: As would I. *Chairete.*

∾

C. S. Lewis is quietly reading a book as a man approaches him.

Ratsach: Professor Lewis, My name is Paraclete Ratsach, and I wondered if I could speak to you about something.

Lewis: Nice to meet you, Mr. Ratsach. I would happy to speak with you. What's on your mind?

Ratsach: I've read your book *The Abolition of Man*, and I'm curious about part of your argument against the use of birth control.

Ratsach: Then, by all means, let us indulge your curiosity.

Ratsach: Thank you, Professor. You make the argument, as many in the Church before you have made, that to use birth control is essentially to take ultimate power over future persons by choosing whether or not they will live at all.

Lewis: I seem to remember quite well. Yes?

Ratsach: Isn't it just choosing to act responsibly over the direction of one's life? Why must it be cast in such a way so as to accuse those who use birth control of idolatry and murder?

Lewis: Do you have any children?

Ratsach: I have two.

Lewis: How old?

Ratsach: One is fourteen and the other eight. We spaced them out that way for financial reasons.

Lewis: Has it been easy to raise them? I mean financially, emotionally, etc.

Ratsach: No. Like everyone, we've struggled with many difficulties, but we're still alive and kicking.

Lewis: You know, I'm a sucker for a good science fiction story.

Ratsach: Who isn't?

Lewis: Imagine, if you will, two years from now someone actually invents a *bona fide* time machine.

Ratsach (*smiling*): Given your love for different realms and theories of time, I should have expected such a scenario from you.

Lewis (*smiling back*): Of course. I have always found that such fantasies are the best method to communicate reality to the masses.

Imagine now that you have the opportunity to go back in time, and knowing the stress and struggles your children have brought to you and how much easier it would have been without them, do you think that you would now decide to use birth control on the days that you know they must have been conceived in order to make your future easier?

Ratsach: Absolutely not! I love my children. They are worth the stress and struggles we've been through. It would be easier without them, but I couldn't trade my children for an easier life.

Lewis: So what is the difference between these children and the ones who you did trade?

Ratsach: What do you mean?

Lewis: I mean that essentially, the difference between the children you had and the children that were not allowed to live because of your use of birth control methods is that you have experientially known your children and come to love them, whereas the others you never knew and grew to love.

Ratsach: They never existed in the first place. They were only possible future persons, not actual ones.

Lewis: What do you mean?

Ratsach: I mean that there is no way to know if a child would have been born through any given sexual act performed. If that is true then it is possible that no future child's existence was extinguished.

Lewis: This is true in theory, but in probability, many have been wiped away.

Ratsach: I'll grant that, but I still would not consider it murder in the same way as if I went out and killed one of my living children now.

Lewis: Then I would ask you to go back to the time machine, and knowing what you know now—about all of the stress and struggles your children have brought to you thus far—if you were to decide to use birth control during the times you figured out they must have been conceived, thus causing them to disappear from your future, would you not consider this the murder of your children?

Ratsach: I said I wouldn't do that.

Lewis: Let's say, for the sake of argument, that you did.

Ratsach: All right, I'll play along.

Lewis: Would you consider it the murder of your now existing children to go back in time and stop them from existing in the first place, so that they will never have lived at all?

Ratsach: I think because I know that they now live, and that I am intending to wipe out their existence, it would be murder.

Lewis: And what is the difference with those whose existence was probably extinguished by your use of birth control and who you have not known?

Ratsach: I am not intending to wipe out the existence of future persons in that case.

Lewis: You're not?

Ratsach: I take it by your response that you see an error in my reasoning?

Lewis: I do. I think we should take a look at the intent of the practice of any birth control method. What is its intended purpose?

Ratsach: To prevent us from having an unwanted pregnancy.

Lewis: And the pregnancy leads to . . . ?

Ratsach: A child.

Lewis: So the purpose of birth control is to prevent a child from existing, is it not?

Ratsach: I suppose so.

Lewis: So you are intending to wipe out a child before it ever exists, are you not?

Ratsach: Yes.

Lewis: And you said that the use of the time machine to wipe out the existence of your children would be murder because of the intent, correct?

Ratsach: Yes, but I also don't know if other children would ever exist.

Lewis: But they are probable, and murder is not in the success of the act but, as we have stated, in the intent. Birth control is not used for children who the practitioner imagines will not exist but for those children he or she imagines will exist if he or she does not use it.

Ratsach: Yes, that's right.

Lewis: Then, whether a future child would have actually come about from any given sexual act or not, according to your own definition, your intent with the use of birth control, whether only in the back of your mind or not, is murder.

Ratsach: OK, well, how is that related to the evil pursuit of divine power over others?

Lewis: Well, I think it obvious that choosing whether or not to murder someone is the ultimate power over an individual. It controls not just behavior but whether or not a person will live. It demands the complete submission of an entire individual's life to the one who wields such power. As such, it is perhaps the greatest act of idolatry, where one steals the very power and position of God over another.

Ratsach: What about human freedom? Why aren't we able to be free in this area and use contraception responsibly at our discretion?

Lewis: Well, first, we must realize that if the use of contraception is idolatry and murder, then I would think that no Christian would make the argument that he or she is free to do so—if by "free" we mean "to be able to practice such and such with God's moral approval."

Ratsach: Understood.

Lewis: Second, it is interesting to note that the argument that one is free to practice contraception is itself an act of idolatry.

Ratsach: How so?

Lewis: Interestingly enough, fallen humans often claim freedoms at the cost of the bondage of others. In other words, if you were going to be the human created through my sexual act, my freedom to practice contraception then limits or annihilates your freedom to exist. I would argue then that it is a blasphemous idolatry because it exalts the freedom and power of the self over the freedom of others. True divinely ordained, human freedom is limited by the existence of the freedom of others. Therefore, I would not have freedom so overarching to the extent that it wiped out all other freedoms of another individual—even their very right to exist, their right to life.

Ratsach: I see. I don't think I wish to indulge my curiosities any further, Professor.

Lewis: I completely understand.

Ratsach: Good day to you, Professor Lewis.

Lewis: Cheerio.

IS CONTRACEPTION SEXUAL IMMORALITY?

Martin Luther is speaking at a university forum on the importance of Christian education in a child's life when he is approached by a man with a question concerning contraception's link to sexual immorality.

Akrates: Professor Martin, may I ask you a question?

Luther: Sure. What's on your mind?

Akrates: You call contraceptive practices sodomy. How is contraception equivalent to the sin of sodomy?

Luther: I equate it to sodomy in that both are sexual acts that are not performed, nor could they be, for the sake of creating a human child to be raised in the Lord.

Akrates: So it is the deliberate waste of the sexual act?

Luther: Yes.

Akrates: But if two people love one another and seek intimacy with each other in a committed monogamous relationship, why can't sex be enjoyable in this scenario without it being condemned as evil?

Luther: You've made a great case for the homosexual position.

Akrates: Well, I believe that homosexuality is wrong.

Luther: Despite the fact that you have now justified the practice of it?

Akrates: When have I justified its practice?

Luther: When you stated that two people who love one another should be able to seek intimacy within a monogamous relationship in which they also can enjoy the sexual act without condemnation.

Akrates: How did I justify it with that statement?

Luther: Is it possible for two homosexuals to love one another in a similar way to the way a non-Christian man loves his non-Christian wife and vice versa?

Akrates: Yes, I think so.

Luther: Are they able to seek intimacy and pleasure through the sexual act?

Akrates: I imagine so. They must, since that often is done.

Luther: And you just stated that as long as the individuals fulfill these uses of the sexual act it should be without condemnation?

Akrates: Yes, that's right.

Luther: Then what are we to conclude but that homosexuality fulfills your only required purposes for the sexual act. One can participate in a homosexual act as long as he is being loving, seeking intimacy, and having pleasure in it.

Akrates: Well, the Bible says it's wrong, so I don't believe it is morally acceptable.

Luther: In other words, you believe *that* it is wrong because the Bible says so, but you have no clue *why* it is wrong. Do you think the "Bible says so" argument will stand the test of time? Or will it fall to "reinterpretations" of those passages that, in your mind, so clearly condemn it?

Akrates: Many can interpret the Bible differently, so I suppose an argument that "the Bible says so" can be undermined by a reinterpretation of what the Bible says.

Luther: A reinterpretation that contradicts the historic Christian Church's position?

Akrates: I don't know about that.

Luther: It's already been done with our present subject. Some who stood against contraception stood on the credo that the Bible said so in the case of Onan and Tamar. We see now how that has been undermined to the point that almost the entire evangelical Church has turned away from the historic position.

Akrates: I guess it could happen the same way then for homosexuality.

Luther: If you continue to define the purpose of the sexual act apart from the primary purpose of procreation, it's not a matter of "if" that will happen but "when."

Akrates: So the modern-day problem we have in defining boundaries for the sexual act is really a problem of defining the primary purpose of the sexual act in the first place?

Luther: Yes, you've got it. If one defines the primary purpose of the sexual act to be procreation, then any support for homosexuality as a legitimate form of the sexual act disappears.

Akrates: But to define it that way is to condemn also any use of the sexual act that is non-procreative.

Luther: Hence, a primary reason why distortions of the sexual act thrive in modern evangelicalism—because to condemn homosexuality through the historical Christian line of reasoning is to condemn the use of contraception through the historical Christian line of reasoning. A man must condemn himself before he condemns another first, and that is much more difficult to inspire fallen, self-justifying humans to do. We love to throw stones at others, but don't appreciate it as much if they are thrown at us.

Akrates: So sodomy is the same type of sin as using birth control in that both of them are sexual acts which prevent the procreation of children.

Luther: Yes. We could pursue another route as well, but that should suffice for now.

Akrates: Thank you, Brother Martin. Goodbye.

Luther: Don't mention it. Auf Wiedersehen!

IS CONTRACEPTION IDOLATRY?

John Chrysostom and C. S. Lewis are sitting in the park discussing the use of allegory in communicating biblical truth. A man approaches and asks if he may speak to them concerning the contraceptive issue, specifically concerning whether it is an act of idolatry.

Philedonus: Professors, how is the use of contraception an act of idolatry? I'm not worshipping contraception.

Chrysostom: To seek sexual pleasure as the end result of the sexual act is to worship the self.

Philedonus: How so?

Chrysostom: It ignores any eternal purpose to the sexual act and therefore ignores any external God for its purpose. It exists solely to please the individual who engages in it.

Philedonus: Well, I believe that God wants us to enjoy life.

Chrysostom: No one said He didn't. However, to say that God's primary purpose in anything that we do is simply for the sake of our enjoyment alone is to be atheistic in our practices.

Philedonus: In what way?

Chrysostom: Because it seeks the pleasure of the human against the pleasure of God. It is self-focused, rather than God-focused. It acts as though all that exists is the human, and God is not. Since only humans exists, only human purposes need to be explored. In a biblical worldview, however, God is the center of our concerns together with any practice in which we choose to participate. The goal, therefore, is to discover what pleases Him.

Philedonus: But maybe God has pleasure in the fact that we have pleasure.

Chrysostom: It then acts as though God has pleasure in what is temporal and passes away. I would argue that this is contrary to the nature of God, who is eternal and has eternal purposes in all things. I would further argue that your statement would imply that God exists as our worshiper, since He is pleased with whatever pleases us. This is backward. We are His worshipers and as such should be pleased only with what pleases Him.

Philedonus: I see.

Chrysostom: One could also essentially make that argument to justify any practice in which someone had pleasure. I could say that I enjoy food and therefore so does God. Since God enjoys my eating food in pleasure for pleasure's sake, I can eat it to all my delight, and therefore gluttony would not be wrong. Do you think that would be a biblical argument?

Philedonus: No, it's clearly not biblical, since many practices in which we would have pleasure also have boundaries that are defined by that which pleases God in their use.

Chrysostom: That's right. And food is a means by which we continue to live and glorify God. If I use it as a glutton, however, I failed to use it for its primary purpose. I have, therefore, sinned against God by seeking my pleasure over His.

Philedonus: But does Scripture tell us what is pleasing to God in the sexual act? If we don't know, then maybe we can just practice it for pleasure's sake and hope that God also has pleasure in it.

Chrysostom: We really can't say that we don't know what pleases God in the sexual act. Clearly, even apart from Scripture, nature tells us that the sexual act has its goal in procreation. Humanity lives on through it. This has an eternal weight in that it creates a human person who glorifies God in one way or another. Ultimately, it is supposed to lead to another human who represents and worships God. The same cannot be said for an idolatrous view of the sexual act that gives temporal pleasure to people.

Philedonus: That makes sense.

Chrysostom: Secondly, Scripture identifies from the beginning that the male and female relationship is created to "increase and multiply."

Philedonus: Hasn't that been accomplished already?

Chrysostom: If the male and female relationship was created for that purpose, then saying that it is accomplished already is the same as saying that there is no more need for the male-female relationship. Did you want to make that argument?

Philedonus: No, I don't believe I want to be a Montanist today.

Chrysostom: Good decision on that one.

Philedonus: One could argue, though, that the male-female relationship perseveres in its secondary functions.

Chrysostom: It could be argued this way, but I think you will run into what we discussed above: a relationship that exists primarily for a person's purposes instead of primarily for God's. I would also like to know just how a male-female relationship that is not procreative functions any differently than a male-male sexual relationship or even a non-sexual partnership?

Philedonus: I admit it would be difficult to argue this way if one desired to remain biblical in one's beliefs.

Chrysostom: I agree. The simple conclusion then is that any use of the sexual act contrary to the primary procreative use is idolatry because it merely seeks to worship the Self.

Philedonus: Do you agree, Professor Lewis?

Lewis: I do. The person who practices contraception has really placed him or herself in the position of God.

Philedonus: So you see it not only as a worship of self through sensual pleasure but also as a lust for power?

Lewis: Yes. The individual who practices it is seeking control of not only his own life but the lives of others.

Philedonus: How so?

Lewis: By seeking to control whether a person exists or not, the individual takes divine power over both him or herself and those who would exist from him or her.

Philedonus: So humans make themselves God by determining their own destiny and the destinies of others.

Lewis: That's right. And if giving and taking life is how God describes His exclusive right and position of what makes Him God?

Philedonus: Then the use of contraception is one of the ways mankind deifies itself.

Lewis: That's correct.

Philedonus: But what if people are doing it to glorify God? What if they practice it because children may get in the way of ministry?

Lewis: For what reason the person may practice contraception in any given instance is irrelevant, since the usurping of power that belongs only to God is an act of self-worship. One could not, therefore, make the argument that he or she disobeyed God in order to glorify Him. This is either misguided thinking brought about from a genuine mistake, or misguided thinking brought about as an excuse to give the self that divine power. Either way, it is misguided.

Philedonus: I see. Thank you for the stimulating discussion, Professor. I must go now. Goodbye.

Lewis: Anytime. Cheerio.

IS CONTRACEPTION CONSISTENT WITH CHRISTIAN DISCIPLESHIP?

Augustine and Martin Luther are sitting in the library discussing the nature and role of grace in salvation, spawned by Luther's book entitled, The Bondage of the Will. *A man approaches and begins to engage them in a conversation.*

Astorgus: Hello, Professors. I was wondering if I might speak to you about an issue I've heard you both address.

Augustine and Luther: Sure.

Luther: What subject did you have in mind?

Astorgus: I was thinking about the issue of contraception. I've heard both of you state that you saw it as contrary to the spiritual growth of both those who practice it and those over whom it is practiced.

Augustine and Luther: Yes, that's right.

Astorgus: How is contraception opposed to Christian discipleship?

Luther: How is it not?

Astorgus: I can evangelize the world that exists already, and hence, fulfill Christ's command.

Luther: True, but you alone cannot do it; nor can you do it as fully as you can if you have as many children as God gives you.

Astorgus: How so?

Luther: Well, first of all, the more children you have and disciple, the more Christians there are to go into the world to disciple others. One person cannot disciple the world, but thousands who are eventually brought forth from that one person, joined to the millions of children from other Christians doing the same, can in fact accomplish that goal.

Astorgus: I see, but how is it that you say I cannot disciple others as fully as if I have many children?

Luther: You cannot do it as fully because the Great Commission is about discipling many people with all that Christ commanded. No person is going to give you the amount of time and energy toward your teaching that your children will give you. They will give you their entire childhood for you to teach them. They are, perhaps, the only people you will ever be able to disciple to the fullest in your lifetime. Is that something you really want to give up or even to limit? Do you really want to miss out on the opportunity, even with a single one of them you could have?

Astorgus: I could adopt and accomplish the same.

Luther: You could, but why pit one against the other? The truth is that there is no reason to turn down discipling one child because you can disciple another. In fact, it would be a great evil to say that you will wipe out the existence of a future disciple of Christ in order to disciple someone else. Why not adopt *and* have your own children, or have your own children and disciple other children in the manner that you may disciple adults? There is no reason to create such a dichotomy.

Astorgus: Well, I don't have enough time to disciple a bunch of adopted children and my own, so I would have to disciple them in the lesser manner.

Luther: The Lord will surely give you and your wife a time of fruitfulness and unfruitfulness, and it is in the times of unfruitfulness that you may want to consider adoption. My only point is that your biological children ought to be brought into the world and discipled regardless of your decisions concerning the others.

Astorgus: I see.

Augustine: Furthermore, I wanted to say that having children also increases good in the world.

Astorgus: How so?

Augustine: The more you accomplish that which we have already considered, the more Christians, or those who have been influenced in Christian thinking and love, go out into the world and become influences for good. The truth and the Christian witness is increased with the increase of children from Christian parents, who genuinely disciple their children in love.

Astorgus: There is no guarantee that those children will become Christians though.

Augustine: That is why I said that there are both Christians made from this parental discipleship and those who are influenced by it. Not everyone will become a Christian, but if everyone is discipled in Christ's love, there is a greater Christian influence set out into the world.

Astorgus: They could always rebel.

Augustine: Of course, but those raised as non-Christians will never depart from it unless they later become Christians, whereas those who were raised as Christians have a greater chance of influencing others with that which they have been raised.

Astorgus: Is this an argument for why contraception is morally unacceptable?

Augustine: I would say it is more of a benefit derived from those who listen to the other arguments against contraception. In other words, it is a good thing to do, and Christians always ought to do good; but it is more a reward than a commandment.

Astorgus: Understood.

Augustine: To argue further, it is also a bad thing to purposely limit your children because it disturbs the discipleship of your existing children.

Astorgus: How so?

Augustine: While telling them that God loves children so much, you communicate that they are not worth having in some instances and, hence, that you do not love them too much. While teaching them to obey God's will, you consider only your own will when it comes to having more children. While teaching them that they are to think of themselves as part of God's community, you hinder their learning to be content with a limited amount of food, or their ability to share and think of themselves as part of the group rather than as an individual because you yourself put your concerns over those of the community. While teaching your children to not murder, you do not allow the existence of future persons. While teaching them to obey God in their sexuality, you do not obey God in yours. While teaching them to worship God, you place yourself on the throne of your own life. I would say that discipleship for someone who uses contraception is not only a major hindrance to existing children, but if they see this hypocrisy, it is virtually impossible. The only thing that makes it possible is the child's ignorance of the contradiction.

Astorgus: Ultimately, then, it is only a problem if the child believes contraception to be wrong.

Augustine: I wouldn't say so. The child is sure to connect, even if only in the back of the mind, that if the parents loved her or him and truly saw in children a great value, they would seek to have more. The fact that the parents decide to limit their children sends a message to the child that there is something, even if ever so small, burdensome, or even loathsome, about him or her. Discipleship in this atmosphere is difficult to say the least.

Astorgus: So someone who uses contraception can't disciple children properly?

Augustine: I didn't really say that. My point was that it is a contradiction to discipleship, and if the child somehow becomes aware of it, it can have a negative result. Ultimately, if we simply see children as the greatest good, and their existence and discipleship as our purpose for being upon the earth, we won't have to concern ourselves with such a contradiction, largely because we won't want to practice it in the first place.

Astorgus: So you are basically saying that the use of contraception is contrary to loving our children?

Augustine: I would definitely say so, yes.

Astorgus: I can love my children without wanting more of them.

Luther: Yes, but not without contradiction, and not to the fullest that you could love them.

Astorgus: In what way is that true?

Luther: Let me give you an analogy. A certain man claimed his entire life that he loved gold. He spoke of it all of the time, and claimed that it was his one desire. He thought of it continually. One day he came upon a treasure chest filled with it. He took only a few pieces, but left the rest because he wanted only a little. Do you think that man really loved gold more than anything? Wouldn't his claim have been true if he had eagerly grabbed all of it?

Astorgus: What's your point?

Luther: My point is that our claim to love our children, and the cold fact that we really have been trained by our culture to see them as obstacles in our lives, has turned our claim into a lie. If we loved them more than anything, we would want more of them. The fact that they are seen as an obstacle shows us that we don't really love them but simply use them as means to love ourselves. When they are not burdensome, and we see having a child as fulfilling, we'll have them. When we see them as burdensome and an obstacle to fulfillment, we blot out their future existence. We are taught to love ourselves and use our children as a means to do so. We are not taught to love our children at the sacrifice of the self. There is a big difference, don't you think?

Astorgus: I think people place great value on their children, so I don't see that they have been trained to see them as obstacles.

Luther: It is not that children are not seen as valuable, but that they are not seen as *more* valuable. During the times of Israelite idolatry, the people would trade their children to the gods in order to receive something from them precisely because children were seen as a value to trade for what was thought of as more important—more valuable. The issue then is not that society views children as worthless, but that they view them as less valuable than the other things that a commitment to materialism, a less stressful life, or just plainly to the self, can give them.

Astorgus: I see. So you are saying that our love for our children is secondary to our love for ourselves, and we treat children as possible obstacles to the fulfillment of love for ourselves.

Augustine: Yes, and the Scripture speaks of any love that is secondary to another as hatred when in contrast to the object of our greater love. When Christ tells us that we are to hate our parents, He is telling us that as a comparison to our love for God. Our parents are to have less of our love than we give to God. Likewise, the Apostle John tells us that to love ourselves more than a fellow child of God is to hate that child of God, not because we have no love for him, but because our love for ourselves is greater than our love for him. In this way, we have loved ourselves and hated our children because we see them only as a means to our fulfillment, not as God's children for whom we ought to subject our goals to their existence and discipleship.

Astorgus: I see. But what if people practice contraception because they feel too many children would hinder their service to God?

Luther: How can that which is service to God in the utmost be a hindrance to the service of God? Our very work in this world is to make covenant children. One, therefore, is essentially arguing that serving God with something else allows him or her to disobey God by refusing to serve Him in this area. We have argued here that true obedience doesn't contradict itself. There is no way that God would sanction an evil act because it supposedly allowed a person to do ministry. Obedience is better than sacrifice, and we need to see ministry as that which God sets for us in the Scripture and cease in our attempts to trump that with our human-made ideas of ministry that counter it. The making of covenant children in every way is our ministry, and all other ministries are either to be complementary or in subjugation to it.

Astorgus: Well, I'm still not convinced that it is wrong.

Augustine: Convinced? Do you think that we've been trying to convince you?

Astorgus: Well, sure. Isn't that the point of the conversation?

Augustine: No. The point of the conversation is to give clarity to what is being said, not to convince you of its truthfulness. No one can be convinced of the truth, nor can he or she understand how true and important it is by mere logical argumentation.

Astorgus: I don't understand. Why discuss it with me just for the sake of my comprehension of what is being said? Don't you want me to believe it?

Augustine: Ah, in fact I do. The problem is that *you* don't want to believe it. The problem is that faith must precede understanding, but you want someone to convince you before you will believe. Your entrance into the discussion is one of doubt, and the Scripture is clear that the one who comes to God in order to gain understanding, but who has a disposition of doubt, will not receive it (Jas 1:5-8). You may understand what is being said, but you will not understand why it is true. The understanding of the *why* only comes from believing the *what* first. Apart from faith in the consistent testimony concerning children by the Holy Spirit, through the Scripture and the Church, you will neither understand why this issue is so important nor why it is true. That type of understanding is the reward of faith. That is why the Apostle Paul said that the Gospel eluded the Greeks. They sought for the wisdom to understand why it was true first. Without faith, however, the truth always sounds absurd to those who are unaccustomed to it. Therefore, belief does not follow argumentation, but rather must precede it for the truth to be confirmed within you through the divine gift of understanding.

Astorgus: I see. Thank you for the discussion, Professors.

Luther and Augustine: Any time. Vale!

BEFORE WE GO: ONE LAST CONVERSATION

As I sit in my office reading Jonathan Edwards' A Treatise On Religious Affections, *a man knocks at the door and asks if he may converse with me concerning my book about contraception.*

Kain: Hello, Mr. Hodge, my name is Elpis Kain. I was wondering if I might have a chat with you about your book dealing with the issue of contraception.

Hodge: I'd be happy to oblige. Is there a starting point from which you wanted to begin?

Kain: Yes, I want to start off by pursuing whether the sexual act is legitimated by the boundaries of marriage.

Hodge: What exactly do you mean?

Kain: Well, I believe that if a person is in a legitimate marriage, between a man and a woman, then the sexual act can be used for a variety of reasons.

Hodge: Well, I didn't say it couldn't be used for a variety of reasons. I said that it shouldn't be used for a variety of reasons contrary to the procreative one, which is primary.

Kain: What do you mean?

Hodge: I mean that the sexual act has many benefits to it but that one ought not to use it for those benefits alone and, thus, hinder the primary purpose of the act that God has set for it. That would sort of be like the Apostle Peter, who was given the gift of tongues, using it mainly to pass his school language exams, when in fact it was given to him for another purpose altogether.

Kain: I understand the clarification, but I would simply restate my original argument: Marriage allows the couple to engage in the sexual act for a variety of reasons, even if they hinder the procreative one.

Hodge: Let me ask you question, if I may. Does marriage set the boundaries for the sexual act, or does the sexual act set the boundaries for marriage?

Kain: What do you mean?

Hodge: I mean, is it simply being married that makes a sexual act legitimate, or is it the legitimate sexual act that makes marriage legitimate?

Kain: Marriage makes the act legitimate.

Hodge: Really?

Kain: You don't think so, I take it.

Hodge: No, I don't. Neither has Christianity ever seen it that way.

Kain: Can you explain?

Hodge: Sure. Marriage cannot define the sexual act; otherwise marriage could be between two men, two women, a man and an animal, multiple partners, etc., as long as the sexual act was performed within that boundary.

Kain: Well, I don't believe marriage is legitimate between any other group than one man and one woman.

Hodge: So you believe that the sexual act defines marriage.

Kain: How so?

Hodge: Because your presupposition, that correct genders in the appropriate relationship to one another define who is eligible to create a marriage, is linked to the fact that the only reason those appropriate genders in proper relation to one another make up marriage is because the sexual act between them is procreative.

Kain: I didn't say that.

Hodge: No, but your use of the traditional Christian position assumes it even though you may not see that it does.

Kain: Well, a man and a woman can acceptably participate in the sexual act for other reasons, like pleasure and to express love.

Hodge: Then why does it have to be a man and a woman? Homosexuals can participate in the sexual act for pleasure and to express love. In fact, every group I mentioned above would be able to participate in the sexual act for those reasons in one way or another. According to your requirement for the sexual act to be legitimate, they have all met that goal. In fact, you would be hard pressed to find any sexual act that does not meet that goal in some way.

Kain: So you're saying that if I believe marriage must be made up of one man and one woman, I am assuming that the sexual act must be procreative even though I don't realize what I am saying.

Hodge: Yes. The problem is that you have assumed two positions. The first is the Christian position I just mentioned: that the only legitimate sexual act is between a man and a woman because it alone is procreative in nature. The second is the secular position that the sexual act can be legitimated by all kinds of uses, like pleasure and intimacy. This is why it is so difficult to talk to modern evangelicals about this subject. You are functioning off of two completely contradictory ideas concerning marriage and the sexual act.

I won't go on about it, since I have dealt with it elsewhere; but suffice to say, the problem we now face is that evangelicals have essentially argued that sex must be procreative in order to get to marriage, but have argued the exact opposite once they are married.

Kain: We want to have our cake and eat it too.

Hodge: Exactly.

Kain: Let's turn then to the conception event. You state that modern evangelicals have adopted philosophic naturalism, which stems from their practical atheistic views gained from culture, instead of supernaturalism, or substance dualism, which would be gained from the Bible, when it comes to the issue of conception.

Hodge: I couldn't have put it better myself.

Kain: I believe that God makes children but that the use of contraception is acceptable to God. I don't think that makes me an atheist or someone who believes in naturalism.

Hodge: In what way do you believe that God makes children?

Kain: What do you mean?

Hodge: I mean do you believe that God makes children in the way that the Bible presents Him as doing so, or in the way that modern evangelicalism presents Him as doing so?

Kain: What's the difference?

Hodge: In the Bible, God directly creates children through the sexual act. In modern evangelicalism, God indirectly creates children by giving the man and woman the ability to have children. In the former, God must morally approve of the creation of the child, since He is the one making the child directly. In the latter, however, God may not necessarily morally approve of every child, since He gives only the ability, not the moral approval by making the child Himself.

Kain: I believe the latter.

Hodge: God gives the ability to have a child, rather than God directly making the child Himself?

Kain: I would still use the language that God made the child.

Hodge: Most would, but it really is inaccurate.

Kain: How so?

Hodge: It's like saying that God made your car. He may have given you the means to get it. He may have blessed you from afar, so that He brought about those means; but He didn't make the car directly. You could then speak of God as helping you get a car by controlling circumstances and abilities, but you really can't speak of God making the car.

Kain: Well, He did make the materials that eventual made the car.

Hodge: And I think that is a perfect analogy to what I am saying. When it comes to a child, in the modern evangelical mind, God only made the materials (i.e, Adam and Eve, the biological process, etc.), but did not make the child directly. Instead, His only role today is to oversee and sustain the materials but not to put them together Himself.

Kain: How is this naturalism?

Hodge: It really assumes that God is absent from the direct creation of life. Evangelicals give God a secondary role because they don't want to be full-blown atheists, but they are largely in agreement with atheists on the point of conception. I don't mean by this that evangelicals are wrong to agree with atheists on the physical observations of the natural world (as we all would); but that they also agree with atheists on the metaphysical beliefs about that natural world when it comes to the area of conception; and this is where the error lies. Naturalism is essentially a metaphysical claim about life in the universe. It claims that any supernatural element is absent from the making of that life. This is why I say that evangelicals have adopted naturalism in this specific area of conception. Either the life of a child is being made by natural processes alone (i.e, naturalism) or it is being made by God through natural processes (i.e, biblical supernaturalism). Whether God sustains the natural process is irrelevant, since the point of the question is whether the life is directly made by natural processes alone or if they need God to intervene in some way for the biological processes to bring about life. As soon as a person states that God needs to make the life directly—natural processes alone will not do it—then he or she has come to the biblical position. Consequentially, he or she has begun to argue against the use of contraception, since it is then seen as a tool used to counter God Himself.

Kain: I see, so the people who use contraception assume that the conception they are countering is simply that which was brought about by their own bodies.

Hodge: Yes, these people then see only that they are holding their bodies at bay, rather than attacking a supernatural, creative act of God.

Kain: But what about the children who are conceived outside of marriage? Surely, God did not approve of their creation. He condemns extra-marital sex.

Hodge: You've confused two things: the sexual means to create a child, which God may condemn if it is outside His moral will; and the goal of the sexual act, as ending in the creation of a child, which is according to God's moral will. We, therefore, have no contradiction in saying that God sometimes condemns the means through which a child is created, but never a child who is created, since the child is His doing. We can no more say that God disapproves of a child made through a disobedient sexual act than we can say that God disapproved of the deliverance of Egypt from the famine (i.e, the end/goal) because He disapproved of Joseph's brother's selling him into slavery (i.e, the means through which the goal was accomplished). To confuse the two is to do a great injustice toward the work of God in the world, since He has chosen to use the evil, which man brings about in a fallen world, in order to bring about His good purposes (Gen 50:20).

Kain: But doesn't the fact that God commands men and women to make children show that it is an ability, rather than a direct interaction between the hand of God and the biological processes?

Hodge: No. You've misunderstood something vital within the text. The command to "be fruitful and multiply" is a euphemistic way of telling the couple to have sex and seek God's purpose through the sexual act. The words $p^e r\hat{u}$ $\hat{u}r^e b\hat{u}$, "be fruitful and multiply," refer to the sexual act and its purpose: to bear children. In fact, because it is progressive, it may take on the subsequent commands as a series of purpose clauses. This means that the text would read, "be fruitful in order to multiply; [multiply] in order to fill up the earth; [fill up the earth] in order to take it over; [take it over] in order to reign over it." Either way, the command conveys that the human couple is to have sex and not hinder the purpose of God, which is to bring forth covenant children from the act. Hence, they are told to fill up the earth. The mistaken idea that this somehow means that the couple

make children themselves, apart from God, is a naturalistic inter-
pretation foreign to the Bible. The command says nothing like this.
Instead, it tells the couple to participate in the sexual act and to be
instruments of His purpose in creation, rather than obstacles to it.
In other words, it is telling them to do the exact opposite of what the
Babylonian epic of *Atra-ḥasīs* tells them to do.

Kain: Interesting. So the people who believe that God gave them their
children and then turn around and use birth control, because rather
than seeing it as countering God's actions they see it as only hindering biological processes from making a child, are a walking contradiction and do not know it.

Hodge: I think that is true.

Kain: What does that say for the natural family planning people, who
say that as long as one engages in the sexual act at times when it can't
produce a child, and avoids engaging in the sexual act when it can
produce a child, one is free to limit his or her children in this way?

Hodge: There really is no moral difference between the NFP position
and that of artificial contraception.

Kain: How so?

Hodge: Well, if I am supposed to do A in order to produce B, but instead
do C in order to avoid the production of B, then the means through
which I choose to avoid the production of B are irrelevant. If someone comes to me and says that I can do D instead of C in order to
avoid the production of B, I have still sought to avoid the production
of B regardless of the path I took to avoid it. One might argue that
method D is more beneficial to me, and more natural, than C, but it
is in no way more beneficial to the production of B, which was what
I was told to produce in the first place. I am, therefore, still guilty
of the willful decision to not engage in A (the fertile sexual act) *in
order* to produce B (the creation of a child). I was not told to engage
in A (the sexual act which is fertile) when A had become D (the
sexual act which is not fertile). Waiting until A becomes D, so that
I can engage in the sexual act for my personal purposes rather than
for the purpose God set for it is no more pious than waiting for the
food to spoil before I serve it so I won't be condemned for poisoning
my guests.

Kain: My head is spinning. Can you clarify?

Hodge: Sure. Let me give you an analogy. A father decides to buy a car for his son because he wishes his son to have transportation to school. The son is not to avoid going to school by driving to the movies instead, as other kids often do. One day the son decides that he wants to go to the movies, but he doesn't want to disobey his father by skipping school in order to drive to the movies. The son decides that he will not drive to school during school hours, but as soon as school hours are over, he will then drive to the movies. He pats himself on the back for not disobeying his father, but has he really prevented an act of disobedience? Wasn't it the purpose of the car that the son drive it to school? Why was the act of avoiding school somehow made morally acceptable because he didn't drive the car during school hours? Would he honestly answer that it was because he waited to misuse the car until he couldn't have used it correctly? Waiting until the point that one cannot obey somehow lessens the act of disobedience when one can no longer perform it? This scenario is, of course, an absurdity of logic; yet, this is precisely the reasoning of NFP advocates. Somehow, avoiding participation in the sexual act during times it functions for that purpose for which it was made (i.e, procreation) legitimizes the act of avoiding the creation of a future child. Then to argue that to use the sexual act during times one could not use it correctly is legitimized because the couple waited until it no longer functioned toward the purpose for which the sexual act was made is of such a greater absurdity that one wonders whether any immoral act could be legitimized with the same sort of temporal manipulation.

Kain: So your point is that one is still trying to avoid the creation of a future person, misuse the sexual act, and take the control and worship due only to God even if one practices the NFP method?

Hodge: Precisely.

Kain: Do you see any other downfalls to the use of contraception? I suppose murder, sexual immorality, and idolatry are reason enough to condemn it, but I was wondering if there are any other issues involved as well.

Hodge: There are of course other consequences of the contraceptive view in general, as we also witness among the non-religious in our society.

Kain: Like what?

Hodge: Well, if children are only a result of natural processes, and we alone make them, then they not only belong to us but they also, therefore, exist only because we let them. They exist because we decided we wanted them for various reasons.

Kain: What's wrong with that?

Hodge: When children are allowed to exist based on our whims, they are seen as subordinate to our purposes. In other words, a child brought into the world because I choose to have him in order to have a sense of fulfillment in life is subject to my sense of fulfillment. This means that the child is a means to my end, not the end himself.

Kain: Well, God is our end, isn't He?

Hodge: That's not really what I mean. I don't mean the end of all being, but the end for my purposes of having a child. In other words, our end is to glorify God. Having a child is a way to glorify God. But the end I am talking about is the primary work God has set forth as our priority in life in order to achieve that ultimate end of glorifying Him. The child is the end work (i.e, the primary means), if you will, in order to achieve the end goal of glorifying God and fulfilling our purpose upon the earth.

Kain: Can you explain that a little more?

Hodge: Sure. Let me put it this way. We tend to see children as a secondary occupation for us. They are something with which we occupy ourselves along the way to our other goals in life. In this way, they are almost like a hobby, rather than the primary reason we are on this earth.

Kain: Where are you getting the idea that they are the primary reason we are on the earth? Our primary reason for being here is to glorify God.

Hodge: Actually, our primary reason for existing is to glorify God. Our primary reason for being *on the earth* is to glorify God through having and discipling covenant children. Everything else can be accomplished in the world to come. God could just end it all now and we could glorify Him in other ways in the world without end. He has placed us here at this time, however, to have and disciple covenant children.

Kain: I understand the point, but don't see where that is in Scripture.

Hodge: Well, what is fascinating about that statement is that it is in the very first chapter of the Bible. If a person wants to know the purpose of earthly existence, all one has to do is ask, What does God tell the man and woman to do when He makes them in the first place? Whatever God wanted them to accomplish on the earth was told to them when they were made. The rest of the Bible is just filling that out. Of course, that means that the man and woman's purpose as a couple is to have and raise up children to the Lord, which also assumes their commitment to God. Children are not, therefore, a side occupation or distraction; they are the very divine purpose God set in place for the human couple to fulfill. All else, ironically, is the distraction. Anything that hinders this goal is the obstacle to be overcome. Modern evangelicals have really lost their way in this respect.

Kain: So we have become twisted in that respect due to our unholy alliance with our culture's views of what is ultimately important.

Hodge: Yes, and it is no coincidence that if God set that as the purpose of the human couple, that the devil has set the world to argue against it from the beginning, and indeed, works hard to convince the Church that the world is going down the right path on the issue.

Kain: Is the whole world, along with modern evangelicalism, wrong?

Hodge: I think you should rather ask, Is the whole historic community of God, throughout its entire existence, wrong and twentieth-century evangelicalism right?

Kain: So what you're saying is that you're right and everybody else in modern evangelicalism is wrong.

Hodge: Well, there are actually a lot of evangelicals who believe what I've stated, so I wouldn't be so free with hyperbole; but does majority rule when it comes to morality?

Kain: I would think that the Holy Spirit would lead His people in the same direction.

Hodge: Are you stealing my historical argument? The number of Christians throughout church history outweighs the number of evangelicals today, wouldn't you say?

Kain: I suppose that's true.

Hodge: My argument, however, is not that the majority rules. Instead, it's that Christian teachers studying the Bible throughout variations in language, culture, time, hermeneutic, etc. were led by the Holy Spirit in this area and all concluded that the practice of contraception was a definite evil. We know from the Bible that God leads His Church; and to have the Church, throughout cultures that advocate the use of contraception, uniformly condemn the practice, while coming at the issue from different directions, is no small amount of significance.

Kain: But that means that modern evangelicalism may not be the Church.

Hodge: Not necessarily.

Kain: Why not?

Hodge: Because modern evangelicalism may simply need to be awakened in this area by the Holy Spirit. It's not as though all believers are immediately ushered into truth at their conversion. Learning that certain things are right or wrong is something that must come through the Spirit of Christ's teaching. Whether they are the Church has more to do with how they respond to God's lordship as He seeks to exercise it over such a crucial area of their lives more than whether they currently have a perfection of knowledge and practice.

Kain: Well if the Holy Spirit needs to awaken them, why write this book?

Hodge: Because the Holy Spirit has chosen to speak primarily through our teaching, not apart from it. He has chosen words to be His means. We are, therefore, told to convict, rebuke, instruct, etc. even though the Bible also tells us that conviction, rebuking, and teaching are the role of the Holy Spirit. Only He, however, can use our proclamation of the truth in a convincing way to His regenerate people.

Kain: But you seem to be judging others for their contraceptive choices.

Hodge: I don't think I personally am judging anyone; but even if that were true, I'm the least of your worries.

Kain: What do you mean?

Hodge: I mean that it doesn't matter what I think about you. I would be far more concerned, if I were you, that the entire Christian Church, which holds the authority to judge believers, and when two or three are in agreement on a disciplinary decision Christ is in agreement with them, condemns you. That entire Christian body with all of its authority and backing from Christ does not believe you are a Christian if you willingly practice contraception after being told it is wrong. Doesn't that concern you?

Kain: Not really. I have my Bible and I know my God loves me no matter what.

Hodge: So it doesn't give you the least amount of pause to know that every Holy-Spirit-led, Bible-centered, Christian teacher, elder, pastor, bishop from the first to the twentieth century would excommunicate you and declare that you are not a Christian if you rebelliously persisted in the practice?

Kain: I don't necessarily believe they would say I wasn't a Christian.

Hodge: Well, they would say that what you are unrepentantly practicing is murder, sexual immorality, and idolatry, correct?

Kain: Yes.

Hodge: And they also say, along with the Bible, that someone who practices unrepentant murder, sexual immorality, and idolatry will not enter the Kingdom of God, correct?

Kain: I suppose so.

Hodge: And do you think that they believe that there are Christians who won't enter the Kingdom of God?

Kain: No, of course not.

Hodge: Then if they believe you are going to hell, do they really believe you are a Christian?

Kain: I guess not.

Hodge: So doesn't that give you pause? Doesn't it give you a sense of fear and humility to know that, if the Holy Spirit has led His Church on such an important issue as this, such a great cloud of witnesses stands against you on judgment day?

Kain: So you think everyone who practices contraception is going to hell?

Hodge: I didn't actually say that. I stated that contraception is the practice of sins that are damnable, and that the Bible says that those who unrepentantly practice these things will not enter the Kingdom of God. To be very clear, I am not talking about someone merely sinning, but those who persist in sin without seeking to do what is right. I also said that the Church has been led to conclude the same, and that those conclusions should at least cause you to think twice about your position.

Kain: Well, I don't believe the Holy Spirit has led the Church in this area.

Hodge: So your entire hope is that He has led you, and the modern religious culture in which you reside, into the truth instead of the entire historic orthodox Christian Church?

Kain: Yes.

Hodge: My question to you then is this, What separates your mindset on this issue from the mindset of a cult in reference to any other issue?

Kain: It may seem similar, but I am not denying one of the essentials of the Christian faith.

Hodge: So it is not essential for Christians to abstain from forms of murder, sexual immorality, and idolatry?

Kain: I don't believe that the use of contraception is any of those.

Hodge: So your denial is that what the Church has seen as essential (i.e, seeing contraception as a form of murder, sexual immorality, and idolatry) is in fact essential in the first place.

Kain: Basically, yes.

Hodge: Could not the follower or leader of any cult or apostate movement say the same?

Kain: I suppose so.

Hodge: So there is really no difference between your mindset and theirs, is there?

Kain: Logically, no. But I would still want to make the distinction.

Hodge: I would as well if I were in your position, but in the end, there really isn't a distinction to be made.

Kain: Well, I don't feel like a member of a cult.

Hodge: OK. Let's look at something a little more objective though.

Kain: Like what?

Hodge: How about the biblical judgment concerning false believers.

Kain: You mean hell?

Hodge: No.

Kain: Then what do you mean?

Hodge: In the Bible, from Genesis to Exodus, from the Exodus to the Conquest, from the Conquest to the Exile, the Lord causes the godly to increase in number.

Kain: Well, that was just an Israelite promise. I don't see how that relates to any sort of biblical judgment.

Hodge: Give me a moment to explain, and I'll show you how it does.

Kain: All right.

Hodge: First, the revealed will that God wants His people to increase is given before Israel is created. If you read the New Testament, you'll see that whatever commands precede those given to Israel are also for the nations (i.e, the Gentiles), and according to New Testament teaching, that means it is for the Church. This is especially true when something is set down at creation.

Kain: OK.

Hodge: So the procreation command is for the Church as well, not just Israel.

Kain: Keep going.

Hodge: Conversely, those who reject God are said to be handed a judgment by God that decreases their number. In other words, a judgment that either ends or limits their lines.

Kain: Like whom?

Hodge: Well, in the Old Testament, there are the examples of Onan, who, through his sexual distortion, ends his line. We could also mention the Canaanites, whose line ends because of their sexually immoral practices. In Psalms 21:10 and 37:38 the Bible says that "their offspring you will destroy from the earth" and "the posterity of the wicked will be cut off." In Job 18:5, 19, the text states, "Indeed, the light of the wicked goes out . . . he has no offspring or posterity among his people, nor any survivor where he sojourned."

Kain: What about in the New Testament?

Hodge: In the New Testament, we are told in Romans 1 that God gives certain people, who have rejected revealed truth, over to nonproductive sexual acts as a type of judgment against them. They sin against their own bodies by not reproducing themselves. Likewise, the characteristics of false teachers in the New Testament almost always include the fact that they are sexually immoral, which means that they practice unproductive or non-covenantal sexual acts. A few passages that indicate this are 2 Peter 2:1–10; 1 Tim 4:1–3; 2 Tim 3:1–7, 13. It is a judgment because the person's earthly existence, which would have continued through his children after the person died, is instead diminished and, eventually, brought to an end.

Kain: So your point is that sexual distortion, like that found in the use of contraception, could very well be a judgment of God placed upon a wicked culture and a wicked religious movement.

Hodge: It is not for me to say whether that is true. I am only suggesting a possibility and, in light of such, asking for greater humility on the part of those who represent your position. In the end, that is something for each individual to think about. I really don't know if that is the case with the modern evangelical movement or not. In fact, I want to be very clear that it is not mine, nor any other person's, to judge another person; but we are to warn people of the judgment God has declared. Whether someone is ultimately condemned by any given practice or lifestyle is up to God. We must simply warn people that God has said that those who unrepentantly practice *sin* A will be given *judgment* B. Our task as Christians is to call out from Ezekiel's watchtower of the impending judgment that is coming. It is not our job to join the oncoming army and strike down people ourselves. I'm not, therefore, going to say this person is saved and this person is damned. I am simply going to preach repentance from sin and the gospel of salvation, which leads us away from loving our "fallenness" toward a love for Jesus Christ and His life-giving work in the world.

Kain: Understood. Do you think that your arguments will end the practice among evangelicals?

Hodge: I believe it will help some. Will it, once for all, do away with the practice? No, most people are comfortable in the boat, and the waters look too scary; but I do believe that it is the beginning of a discussion that has been pushed aside far too long. This is only the starting point, however, not the finish line.

Kain: I see.

Hodge: Well, Elpis, it's getting late; and you have a lot to think about. I hope our conversation is of benefit to you. May God grant you, and those with you, clarity of mind and purity of desire as you seek the truth of these things. Amen.

Conclusion

THIS BOOK HAS ARGUED that the use of contraception ought to cease being a viable option for a Christian. It has put forth the historic Christian arguments that see the practice as a form of murder, sexual immorality, and idolatry. I have also sought to show that it is not only the content of the arguments that matter, but the nature of the argumentation itself. Hence, I have presented the two contradictory trajectories taken by historic and modern hermeneutics in evaluating sexually moral issues.

This study has further put forth the argument that the use of contraceptive measures is contrary to Christian discipleship, love, and the preserving of life. In fact, these elements are really all different components of one another. Contraception, as murder, is the hindrance of the production of life; as sexual immorality, it is the means through which that life is hindered; and as idolatry, it is the audacity to partake of the divine right to use such means to hinder that life. Finally, as contrary to Christian discipleship, love, and the preserving of life, the sins of this one event culminate to negate the rearing and sending out of a covenant person and his or her further life-perpetuating influence in the world.

Furthermore, it has been argued that this position is counter-cultural, and has always been so. Only a genuine submission to Christ as Lord will bring about an honest evaluation of this subject. Hence, only a true Christian will give it a just trial within his or her mind. I am confident that, when he or she does so, the Spirit of God will bring that person to the same understanding He has always graciously granted to those who seek Him with the whole of their lives. If Christ is allowed to change the thinking of a person in this area, He most certainly will change also his or her life for the glory of God. Such a discovery, therefore, can be made only by those who genuinely seek to be changed; and in a church filled with easy-believism and false piety, such may be indeed rare gems to find; but I am confident that they are still to be found.

I have no illusions that the evangelical community will suddenly turn around and see the shunning of all forms of contraception as the ultimate good of the sexual act, which glorifies God and fulfills its purpose in the world. It is a long road ahead, and this book is meant to provide a starting point for discussion. There are many details that are still left to explain but which had to be omitted to keep the book at a manageable level. As such, much of what is said here will have to be fleshed out in further discussions. It is my hope that this book will simply provide the needed aid for any Christian couple seeking to come to terms with what is pleasing to God in this extremely important area of their lives.

Finally, I want to conclude by saying that I did not write this book to argue that everyone on earth should have more children. The goal is not that the earth should have tons more people on it just for the sake of it. The goal is that more covenant children be born and raised to the glory of God through the gospel of His Christ. My argument, then, is to the Christian community. It is a plea for God's people to do what only they can do (i.e., to have and raise up children to the Lord). The unbeliever, whether holstering a claim to a Christian identity or not, cannot do this. Hence, the Lord's purpose in the sexual act cannot be completely fulfilled through the unbeliever. It can be accomplished only through God's people, through those who truly believe. It is time for the modern evangelical to turn away from the pattern set down by the demonically influenced culture and to embrace the pattern God set down in Scripture for His people to follow. It is my hope that the Christian, who seeks God's desires for his or her life, will hear the voice of God and seek His purpose through the sexual act by giving God the continual opportunity to create a covenant child, who will not only glorify God through the couple's family, but also change for the better the Church and the world for ages to come.

It is further my prayer that one day the *right to life* will include in the Christian mind, not only the young, nor only those who have made it out of the womb, nor solely those in the womb, but all people present and future. May God grant us the courage to bring the case of those with no voice into the assembly of the God who knows and desires to create each and every one of them.

> "Now the God of peace, who brought up from the dead the great Shepherd of the sheep through the blood of the eternal covenant, Jesus our Lord, equip you in every good thing to do His will, working in us that which is pleasing in His sight, through Jesus Christ, to whom be the glory forever and ever. Amen." (Heb 13:20–21)

Appendix A

The Christian Case against Sterilization

CASTRATION, WHAT NOONAN CALLS "an extreme form of contraception" simply because it was often done not to curtail lust so much as to deny any future possibility of having children, was overwhelmingly condemned by the early Church. Often castrated individuals still performed sexual acts but without the result of offspring. The Council of Nicea (AD 325) stated that an individual who castrates himself is to be denied a ministerial office (perhaps taken from Deuteronomy 23:1). Its decision is as follows:

> If anyone in sound health has castrated himself, it behooves that such a one, if enrolled among the clergy, should cease [from his ministry], and that from henceforth no such person should be promoted. But, as it is evident that this is said of those who willfully do the thing and presume to castrate themselves, so if any have been made eunuchs by barbarians, or by their masters, and should otherwise be found worthy, such men this canon admits to the clergy.[1]

Chrysostom then calls those who castrate themselves murderers as well[2]—most likely due to the intended purpose of seeking to wipe out the possibility of future children coming into existence.

It must be argued that the prohibition in Deuteronomy 23:1 is in the context of whether someone is a covenant child, or can have covenant children. The two other groups that are prohibited to be a part of the assembly are (1) someone who could not verify that his father was an Israelite and (2) the Ammonites and Moabites, because they sought to

---

1. Canon, 1.
2. Chrysostom, *Homily 62 on Matthew*, 19.

mix Israel's children with non-covenant children in an effort to make God angry with Israel. If Egyptians or Edomites, however, become a part of the covenant, their children could enter the assembly after three generations (apparently because religious assimilation into the worship of YHWH would have taken place by then). There seems, then, to be a concern with whether covenant people are entering into the assembly, and this probably does speak to our issue in respect to covenant children.

Having said this, however, the main argument I would level against permanent sterilization is the same as I would level against temporary sterilization. It may be that the Deuteronomic passage is concerned only with issues of circumcision (i.e., only non-covenant issues) irrespective of the procreative aspect. It may also allude to the holy and the profane as illustration, rather than arguing for a particular moral *per se*. It, of course, can include all of these together with the non-procreative possibility on the part of the castrated as part of the exclusion from the assembly; but it is not necessary to pursue that route here.[3] The preceding book explains why God would not find the practice acceptable. Hence, using this passage is not central to the argument against permanent contraception (i.e., sterilization). If temporarily hindering the creation of a child through the sexual act is an evil, how much more so is the permanent hindrance of that sacred event?

Dietrich Bonhoeffer argued against permanent sterilization when he stated, "Neither I nor the state can lay claim to an absolute right of free disposal over the bodily members that have been given to me by God."[4] Such a sentiment directly counters the self-focused reasoning a person usually uses when deciding to permanently sterilizes him or herself. Even those in favor of the practice admit that most evangelicals do not really even consider biblical ethics and God's thinking about the subject before entering into such a permanent decision.[5] (Indeed, I have argued here that most evangelicals don't think seriously about *temporary* sterilization

3. Having stated this, however, the case for the Deuteronomic relevance to this issue is largely underestimated by the dismissive, and largely false dichotomistic, arguments made by advocates. See the less-than-thorough treatment of this text given in Feinberg and Feinberg, *Ethics*, 176; and the arguments concerning Deuteronomy 23:1 cited in Davis ("Theologically Sound," 70), which attempt to bypass the immediate context for the statement concerning eunuchs by alluding to doubtful Mesopotamian origins and later Jewish interpretation of the text.

4. Bonhoeffer, *Ethics*, 181.

5. Orr, "Ethically Defensible," 47–61.

in their use of contraception. The lack of thought that goes into permanent sterilization is simply a logical outflow to the thoughtlessness that goes into both this and Christian ethics in general.)

If one sees any individual non-procreative sexual act as an act of murder, sexual immorality, and idolatry, then there is no longer any foundational reason for believing that a purposeful act that makes all other acts non-procreative would be a morally acceptable option for the Christian.

Appendix B

The Propagandistic Myth of Overpopulation

MUCH OF THE ACCEPTANCE of contraceptive practices came about
from the idea that the world was becoming vastly overpopulated.[1]
I do not wish to go in depth on the subject of overpopulation arguments
(which are made as excuses as to why one might practice contraception,
not why it is a morally acceptable solution to overpopulation); but I do
want to say a few brief words concerning Neo-Malthusian overpopulation arguments.[2]

Throughout the Book of Genesis, standing side by side with the
promises of children, are the promises of land to sustain them. In fact,
the dominion of mankind over the animals in Genesis 1 is a promise to
give mankind all the land needed to support the children God is giving.
Note that the land animals (specifically predators) are not blessed with
the command to be fruitful and multiply as are the birds and fish and
lower land animals. This may be due to the fact that humans will one
day take over their land. It is possible that these predators were made by
God simply to maintain the environmental eco-system until humankind
became numerous enough to cultivate and take over the predatory role.

---

1. See the comment by Bart Garrett (*Christians and Contraception*, fn. 16) "It is note-
worthy here to mention that particularly in the 1950s and 1960s when much attention
was given to the scare of overpopulation, many theologians strongly advocated birth
control in an effort to control the rising population. See for example: Jewett, Paul King;
"A Case for Birth Control," *Christian Century,* May 24, 1961. Volume: 78: 651, 652. New
statistics of the 1980s and 1990s would lead us to believe that the world is really not in
danger of becoming overcrowded as some once thought."

2. For definitions, a summary and critique of Malthusian theories, see Wolfgram,
Population, Resources and Environment.

In any case, the answer to overpopulation of an area in the Book of Genesis, rather than being one of limiting children, is to spread out. Instead of congregating in cities, which is from whence the bulk of over-population arguments come, Genesis tells us that God wants us to fill up the earth, to spread out over it. Disobedience to this command often leads people to argue that there are too many people on earth, even though acres and acres of uninhabited land scream out to us otherwise—hence, the book's lack of enthusiasm toward the building of cities,[3] culminating in its condemnation of people living in one place at the city of Babel.[4]

One of the experiences in my life that will always amaze me is a missions trip I took to China. I had been taught, from the time I was very young, that China was vastly overpopulated. Along with this, I had been taught that the government had rightly mandated that only one child was allowed per family because of this overpopulation and the fear that it would limit all of the resources. What shocked me, when I actually went there, was the thousands of miles of uninhabited country that was rich in resources. Flying from Southern China to Beijing, I realized that these overpopulation arguments stemmed from the *sense* that there were too many people derived from the overcrowding of cities. Beijing (as well as cities like Hong Kong) itself was overcrowded because people congregate toward that major cities for various reasons (e.g. perceived protection, resources, jobs, convenience, etc.); but the country as a whole has the land, and consequentially, the resources, that are able to support large numbers of people. I soon realized that the perceived global problem with overpopulation was intrinsically connected to the city. Very few country folk wake up in the morning, go outside, look right and left at their hundreds of empty acres of land or forest, and conclude, "There are too many people around here." The argument in Genesis seems to be aware of not only the falsity of the overpopulation argument but also of its lopsided origins, which stem solely from overpopulated urban life.

There is, of course, nothing wrong with living in a city as long it does not drive one to disobedience. If one seeks to obey God in sexual activity and acknowledges the biblical solution to overpopulation, then one will have to decide what to do depending on one's respective situation. If God

3. See Kikawada and Quinn, *Before Abraham Was*, 54–82, for a further analysis of the Genesis antagonism toward the city.

4. Note that the emphasis in Hebrew is on the city, not the tower, as is often assumed. See Westermann, *Genesis 1–11*, 547.

has not given many children, or He has given the finances to support those that He does give, staying in the city might be fine for some. If He decides to give many children to a couple, however, and less finances for city living, that couple ought to consider spreading out. Note that the freedom to decide what to do in a given situation is a freedom of where to live, rather than the freedom to prevent human children from existing.[5]

It should also be noted that the command is to be fruitful and multiply and *fill up the earth* in order to subdue it. In other words, whether one is obeying the command to fill up the earth and subdue it may become a factor when one ponders whether spreading out is appropriate.

One might object to such an inconvenient answer to the problem, but such an answer is biblically faithful and has always been the Christian response to the objection raised. C.H. Spurgeon commented beautifully as he stated:

> Children are a heritage which Jehovah himself must give, or a man will die childless, and thus his house will be unbuilt. And the fruit of the womb is his reward, or a reward from God. He gives children, not as a penalty nor as a burden, but as a favour. They are a token for good if men know how to receive them, and educate them. They are "doubtful blessings" only because we are doubtful persons. Where society is rightly ordered children are regarded, not as an incumbrance, but as an inheritance; and they are received, not with regret, but as a reward. If we are over crowded in England, and so seem to be embarrassed with too large an increase, we must remember that the Lord does not order us to remain in this narrow island, but would have us fill those boundless regions which wait for the axe and the plough. Yet even here, with all the straits of limited incomes, our best possessions are our own dear offspring, for whom we bless God every day.[6]

However, the inconvenience of such a solution to overpopulation in an area drives us to make alternative arguments—even to the point of arguing against God. In this way, we no longer live to seek the divine promise of the Garden, but the earthly focused desire of Babel.

---

5. Note that the solution advocated in Genesis is to spread out in the cases of both urban (e.g., Babel, where too many people have gathered in one place) and rural overpopulation (e.g., when Abraham and Lot decide to spread out from one another because there are too many people in one place).

6. Spurgeon, *The Treasury of David*, comment on Psalm 127:3.fch.

Appendix C

Seven Tough Questions from Friends

THE FOLLOWING QUESTIONS WERE proposed by some friends who reviewed the book for me. As these were developed from personal correspondence, they have taken upon a much more conversational tone. None of the following is meant to be the definitive answer to each question. They are only meant to be a starting point and initial advice in what will hopefully be a larger continued conversation. I have edited and organized these questions as follows:

1. *How would you address health concerns for the mother? I am not speaking of an average, healthy woman, but of a woman, who although does not have problems conceiving, would be jeopardizing her health with pregnancy/childbirth?*

It should be understood that this is essentially an argument from situational ethics, which would be specifically classified as an argument from pity.[1] It is a powerfully emotional argument precisely because it involves the possible giving of the mother's life. Therefore, the threat to a woman's health has been used often as a red herring for the abortion issue as well. It is often meant to trump or shame any argument suggesting that abortion may be wrong.[2] As such, it is also an argument from pity in that it seeks to gain the upper hand in an argument through emotion rather than through reason.[3]

---

1. See Francis J. Beckwith, Politically Correct Death, 53–54.

2. For discussions of the health issue in the case of abortion, see Ibid. 31–32, 125–26.

3. Ibid., 53–77.

It should first be acknowledged that a doctor claiming that a woman should not have any more children ought to be critically evaluated in the same way that anyone suggesting such a life changing alternative should be scrutinized. It is possible that the climate of our current culture may gear itself to recommendations that are biased in a particular direction.[4]

Having said that, let's say that the health risk is genuine. Some would answer that, in cases where the woman's health is at risk, the use of contraception (and abortion) is justifiable. Ultimately, in decisions of life and death, the only person who should decide such things is the very person at risk. Hence, the decision does not belong to anyone else but to the mother alone. With that understood, there are some Biblical issues to consider when making that decision.

The first is to acknowledge that no one is psychic and knows for sure what will occur if a woman decides to let God give her a child.

The second is that God is the one giving her a child. Do we then say that God is unaware of what may happen to her? A person ought to also scrutinize her view of the conception event in that such reasoning may indicate the unbiblical adoption of philosophic naturalism. The person should realize that she is countering an act of God in order to save her life. The same is true in the abortion debate. There needs to be an acknowledgement that God's work to create a child is being countered. Now, it may be the case that because other factors are ultimately countering it, even though the woman herself would not want to do so, but is forced to do something about the child due to those forces, is morally allowed to counter it; but I would still not say that this justifies the use of contraception. If the woman is of such a weakened state that she cannot go through a pregnancy, why is it that she does not simply decide to abstain from the sexual act in her frail condition? As long as she abstains because she is sick and not because she wants to avoid having a child that would endanger her health, there would be no immorality in it. If she is able to participate in the sexual act, but not able to endure a pregnancy, it is at this time that she will have to make the decision whether or not to use a contraceptive measure or abstain from the sexual act, exercising self-control. One must also ask what moral choices she is going to make if the contraceptive measure should fail. What if God overrides it? Will abortion then be an option because the deliverance of her physical life is seen as the ultimate good? She may conclude that it is.

4. See Rick and Jan Hess, A Full Quiver, 95–101.

She must further ask herself whether it is moral for her to engage in a purposeful unproductive sexual act instead of abstaining even if she is strong enough to do this, but too endangered by the state of pregnancy.

I do not, however, believe that she is just as moral to destroy another's life in order to save her own as when she sacrifices her life for another. One is still an unchristian response and one is a Christian response. I often think of Rachel, and wonder if she would have known before she conceived that she would die from Benjamin's birth, whether she would use contraception (which was available to her) in order to save her own life. If she would have, not only a little boy, but an entire tribe, including the Apostle Paul, would have been extinguished from existence. On a personal note, my mother was told this same thing, and luckily for me, she didn't use contraception to wipe out my existence either.

To use a difficult analogy, imagine if you and your husband were chained to each other and thrown into the ocean with nothing else around you, left only with a single life-preserver. He is able either to weigh you down and sink you (hence, both of you may sink or he may survive and you drown) or you can push him down, use him as a floating device and save your life instead.

Now, even though I'm sure you love your husband, imagine it was one of your children to whom you were chained in the ocean instead. I'm sure as a mother, you would sacrifice yourself for your child. The only reason, then, that we think differently when it comes to the subject of contraception is that we don't know and have not yet come to love the child who would have existed if only we had given him or her a chance to live. I think if people were to see it this way, they would perceive contraception much differently than they do.

The question becomes: "Is it moral to take a life in order to save one's own?" Most people would answer, "Yes," and see my response as an irresponsible burden placed upon the woman. Religion, including Christianity, in our culture is primarily used for the enhancement of a person's physical and temporal life, not the risk of its loss. We, therefore, see any teaching that would risk our lives as radical and irresponsible. But the core of genuine Christianity is the sacrifice of the temporal physical life for the glory of God. True Christianity lives in this world, but not for this world. Instead, it lives for the world behind, and beyond, it. Therefore, the Christian says with Paul, "For me, to live is Christ and to die is gain" (Phil 1:21). For the average Westerner, however, his theology is one of "For me, to live is gain and to die is loss." Therefore, we seek to prolong our lives through whatever means necessary, and give little thought to Jesus' statement, "But who among you through worrying can add a single hour to his life span?" (Luke 12:25). In Job, we understand that God has already set how long we will live: "Since his [a person's] days are determined, the number of his months are with you; and his limits you have set, so that he cannot pass them" (14:5). This does not mean that these things are not worked out through the decisions we make, but only that if it is a choice between doing what is right and saving one's own life, then such a decision should be made in light of the brevity, providentially determined, and eschatological orientation of the Christian's life. In other words, the question we should always ask is not, "What will happen to me if I do X?", but instead, "Is X the right or wrong thing for me to do?" If Christianity is about trust in God even to death, believing that God has decided already when and how we will die, and that He has given us the spirit of Christ and the power to go to our deaths for the love of another, then the Christian response seems to be one of sacrifice to preserve another, rather than the selfish preservation of self (the Atheist's "survival of the fittest") at the sacrifice of others.

The real problem most people have with this answer, then, stems from a "this worldly" focus of religion in our culture, a view that leaves little hope for a humanity whose "days are but a breath" (Job 7:16). But even though Christians live here on this earth, seeking to preserve the lives of others and their own lives, we do so with the understanding that this preservation is but a foreshadowing of a kingdom that is "not of this world" (John 18:36), and a life that is "yet to be revealed with Christ in God" (Col 3:3).

Of course, if both mother and child are definitely going to die (although I've seen so many doctors that are wrong on this, so I would not trust mere human estimates all of the time), it may be a different story in that the preservation of one life is better than the destruction of two. However, this is more of an issue for abortion than contraception as no one is really able to predict with certainty that both mother and child will definitely die if the woman conceives. We don't usually make good psychics, and mothers who are told that both will die have had children and lived as well many times before, so it all has to be taken with great care, and the possible intervention of God can never be left out of the mix.

2. *I understand the idea that Christian couples should not do anything to prevent God from creating a life if He chooses to do so. Since the primary objective of the sexual act is to procreate, does not your argument suggest, therefore, that sex during times of the month the woman cannot conceive, sex during pregnancy, or sex after menopause is sinful?*

Well, first, I would distinguish between the former issue and the latter two. Remember that the argument presented here concerns the misuse of the sexual act, which could be otherwise used as productive. In other words, a person is able to participate in a sexual act that is productive, but instead chooses to participate in one that is not. Thus, there is the wasting of semen, which could have resulted in life, but will now end in non-life (i.e., death).

Second, I would want to point out, concerning the first issue mentioned, that it is not necessary to try and figure out the woman's cycle and become the oracle predicting times of fertility versus non-fertility. It is enough to know that a person should participate in the sexual act for productivity, and do so freely without worrying about what days of the month could be better or worse for such.

Now, having made that clear, if a person absolutely knows for a fact that the sexual act at that time will be unproductive, with the possibility of it being used as productive later, then he or she should exercise restraint, and wait until that unproductive time has passed. Some may object to this statement, but if a married couple is willing to tell their unmarried Christian teenagers that they should abstain from the sexual act for years to come until married (i.e., until it can be practiced within the appropriate boundaries for which God purposed it), then that couple can exercise a more mature Christianity and abstain for a few days for the same reasons.

I do stress, however, that I personally don't think it is necessary to try and figure it all out, but instead would seek to obey the command given. God tells us to "be fruitful and multiply." He does not tell us to "become scientists and figure out the inward workings of the woman's anatomy and cycle in order to hypothesize the likely result of pregnancy through the sexual act." The use of the sexual act as a tool to bring forth children is His job. The command given is that with which we are to concern ourselves. He will work out the rest. Therefore, this ought to give a couple the relief of the burden that really only God can bear.

Concerning the latter two, the Fathers had concluded that a person ought not to participate in the sexual act if the woman had already conceived or was post-menopausal. Now, I do think this is a viable option and no more absurd than suggesting to a young single person or a widow that they ought to exercise restraint and abstain from the sexual act by the power of the Holy Spirit given to them. However, I think the Patristic view here stemmed both from a consistent logical reasoning and a lack of the appropriate knowledge of biology in this case. Had they known the biology, I don't think they would have concluded the same. So I do think that science in this area can help in this issue.

If the evil of an unproductive sexual act is due to the fact that the semen can be used in a productive sexual act, then there is no evil in participating in the sexual act during times of pregnancy or menopause because sperm within the male body will only last for three weeks before it dies on its own. In other words, it will end in death/non-life either way. No life can spring forth from it regardless as to whether an individual has sex with his wife or not.

Although I have maintained that the sexual act is to be fulfilled in its primary purpose of procreation, I have also maintained that there are numerous secondary benefits to that sexual act. Now, if a person has entered into a marital relationship for the purpose of having children through the right use of the sexual act, and the sperm will die before an act will become available for that use, then seeking to fulfill the secondary benefits of the sexual act is better than gaining nothing at all through it. In other words, the person has not made the sexual act unproductive, the situation has. The sperm will die either way. Therefore, in these cases, it is not an evil, and indeed may even be a good, to participate in the sexual act with a person's spouse during these longer, and possibly permanent, times of infertility.

It should be remembered also that God still brought about a child through post-menopausal women like Sarah and Leah.

This argument, therefore, assuming both that the act cannot be used for its primary purpose otherwise, and that God, as the one who gives children, may decide to use it anyway for the primary purpose, can also be applied to other situations where the couple are infertile.

In summary, then, one should participate in the sexual act freely. If it is known that it can be used productively instead of unproductively, then the couple should wait for the productive period. If it cannot be used productively, and the sperm will die either way, it is better to fulfill one of the secondary benefits within the Biblical marriage between a man and a woman than to fulfill nothing at all.

3. *Should Christian couples be actively trying to get pregnant? Should they attempt to determine times of fertility and only have sex during those times?*

I think Christians ought to simply be engaging in the sexual act as normally befits them (unless they are not engaging in it very much at all). We are simply told to have sex by God, but not really told how much to have; nor are we told to try and scientifically calculate a woman's cycle. I would say that it is not necessary to try and figure out when one is most fertile, etc. largely because it isn't the person's fertility, but God's decision that will bring about a child. Hence, this perspective should actually bring about a lot of freedom from trying to be God (something Genesis tries to convey to us) and control the conception event either way. Instead, we need only to be obedient in marriage by not hindering the sexual act and engaging in it in what is determined an appropriate manner by the couple in light of their duty to be fruitful and multiply.

If a certain time is known to be unproductive for a fact, then restraint should be employed to keep the sexual act within the boundaries God has set for it. This, of course, is nothing different than saying to an unmarried couple that restraint should be employed to do the same. There is no Biblical reason that I can see that would tell us that restraint is for the unmarried person only. But I would emphasize again that it is not necessary to try and figure everything out. The command God gives is that we are to participate in the sexual act as a means to productivity. So the weight of the figuring out the mechanics of the act are left on God's shoulders, and freedom in which the act can be performed should bring about the greater joy that comes in assigning divine decisions to the only one who can handle them adequately.

4. *Should Christians use artificial means to conceive, such as In Vitro Fertilization (IVF), artificial insemination, fertility drugs, etc.?*

Although the book is really about issues surrounding the countering of the conception event, I wouldn't advocate certain artificial means, as many of them include the bringing about of life, which in all likelihood will be destroyed (I'm thinking of In Vitro here). As for artificial insemination, I probably wouldn't take as much of an issue with it, since it does not involve the creation of "disposable" embryos (even though there are other issues to consider). As for fertility drugs, Christianity doesn't seem to ever have a problem with fertility drugs when they are procreative. It only seems to take issue with drugs that are contraceptive or abortive, so I don't see any reason I would take issue with them. In fact, the mandrake root, mentioned in a few places in the Bible, is an ancient form of a fertility drug, and the Bible doesn't seem to place it in a negative light at all (Gen 30:14–16; Song 7:13). I certainly would take issue if any artificial means replaced the natural means, since the sexual act is the primary means through which procreation should take place; but as long as it didn't replace it, I can't see that I would take much of an issue with those methods that are procreative without including anti-creative results, such as knowingly making human embryos which in all probability will be disposed.

5. *Also, would you have any advice for people who have already taken permanent measures to prevent conception of a child (i.e., those who have already had a vasectomy or tubal ligation procedure performed)?*

I would say to the person, who already had a vasectomy or tubal ligation procedure performed, that he or she should see if it can be reversed, since they have committed a great sin. In fact, most modern theologians and ethicists who don't hold the position I do about temporary contraception would be in complete agreement with me on that one. Marriage needs to be open to having children. Now, if the person is not able to reverse it, then I would say he or she at very least needs to ask for God's forgiveness for the sin, which they now acknowledge. Who knows? Perhaps, God will even override the natural obstruction of the surgery in the sexual act. In any case, the great thing about repentant faith is that anyone who exercises it can be redeemed.

6. *Doesn't the argument here indicate that people who use/used birth control are going to hell? If so, does this mean that the bulk of evangelicals in our time are going to hell, and others who have died are already in hell because of this issue?*

There are few things here. If the use of birth control is to be identified as types of sin, such as sexual immorality and murder, then we must somehow make sense of the Bible's statements that those who practice such things will not enter the kingdom of God. When the great theologians of the Church make these condemnatory statements concerning the issue, we need to understand that they are not simply being legalistic, but are genuinely concerned for the eternal well-being of people within the Church.

We are all guilty of these sins in one way or another; but there are two types of people who sin: repentant and unrepentant. Now, if by "repentant" you think I mean the ceasing of all sin in perfection, then you're right, no one is going to make it. We're all in trouble. But if you understand repentance as striving to lead lives that are pleasing to God, then this would indicate that a person ought to seek to give up the contraceptive and murderous lifestyle and should seek to do otherwise.

We need to see grace as coming only through a repentant faith (as the Scripture states) and apart from that kind of faith, there is no grace for that person. Different sins are brought to our attention at different points in our lives, so immediate perfection is not required. However, I do perceive repentance as the journey away from sin, rather than the perfection of life, so that when a sin is brought to the person's attention, their true disposition toward God is revealed. We are all sinners, but those who belong to Christ seek to "sin no more" as opposed to those who are justifiers of the self. We all may be in the same cesspool, but there is a difference between those who are struggling to get out of the cesspool and those who are lounging in it, willingly soaking it up.

My issue then would be with people who are not going to journey away from the use of contraception. And that is the issue the Church takes with people and becomes a subject of discipline throughout its history.

If the question is whether a person will enter heaven in willful rebellion against Christ's teaching in the Scripture, I would simply warn that the Bible doesn't present that person in a good light. Either severe discipline is brought about by God (either through the Church or directly) or no discipline is brought about by God because the person does not really belong to Him (Heb 12:4–11).

Having said all that, it may be that God gives people time to grow and learn on this issue because there has been such a blinding on the issue. This should not be taken as an excuse to remain in sin, as He doesn't seem to be so lenient in Scripture even when the surrounding culture may have persuaded individuals from practicing what was right or even seeing that it was an issue in the first place. The person who knows the truth and does not do it receives many lashes, but the person who does not know still receives lashes for it. So it really is a much more serious issue to God (as I tried to demonstrate in the book) than we may realize. My only point is that I would not rush to excommunicate someone from fellowship because the cultural barrier is thick, and we need to give God time to break through it with His Word.

7. *If I am correct, that the practitioners of birth control are going to hell, then does this not imply that a person cannot have sin in his or her life in order to go to heaven? I'm not advocating the "I'm saved by grace, so it doesn't matter what I do" position; but instead asking whether this means that a person must have all of his or her "stuff" together in order to be accepted by God into His presence? It would seem that the element of grace would come in at that point. I've never understood the Bible to be saying that someone had to be sinless in order to enter Heaven, but more that we should be striving to lead godly lives. Most evangelicals don't even consider this to be a controversial issue, and are completely unaware that they may be doing something wrong. As you addressed, it is relative (i.e., "to each his own"). Since most evangelicals are only taught this one view by the modern church (i.e., that the issue is relative to the person), then how can we expect repentance, and therefore, salvation for these people? If this is all true, then it would seem that salvation is really works-based, is it not?*

Let me say this as clearly as I possibly can. Salvation is, from beginning to end, start to finish, grace-based, not works based (Eph 2:8–10). But there is one correction I want to make here. We must enter the eternal presence of God sinless (Matt 5:20; Heb 12:14). That is absolutely true. That is why Christ must place His sinless life upon us (Rom 5:10). Otherwise, not a single soul would make it. So we enter into the presence of the Father through the righteousness of the Son, not through our own righteousness. He takes away the sin of the world that we might enter into eternal fellowship with God.

The confusion comes in when evangelicals have not been taught the means through which Christ transfers His life to ours. He does not simply give grace apart from Biblical faith; and Biblical faith consists of a trusting relationship with Jesus Christ, which carries with it a submissive attitude toward Him as Lord and a desire to turn away from what is evil. Repentance for me is not the perfection of our own lives, but it is an attitude/decision that marks the beginning of the journey away from sin and toward the mind and life of Christ in all things. It is through this relationship that Christ transfers, by grace, His perfect life to ours. Notice that those who do not have this type of relationship with Christ, even though they have an unrepentant version of "faith," are told by Christ that "I never knew you; depart from Me, you who practice lawlessness" (Matt 7:22–23). In the context, the Lord defines those who practice lawlessness (anomia "without external government") as those who do not belong to the group who "do the will of the Father" (v. 21). These people have a form of belief, but it is not the Biblical faith which includes a turning away from self-worship to the worship of Christ as Lord. So I agree with you that none of us has our "stuff" together, and all of us need grace to be saved; but that grace comes through the means of saving faith, and that saving faith relationship carries with it the desire to journey away from the love of self to the love of God that then produces actions/works that express this change in trajectory. The former is what saves; the latter is the product of that genuine saving faith.

What I have talked about in this book, then, is the recognition of, and repentance from, the sins of murder, sexual immorality and idolatry, which are inherent within the contraceptive mindset. A call to repentance is really a wake up call to the community of God, which declares, "Thinking or Action B is not consistent with Claim A;" or, in John the Baptist's words, if you are the people of God, "bear fruit that is consistent with repentance" (Matt 3:8). In other words, if we have truly repented of our sin, then we will live the lives that are consistent with that claim (i.e., we will worship God instead of self; use our temporal pleasures for God's ultimate purposes; and become life-givers instead of hoarders of life).

Does a consistent, unrepentant lifestyle indicate that a person is not saved? Here I want to be cautious. What I would maintain is this: the Bible states that those who practice idolatry, sexual immorality and murder will not enter the kingdom of God. I tried to be very clear that this is what the Bible (and consistent with the Bible, it has been the continual declaration of God's historic Church) has said, not me. The issue is, therefore, not with me, but with the Bible as seen through the eyes of the Church. I do, however, believe these passages of condemnation to be talking about people who do not repent of these sins, not just anyone who has ever committed them.

The second thing I wanted to be clear about is that I can't go around judging the servants of another. I can't say upon whom God will have mercy, upon whom He will not, who is going to hell and who isn't. That's not my right. As a shepherd, I do have the responsibility to warn people that God has said He is going to do A apparently to the people who practice B, and urge them then not to do B, but the rest is in God's hands.

I would also want to steer evangelicals away from the argument that stems from the wrong-headed idea that all of these people couldn't possibly be wrong and go to hell. This is itself a dangerous argument in that God most likely has sent entire religious cultures into eternal judgment (Rom 9:27–10:3). There is no reason to suppose that a self-focused religion like modern evangelicalism should be any different. In fact, the religious culture we see being sent most into eternal judgment in the Bible is that within the visible church itself (Matt 25:41–46). The idea that those who believe they have a genuine relationship with Christ couldn't possibly be going to hell runs counter to the Bible's teaching that they do. This presumptuous argument that is often made needs to be replaced with humility and a testing to see if we are "in the faith" (2 Cor 13:5).

However, I am hopeful that many evangelicals simply may be ignorant instead of rebellious. I say this with some care because many times ignorance is rebellion, and people are judged for not seeking out the truth as well; but I have high hopes for repentance in this area as the truth breaks through the cultural darkness. Anyone who preaches repentance in any area of life should be hoping for the repentance and salvation of those to whom he or she is preaching. It is an awful thing for any preacher to have his ministry result in further condemnation, rather than in life and salvation; so ultimately I'm hoping for repentance rather than condemnation with what I know will be perceived as a severe warning.

Appendix D

The Alleged Stoic Background of the Patristic Attitude toward Sex

ONE OF THE MAJOR tactics used to undermine the Church's view of the purpose of the sexual act concerns a claim that the Church has been influenced by Stoic ideas; and that these ideas, therefore, are not really Biblical at all. This sort of thinking stems from the idea that a person can refute certain arguments presented by the historic Church's position, then the position itself will be refuted.

This, of course, is not necessarily the case. Even if a person could refute a bad argument offered as a support of a particular theological or ethical issue, it does not logically follow that the position itself is wrong.[1] As an example of this, the main argument for why the Early Church accepted the book of Hebrews into the canon of the New Testament was because they believed it to be Pauline. Here we are able to see how the Holy Spirit might bring His Church into the right conclusion and practice even through a wrong argument made to support that conclusion. It takes faith of course to believe that the Church made the right decision even with a bad argument, but there are numerous instances where one can observe the same phenomenon occur throughout Church History up to the present day.[2] Of course, the real issue is whether the conclusion made is consistent with the rest of Scripture and its interpretation as the Holy

---

1. The attempt by Boswell (*Christianity, Social Tolerance and Homosexuality*, 137–43) to undermine the entire historic Christian position on homosexuality by dismissing Epiphanius' argument concerning hyenas comes to mind.

2. This is particularly true of the modern evangelical, "linguistically-challenged" use of word studies. Often extremely bad arguments are made to support a very correct theological position.

Spirit has led His Church into the same conclusion throughout history, regardless of shifts in cultural and hermeneutical thinking. If a person finds him or herself in the situation where He has not, then he or she may find themselves in an unorthodox cultic mindset, instead of a historical orthodox one.

In any case, the argument concerning Stoic influence is made by various groups, from those who argue that the historic Church's view of homosexuality is wrong to those who argue for a greater tolerance concerning extra-marital sexual relations. Some groups attempt to show that the New Testament itself has this influence, and therefore, in this group's estimation, it cannot be trusted to supply us with an adequate framework for a morally acceptable sexuality. Others, who do not wish to throw dirt on the New Testament, instead, limit this criticism to the Early Church, and any of those theologians who may follow the interpretive trajectory found therein.

What the latter group fails to explain, however, is that if such a claim damages the testimony of the Early Church, how is that the New Testament's testimony remains unscathed when it uses the same language and concepts that can be observed in the Fathers? In fact, what we will see is that the Fathers gain their concepts and terminology of the sexual act from the New Testament. If this is true, what is said of the one may also be said of the other.

THE CLAIM OF STOIC INFLUENCE

H. Wayne House argues:

> History reveals that such notions owed more to Greek Stoicism than to the New Testament. In Stoicism, emotions were downplayed and self-control was exalted. This even became true in marriage, where passion was considered suspect. Marriage must have another purpose—namely, the continuance of the human race. In the words of the Stoic philosopher Ocellus Lucanus, "We have intercourse not for pleasure but for the purpose of procreation . . . . The sexual organs are given man not for pleasure, but for the maintenance of the species.[3]

---

3. House, "Should Christians Use Birth Control?"

Noonan argued that "Stoicism was in the air the intellectual converts to Christianity breathed. Half consciously, half unconsciously, they accommodated some Christian beliefs to a Stoic sense."[4]

He further states:

> If one asks, then, where the Christian Fathers derived their notions on marital intercourse—notions which have no express biblical basis — the answer must be, chiefly from the Stoics. In the case of such an early and influential teacher as Clement of Alexandria, the direct descent is obvious; his work on the purposes of marriage is a paraphrase of works of Musonius. In the second century, Origen's standard for intercourse in pregnancy is clearly Seneca's. In the third century, Lactantius' remarks on the obvious purpose of the generative faculties echo Ocellus Lucanus. In the fourth century, Jerome's most austere remarks are taken from Seneca. It is not a matter of men expressing simply truths which common sense might suggest to anyone with open eyes. It is a matter of a doctrine consciously appropriated [from Stoic sources]. The descent is literary, the dependence substantial.[5]

The case sounds so clear as it is argued here by Noonan and House. However, is it really as clear as these statements suggest? Is it the Stoic philosophy of sexual desire adopted by the Early Church, or is it simply the language of their moral culture evaluated by and transformed by Biblical teaching?

THE BELIEFS OF THE STOICS

There is disagreement between Stoic scholars as to the way the Stoics perceived *lex naturalis*;[6] but most would agree that it stems from the perception of the function of nature as it was witnessed contemporaneously by the observer. In other words, a philosopher would observe a pattern within nature that he saw as either positive or negative, and from that, would proceed to pronounce that which he perceived to be positive as virtuous for all human behavior and that which he saw as negative would then be designated as base and contrary to virtue.[7]

4. Noon, *Contraception*, 46.

5. Ibid., 48.

6. See, for instance, Phillip Mitsis, "The Stoics and Aquinas on Virtue and Natural Law," 35–53.

7. For instance, the starting point of debate between the Epicurean use of *lex natu-*

This philosophy held certain philosophical premises about the universe, which saw the physical world as animalistic and the spiritual world as divine (in a panentheistic sense). In this way, the Stoics were much like the sort of Taoism one may observe in the ever popular Star Wars movies, where the force of nature has a positive and negative aspect (i.e., the yin and yang), which is then extrapolated into an ethical code of virtuous and evil behavior. This moving from fact to moral in seeking to live in accord with the ultimately positive aspect of nature derives what is good from the inference of natural events.[8]

The ultimate goal of living virtuous is happiness.[9] The Stoics argue that emotion/pleasure gets in the way of happiness, and in fact, makes a person unhappy. As a vehicle of unhappiness, emotions should be discarded as belonging to the category of that which is irrational.[10] Only reason, which is derived from the observation of what is orderly in the universe, is capable of countering these negative emotions that cause unhappiness.

The perfect example of a Stoic in modern fiction is Spock from Star Trek. The Vulcan must remove all emotion from himself in order to achieve ultimate peace and happiness through pure reason. However, he finds himself in a continual struggle with his human side, which is always interfering with this quest due to its limitations caused by emotion. His ultimate solution is to suppress the emotion of his human side by banishing it from his daily life and replacing it with pure logic.

ANSWERING THE CLAIM

Noonan's examples include four individuals: Clement of Alexandria, Origen, Lactantius, and Jerome. I have not cited Origen in this work largely because many of his unorthodox views were rejected by the Early Church, and in fact, he is condemned as heterodox by the Fifth Ecumenical Council

---

ralis, in observing that animals and babies first seek pleasure before being corrupted by other influences, and the Stoic model of *lex naturalis*, which argued that animals and babies first seek self-preservation, even at the cost of pleasure, displays a reliance upon the observation of nature as it can now be observed as the guide for what should be observed (Diogenes Laërtius 7.85; See also Malcolm Schofield, "Stoic Ethics," 247).

8. Long, *Stoic Studies*, 137–38.

9. Cicero *On Goals* 3.27–28, as it is quoted in Inwood, *The Stoics Reader*, 154; Tad Brennan, *The Stoic Life*, 35–36.

10. Ibid. 95.

(AD 553). I have, therefore, replaced his writings here with two greater representatives of early Christianity: John Chrysostom and Augustine.[11]

In contrast to the Stoic claim, the Patristic idea is clearly put forth by Lactantius:

> No one doubts but that in the former case to rejoice a little, and in the latter to rejoice too little, is a very great crime. We may say the same respecting the other affections. But, as I have said, the object of wisdom does not consist in the regulation of these, but of their causes, since they are acted upon from without; nor was it befitting that these themselves should be restrained; since they may exist in a small degree with the greatest criminality, and in the greatest degree without any criminality. But they ought to have been assigned to fixed times, and circumstances, and places, that they may not be vices, when it is permitted us to make a right use of them. For as to walk in the right course is good, but to wander from it is evil, so to be moved by the affections to that which is right is good, but to that which is corrupt is evil. For sensual desire, if it does not wander from its lawful object, although it be ardent, yet is without fault. But if it desires an unlawful object, although it be moderate, yet it is a great vice. *Therefore it is not a disease to be angry, nor to desire, nor to be excited by lust; but to be passionate,*[12] *to be covetous or licentious, is a disease.* For he who is passionate is angry even with him with whom he ought not to be angry or at times when he ought not. He who is covetous desires even that which is unnecessary. He who is licentious pursues even that which is forbidden by the laws. The whole matter ought to have turned on this, that since the impetuosity of these things cannot be restrained, nor is it right that it should be, because it is necessarily implanted for maintaining the duties of life, it might rather be directed into the right way, where it may be possible even to run without stumbling and danger.[13]

11. This is not to say that Origen's views are what Noonan would make them out to be, but only that there are better representatives of the Christian position. Beside this fact, Origen's views are close to that of his teacher, Clement of Alexandria; and in analyzing Clement, we can understand Origen's views further as well.

12. It is important to remember that the term "passion" in the Patristic writers refers to the uncontrolled, irrational desire which entices a person to foolishly sin against God. This is in contrast here to having desire and being excited by lust, which is controlled by the wisdom of God and expresses itself within the appropriate boundaries God has laid out for it in Scripture.

13. *Inst.* 6.16; *ANF* 7:181, italics added.

He further states:

> There are three passions, or, so to speak, three furies, which excite
> such great perturbations in the souls of men, and sometimes com-
> pel them to offend in such a manner, as to permit them to have
> regard neither for their reputation nor for their personal safety:
> these are anger, which desires vengeance; love of gain, which longs
> for riches; lust, which seeks for pleasures. We must above all things
> resist these vices: these trunks must be rooted up, that virtues may
> be implanted. The Stoics are of opinion that these passions must be
> cut off; the Peripatetics think that they must be restrained. Neither
> of them judge rightly, because they cannot entirely be taken away,
> since they are implanted by nature, and have a sure and great
> influence; nor can they be diminished, since, if they are evil, we
> ought to be without them, even though restrained and used with
> moderation; if they are good, we ought to use them in their com-
> pleteness. But we say that they ought not to be taken away nor less-
> ened. For they are not evil of themselves, since God has reasonably
> implanted them in us; but inasmuch as they are plainly good by
> nature,—for they are given to us for the preservation of life,—they
> become evil by their evil use. And as bravery, if you fight in defense
> of your country, is a good, if against your country, is an evil, so the
> passions, if you employ them to good purposes, will be virtues,
> if to evil uses, they will be called vices. Anger therefore has been
> given by God for the restraining of offences, that is, for controlling
> the discipline of subjects, that fear may suppress licentiousness and
> restrain audacity. But they who are ignorant of its limits are angry
> with their equals, or even with their superiors. Hence they rush
> to deeds of cruelty, hence they rise to slaughters, hence to wars.
> The love of gain also has been given that we may desire and seek
> for the necessaries of life. But they who are unacquainted with its
> boundaries strive insatiably to heap up riches. Hence poisoning,
> hence defraudings, hence false wills, hence all kinds of frauds have
> burst forth. *Moreover, the passion of lust is implanted and innate in
> us for the procreation of children; but they who do not fix its limits
> in the mind use it for pleasure only.* Thence arise unlawful loves,
> thence adulteries and debaucheries, thence all kinds of corruption.
> *These passions, therefore, must be kept within their boundaries and
> directed into their right course, in which, even though they should be
> vehement, they cannot incur blame.*[14]

---

14. *Epit.* 61; ANF 7:247–48, italics added.

He speaks of the boundaries of marriage in which sexual pleasure should remain. When condemning sinful pleasure (i.e., pleasure outside those boundaries) it sounds like he is condemning all pleasure; but this idea is negated by the context. In reality, Lactantius is referring to what he calls "strange pleasure," which tells the reader that when he is condemning pleasure or passion, he is condemning those desires that are fulfilled outside of the boundaries God has placed for them.[15] In other words, humans must guide their emotions, and in fact, already do so, with their minds. Those who are wise guide their emotions in a way that is pleasing to God, but the foolish abandon self control/the control of their thoughts and let their emotions govern them.

Note his argument that sexual desire/passion is given to us in order to fulfill the mandate of procreation. The two go together. He does not caste the two with the *either/or* fallacy, as does the modern evangelical. Sex is not either for the purpose of procreation or for pleasure as a secondary benefit. Instead, he rebukes the person who participates in the sexual act "for pleasure *only*," rather than for a pleasure which works toward God's goals of procreation as well. The Stoics, however, see this sort of pleasure as animalistic, and seek only to perform their duty to nature. For the Stoic, the base sexual desire is to be expunged or limited. In contrast, however, Lactantius states that a person might have great sin with only a little desire, but no sin with great desire. Hence, he rejects the idea that sexual desire itself should be expunged or limited in degree, and rather advocates for a control of all desires, sexual or otherwise, within the moral boundaries in which God had placed their right use.

In fact, he even attributes emotion to God; but not only emotions, but emotions that we even see as less than desirable, such as anger. Lactantius further argues that if God does not have emotions and happiness/pleasure, then He has lost all of His divinity.[16] He mocks the Stoics for attempting to attribute kindness to God, but the emotion of anger as an evil in which God cannot partake.[17]

Of course, God is perfect and perfectly governs these emotions with wisdom and virtue. But this is precisely the point. For the Fathers, God is the model through Jesus Christ. Hence, there is nothing wrong, and in-

15. Ibid., 66.

16. *Ir.* 4, which is a chapter entitled, "Of God and His Emotions."

17. Ibid., 5.

deed, it is even virtuous, in having emotions. The problem is when fallen men twist and apply them to evil vices.

Therefore, when the Fathers make statements like, "not to be angry, not to desire riches, not to be inflamed with lust, not to fear pain, to despise death" are "plainly virtues,"[18] they need to be read within the larger context, which tells the reader that the Patristic author is referring to the sinful use of these emotions and desires, not the emotions and desires themselves.

But is this not what the Scripture itself teaches? Why is this suddenly attributed to Stoicism then? What is with this *pan-Stoicism* that would have us believe that the Fathers did not believe emotion and pleasure were redeemable human attributes? Such myths ought to be purged from our thinking. There is no difference between the general Patristic view of passions and virtues and those one finds in the New Testament from whence the Fathers primarily draw their ideas. When Stoicism, or any other philosophical school, happens to make points toward the Scriptural view, the Fathers will praise it. When it makes points against the Scriptural view, the Fathers will condemn it. Therefore, the Patristic view is gained from Scripture as its source of authority, and this is easily seen due to the fact that the Bible is the final judge that decides whether what is said in the world is good or evil, right or wrong.[19]

So God, man, and animals have emotions and desires; but only God and man have wisdom to govern those desires. God does this in perfection and man strives to be perfected in them through the wisdom that comes from God and culminates in the gospel of Jesus Christ.[20]

Clement of Alexandria argues that we ought to be free from "passions," which out of context, give rise to the common misconception that the Fathers do not believe sexual pleasure is permissible. However, in context, Clement qualifies his statements by referring to these as "unnatural passions," of which Christ does not rid us, but heals within us.[21] He declares that Christ is free from human passions and so we ought to seek to be delivered from these passions as well. He then goes on to couple passions with disorders, showing that he is referring to animalistic lusts and

18. *Inst.* 50.

19. Christian authors, from the Fathers to the Reformers and beyond, have continually critiqued and rejected numerous claims made by Stoic philosophers.

20. *ANF* 7:262–63.

21. *Paed.*, 1.2.

desires, which are not controlled by the wisdom of God, but misdirected and outside the boundaries God has placed for them.[22]

Augustine, likewise, asserted that the passions are neither good nor evil in and of themselves. Instead, the good or evil of a desire exists in how we use them. He, therefore, declares that "they are evil if our love is evil; good if our love is good."[23]

In his commentary on Galatians, he makes it clear that the desires/ passions, to which the Apostle Paul refers, are those that arise from our sinful nature, or the *poenalis consuetudo* "penal habit," which refers to the body's addiction to pleasure.[24] It is clear that Augustine does not view desire as evil, but instead qualifies the term, as do all of the Fathers, by collocating negative words together in order to denote negative desires which tempt a person to sin (e.g. "habitual lusts of the flesh,"[25] "agreeing with carnal passion,"[26] etc.). He neither sees all sexual desire as bad, nor does he see that we will rid ourselves of these *negative* aspects of emotion, contrary to the Stoics, until we are glorified. Instead, the godly have these emotions, but are persuaded by a more powerful desire of love to do what is pleasing to God, and it is through this path that a person assails the temptation to pursue the fulfillment of desires outside the boundaries God has set for them.[27]

Chrysostom, in his commentary on Galatians, is careful to point out that when Paul talks about the "passions of the flesh" that, contrary to the Stoic argument, he is not here referring to the evil of the physical body or physical nature of man, which is determined either for natural or unnatural emotions, depending upon the fate of the individual involved, but to "earthly thoughts which trail upon the ground"[28] and interprets the negative use of the Pauline σάρξ as "evil actions."[29] We see, therefore, that the claim that the Fathers' views were essentially Stoic is contrary to what the

22. Ibid.

23. *Civ.,* 14.7.

24. Eric Plumer, *Augustine's Commentary on Galatians,* 211, fn. 227.

25. In reference to the heavenly state of humans, Augustine declares that only in that state will there be *carnis concupiscentias non habebit* "no practicing carnal desires" (Ibid., 212).

26. *cupiditatibus carnalibus consentientes* (Ibid.).

27. Ibid., 212–13.

28. *Hom. Gal.* 5.19–21 as translated in *NPNF*[1] 13:42.

29. Ibid., 5.24.

evidence itself shows. Sexual desire is not bad in and of itself, nor should it be banished from a person's life, but instead it ought to be mastered by the love of God and expressed within the appropriate boundaries set for it at the creation of the world.

Finally, Jerome's statements concerning the sexual act are in the context of arguing for the abstention of anything that causes a person to stumble. His concern is for the weaker brother of Romans 14 and 15. His words should, therefore, not only be taken in this context, but also observed within the context of the larger Patristic view discussed above. Note that he also is not speaking of all sexual desire when he condemns lust, but instead is talking about "carnal passions," as are the rest of the Fathers.[30] As to Jerome's "stoically" similar language, he is clear to say that his arguments are from two sources: Scripture and philosophy.[31] He does this to show that even through philosophical logic a person can understand why the Scripture presents abstention from sex as more appropriate in certain situations;[32] but never argues that sexual desire itself is an evil to be shunned in all situations. In fact, his *Epistle to Eustochium* is a work attempting to show the virtues of virginity against those who treat it as a common commitment no greater than indulgence in pleasure, not a treatise concerning all aspects of sexual desire. He himself relates in a later letter how he is taken out of context as being too austere on the subject of sex and marriage when he is only addressing a specific argument set against the noble commitment of virginity.[33] He clearly states that sex is to be enjoyed by those who are married and protested any claim that he thought of it as a bad thing.[34]

---

30. He is clear to state that the pleasure to which he refers is "vicious" or "filthy pleasure" (*ad. Jov.* 2.11), not pleasure itself.

31. He presents his argument in *Jov.* 2.6–7 as Scripturally in agreement with certain philosophies, but in rejection of others: "I will meet philosophic argument with argument" and "I have quoted these few passages of Scripture to show that we are at one with the philosophers."

32. See 1 Cor 7; Exod 19:15.

33. *NPNF*[2] 6:71–78.

34. "With my last breath, then, I protest that neither now nor at any former time have I condemned marriage" (Ibid. 78). He then continues to explain that he himself is married and not a virgin, and as such, believes marriage (and for the Fathers that means the joy of the sexual act) is a good thing, as long as it is within the procreative boundaries which God has laid out for it (Ibid., 27).

Therefore, these Fathers are for the most part unified on the subject, and Noonan's claim must be seen as simply confusion between *language* and *concept*. The Fathers surely use the same language that is found in Greek philosophical traditions, but the philosophical concepts themselves are accepted or rejected based upon whether they are in agreement with Scripture.

Even Augustine, the teacher who utilizes Stoic philosophy more than many of the other Fathers, adopts only what can be confirmed by Scripture. Marcia Colish states:

> The natural law of reason to which he refers is both the human intellect as applied to the interpretation of the Bible and the general program of moral education to which the understanding of Holy Scripture leads. Here, then, natural law is a faculty that enables man to move from this world to the next in a specifically Christian manner. Exegesis also provides another setting in which Augustine considers natural law, in this case one that inclines him to shift his attention away from its rationality to its attributes of eternity and ubiquity.[35]

She continues to state that the law of nature, for Augustine, is reinterpreted to mean "the will of God," and Christians know that will through divine revelation.[36] In other words, natural law is not known simply through observation, nor can it be completely followed by the unregenerate person, but instead must be confirmed by divine revelation. Augustine, therefore, sees certain Stoic ideas as compatible with Christian ideas, but not identical to them.

It is without doubt that the Fathers are influenced by the language and categories of Stoicism; and as the main philosophy of the culture, it would be difficult to completely divorce their ideas from that linguistic influence. This, however, is no different than any other truth claim made in any other time period. One cannot divorce the language and categories found within truth claims made by modern evangelicalism from the influence of Modernity/Postmodernity, or the language and categories of the Hebrew Bible from the conceptual universe of the ancient Near Eastern. The question is not whether culture has some bearing on the Bible and Church's ideas and language, but whether it is the final judge of those

35. Marcia L. Colish, *The Stoic Tradition*, 161.
36. Ibid., 163.

ideas. For example, it may be that the New Testament adopts the cardinal virtues of Stoicism (σοφία "wisdom," δικαιωσύνη "righteousness" and σωφροσύνη "self-control"[37]) within a Christian framework, but it is precisely the Christian framework that judges the validity and extent to which these ideas are true, utilizing the special, divine revelation, which is absent from the rest of the world. Paul has the Hebrew Scriptures and prophetic revelation from the Lord Jesus to judge between the rightful and wrongful adoption of these ideas. I see little difference in the methodology of the Fathers, who are continually judging the validity of the philosophical ideas within their culture using the Scripture (both Old and New Testaments).[38]

We are continually doing the same within our culture. We do not reject the culture-wide push against racism because we also see, as Christians, that racism is evil; but we also do not counter racism for the same reasons that culture does. Our culture tends to counter racism on the basis that a particular group has had their "turn" at exercising abusive power and favoritism. The culture then tends to turn racism back upon the empowered race that was considered racist. This is simply reverse racism. We, as Christians, instead, armed with the Scripture, counter racism with the gospel understanding that now we "no longer consider any person according to the flesh" (2 Cor 5:16; also see Acts 17:25–31). We may still, however, employ terms and categories that mimic those utilized by the culture in its opposition to racism. So we do not reject a cultural concept simply because it is either based in a faulty theology or applied in the wrong manner. Instead, we evaluate it according to Scripture. If it is good, we adopt it. If it is evil, we reject it. If it needs to be tweaked, we tweak it, so that it accords with what we have been told in the Scriptures. It is the task of every generation of Christians to do the same, and to reject what the Fathers had to say based on some erroneous view that morals and certain theological concepts are distinctly Christian is to be ignorant of what makes Christianity truly unique, which is the identification of

37. Although the New Testament does not explicitly use the fourth word ἀνδρεία for the Stoic virtue of bravery, it certainly holds up bravery as a virtue in preaching the Gospel and standing against the world's persecution (see Rev 21:8). The concept is also found in the OG: Ps 67:7; and are themes in some of the Apocryphal books: 1 Mac 9:10; 4 Mac 1:4, 6, 11, 18; 5:23; 17:23, etc.; also see Wis 8:7, where all four virtues are mentioned.

38. Note that the Reformers are extremely critical of "Neo-Stoicism" and its adoption of the emotionless *apatheia* in exchange for the Christian virtue of patience through suffering (cf. Calvin in *Inst.*, 3.8.9).

God through the revelation of Jesus Christ, found throughout the theology of Scripture. We, therefore, do not reject the Book of the Covenant at Sinai because it reasons in the same manner as the Code of Hammurapi, but instead see it either as God's divine approval or rejection of the theology and ethics found therein. Therefore, "none of these Christian authors wholly endorsed the Stoic philosophical system. Indeed, they often conflicted with regard to which parts of Stoic philosophy they thought could be reconciled with orthodox Christian teaching."[39]

Having said that, it is my hope to make it clear in this article that, although what is taught sounds similar, neither the New Testament nor the Fathers adopt Stoic views on our present subject. They simply do not believe what the Stoics believe about sexual desire, and hence their arguments do not follow that train of thought.[40] Their views, in following the trajectory of the Apostle Paul in Romans 1, follow the course laid out by Genesis 1:26–28 and Leviticus 18.[41] Whatever language or arguments they may adopt beyond that, no matter how Stoic they may sound, are not, at their foundation, Stoic.[42]

---

39. "Neostoicism," in *The Internet Encyclopedia of Philosophy*.

40. Theophilis (c. 180) maintains that the Stoics teach that incest and sodomy are morally acceptable practices (2.112); but the Fathers argue that "the sin of Sodom is contrary to nature" (*Apost Const* 7.463). Where one may read the appeal to *physis* as Stoic, it is in fact an argument from Paul's interpretation of Gen 1:26–28 and Lev 18 found in Rom 1. The statement, therefore, is not that the sin of Sodom does not accord with the flow of the ordered universe, but that it is contrary to God's purposes for the sexual act related in the creation of the male and female. We see, then, that the Fathers gain their view of the sexual act from Scripture and disagree with the Stoics when the Stoics themselves contradict that Scripture.

41. Of course, the Patristic trajectory of argumentation now includes the argument in the Epistle to the Romans. Hence, the Fathers use the same type of language the Apostle does in referring to *pathēma* ("passions"), *physikos* ("that which is in accord with nature"), *para physin* ("that which is contrary to nature").

42. cf. Paul's statement in Galatians 5:24 with the Patristic view, when he says, οἱ δὲ τοῦ Χριστοῦ Ἰησοῦ τὴν σάρκα ἐσταύρωσαν σὺν τοῖς παθήμασιν καὶ ταῖς ἐπιθυμίαις "But those who are of Christ Jesus have crucified the flesh together with its passions and desires/lusts." Like the Patristic statements concerning passion and desire, although this language sounds very Stoic, it is instead a statement concerning the carnal desires to sin against God, not an adoption of the Stoic philosophy to purge oneself of pleasure and emotion.

A PURPOSEFUL POISONING OF THE WELL

If the Patristic view of sex is not void of pleasure, but instead simply maintains that sexual pleasure must remain within its God-honoring boundaries, a sentiment shared by all Christians of all ages, including our own, why is that they have been painted with a very different brush?

One answer is simply that they have been misunderstood by well meaning individuals, who mistakenly saw a Stoic under every rock and in every mention of "nature." These scholars simply were not careful in distinguishing between the nature that stemmed from *ordo creatus naturalis*[43] and one which stemmed from the Stoic view of *lex naturalis*. The former is based in the divine revelation found in Genesis 1 and 2, and interpreted through Leviticus 18, the latter upon philosophical speculation.[44] It is hoped that the distinction made in the discussion above will help correct such a misinterpretation.[45]

43. Although the concept of *ordo creatus naturalis* often refers to the ordering of creatures, I am using the term to refer to the order of intended purposes for that which is created, specifically speaking here of the primary, divinely instituted purpose intended for the sexual act as it is set down in the creation narrative. Hence, as *per* Paul in Romans, the argument from nature's created order "also expresses . . . the order intended by the Creator, the order that is manifest in God's creation or . . . the order seen in the sexual organs themselves which were ordained for an expression of love between man and woman and for the procreation of children" (Fitzmyer, *Romans*, 286).

44. Malcom Schofield ("Stoic Ethics," 244) puts forth the Stoic idea of *lex naturalis* as follows: "'Nature' here seems then to be 'human nature', as Zeno's book title implies. But it is not *just* human nature. Diogenes Laertius goes on to report as follows (VII 87): 'Further, living in accordance with virtue is equivalent to living in accordance with experience of the natural course of events, as Chryssippus says in *On goals* Book I.'"

45. A good example of this distinction is found in Paul's argument concerning head coverings in 1 Corinthians 11. In vv. 7–12, Paul lays out an argument which I would classify as an argument from *ordo creatus naturalis*. However, in vv. 13–15, he makes an argument from *lex naturalis*. The argument from *ordo creatus naturalis*, or "priority argument," is a foundational type of argumentation for 2d Temple Judaism and New Testament Christianity precisely because the new philosophies introduced by the occupying foreign cultures caused the community of God to ask questions concerning the value of precedence. Is it Greek culture or Israelite culture that should be exalted as morally superior, and therefore, the standard of conduct for the religious community? The answer is found in creation. What God intended at the beginning expresses His ultimate desire for His intended future community. The arguments put forward, therefore, reflected the desire to override any cultural influences and innovations which ran counter to God's desires expressed at the creation event. The *lex naturalis* is, therefore, used only as a supplementary argument to the superior *ordo creatus naturalis*, which although can be seen as a subclass of the former, is considered both logically prior to, and independent from, it.

Originally, however, there may have been a purposeful conflation of the two lines of reasoning, since it is thought that if a person can identify the origins of the Patristic argument as that which stems from philosophy, rather than Scripture, then such arguments concerning the sexual act (whether they be prohibitions against contraception or homosexuality, etc.) could simply be ignored. After all, the Christian source of authority is the Scripture, not Greek philosophy.

As stated before, this genetic fallacy does not hold up even if all of these claims were true.

ISN'T IT IRONIC?

I find it to be of the utmost irony that those who make this argument, then turn to the "pro-creationist's" claim, that the "pro-contraceptionist's" view has stemmed from philosophic naturalism, and attempt to brand this argument as the genetic fallacy as well.

However, there is a major difference between what is being said about the acceptance of contraception among evangelicals and the use of Stoic language and concepts in the Early Church. The genetic fallacy is only a fallacy when unaccompanied with the evidence that such and such a view could only come from the one source. In other words, if a belief in A can come from presuppositions B, C or D, then arguing that A is wrong because B is wrong is fallacious, since A could have come from C or D as well.

However, if it can be shown that presupposition B is needed in order to conclude A, and presupposition B is known to be false, then conclusion A is also false, since it needs presupposition B in order to substantiate its truthfulness.

In the case of contraception, the presupposition of philosophic naturalism (even in its ancient forms, where the biological function of reproduction is a tool to be used by the person at his own discretion) is necessary in order to conclude that the use of contraception is acceptable for the Christian.

However, if a person presupposes the Christian, supernatural view of the conception event, as it is presented in Scripture, then the acceptable use of contraception becomes impossible, as then an individual would be working against the creation and work of God. The claim, therefore, that associating the use of contraception with philosophic naturalism is a use of the genetic fallacy is itself fallacious, as it misunderstands the nature of the genetic fallacy.

The great irony, therefore, is that the ideas presented by Christianity are consistent with its Biblical presuppositions, and although may be consistent with certain positions held by the Greeks, and are able to be presented within the language of those philosophers, does not need to stem from those philosophical worldviews, and indeed, has not done so. The argument, therefore, that seeks to undermine the historical argument against contraception by identifying an association between Christian ideas and Greek sources is the truest form of the genetic fallacy, and as such should be rejected as a viable form of argumentation.

CONCLUSION

The Christian argument against contraception stems first and foremost from its Biblical worldview, not the philosophical culture in which it resides. The attempt to undermine its validity by associating it with the Greek philosophical tradition is nothing more than to commit the genetic fallacy. Ironically, the arguments used to support the use of contraception by evangelicals can only be gained from the non-Christian presupposition of philosophic naturalism, and therefore, is not a use of the genetic fallacy as some have claimed.

Regardless, however, the arguments made by the Patristic authors follow the trajectory of the New Testament authors, and should be classified as primarily arguments from *ordo creatus naturalis* (with the understanding that their arguments from the broader *lex naturalis* are simply supplemental to the *ordo creatus naturalis*, and must harmonize with those Scriptures which are the foundation of that argument).

Due to these three elements (i.e., argument from the genetic fallacy, the confusion between Stoic language and Stoic philosophy, and the further category confusion between arguments from *lex naturalis* and arguments from *ordo creatus naturalis*), the claim of contraception proponents (i.e., that Stoic influence invalidates the historic Christian view of the sexual act) is to be rejected.

Appendix E

An Analysis of James B. Jordan's "The Bible and Family Planning: An Answer to Charles Provan's 'The Bible and Birth Control'"

IN 1989, CHARLES PROVAN published a small booklet entitled, "The Bible and Birth Control," which argued that Christians were not morally justified in using contraceptive practices. Shortly thereafter, James B. Jordan wrote what has been considered the best refutation of Provan's work provided by the opposition. His work is entitled, "The Bible and Family Planning: An Answer to Charles Provan's 'The Bible and Birth Control.'"[1] After reading both works, however, it was evident to me that Jordan had not only misconstrued many of Provan's arguments, but had also presented numerous textbook examples of fallacious reasoning in his quest to refute Provan.

The following is a brief analysis of Jordan's alleged refutation. I have not dealt with everything Jordan has said here for three reasons: (1) Much of what Jordan brings up, I have already refuted elsewhere in this book; (2) I am either in agreement with his assessment of some of Provan's arguments; and (3) some of his critiques are to be considered less than substantial to the core of the debate.

---

1. Rather than reproduce Jordan's entire article, this appendix is meant to be read alongside his article, which can be found online at http://web.archive.org/web/20040803183656/http:/www.visi.com/~contra_m/cm/features/cm09_birthcon.html#fn28 as well as in pdf form at http://web.archive.org/web/20040806061015/www.contra-mundum.org/cm/cm09.pdf.

TRUE LEGALISM

Jordan begins where he will eventually end: with an ad hominem fallacy. The attempt to paint Provan, and other procreation advocates, as legalists only rings true if the position is not a biblical mandate. Hence, Jordan begins his case by arguing the following:

> I need to make this point: *Nowhere does the Bible forbid family planning and birth control.* It is not mentioned in the Law, which certainly mentions plenty of other sexual matters. There are loads of 'thou shalt nots' in the Bible, but nowhere do we find anything like 'thou shalt not prevent conception.' The silence of the Bible on this subject is a pregnant silence, since birth control was practised[sic] in the ancient world.[2]

Let's see how this argument holds up with another unmentioned immoral sexual act:

> I need to make this point: *Nowhere does the Bible forbid pedophilia.* It is not mentioned in the Law, which certainly mentions plenty of other sexual matters. There are loads of "thou shalt nots" in the Bible, but nowhere do we find anything like "thou shalt not practice pedophilia." The silence of the Bible on this subject is a pregnant silence, since pedophilia was practiced in the ancient world.

Does Jordan really want to make this argument? The Bible does not explicitly mention abortion, masturbation, pornography, sadomasochism, pedophilia, sex with inanimate objects, necrophilia, etc. Yet, all of these exist in the ancient world and would have been well known by the ancient Israelites. This is the problem literalists and legalists have when reading the Scripture. The true legalist wants to excuse his immoral practices by limiting the Scripture to the explicit letter. In this very technical reading, many of the things the text was meant to condemn can now be excused as a matter of conscience. True Pharisaic legalism seeks to do away with the larger, expanded intent of the law in order to replace it with culturally-common, human-made practices (Matt 15:2–9). The Lord informs us, however, that our hermeneutics need to see the mindset of the laws which God gave to us in a way that expands the loving reign of God into every aspect of our lives. The explicit laws, therefore, are examples of larger principles, not exhaustive lists of practices with which God takes issue. This understanding is vital to understanding not only the present

2. Jordan, "The Bible and Family Planning," 3.

subject at hand, but the Christian interpretation of the Bible as a whole. Hence, the question is not, "What does the Bible explicitly say?" but instead, "What is the underlying principle of the legal examples the Bible gives to us?"

Jordan wants to argue that the Bible's silence concerning the subject of contraception lays the burden of proof completely upon Provan; but this is not quite the case. The Scripture lays out numerous texts about the productivity of the sexual act, both in commanding and affirming the productive sexual act and condemning the unproductive. To say that an unproductive sexual act should be considered as morally acceptable to God as a productive one, therefore, is to make an argument contrary to the flow of Scripture. The burden of proof, therefore, is actually placed completely on Jordan, who, despite his best efforts, presents no logically valid, positive case for his position.

GENESIS 1:28: COLLECTIVE OR DISTRIBUTIVE?

Jordan then proceeds to argue against Provan's use of the procreative command in Genesis 1:28 by arguing that the command must be taken collectively rather than distributively.[3]

Argument 1

He states:

> If we understand it distributively, it means that every single human being is obligated to try as hard as possible to be fruitful and multiply. This would mean that it is sinful not to marry, and that we must marry as early as possible, so as to have as many children as possible. It would mean that any kind of "natural" contraceptive method, such as the "rhythm method", is sinful. Failing to get remarried after being widowed would be a sin. Perhaps a man could divorce a sterile wife, or divorce her after she reaches menopause, so that he could continue to "obey God and multiply".[4]

Jordan argues that the command is given to individuals rather than to couples. Hence, the command is not meant to be applied to everyone, since Jesus and Paul, etc. do not obey it. (See the refutation of this argument on pp. 137–38.)

3. Ibid.
4. Ibid.

Argument 2

Based upon Jordan's assumption that the command is to individuals apart from the male-female relationship, Jordan argues that the command would imply that we are to try as hard as possible to have children.

But where is this assumption? Is it in the text or in Jordan's importation of philosophical naturalism? Nowhere in the text does it say, "try as hard as you can to be fruitful and multiply." That absurdity is imported into the text by Jordan. Instead, the text is simply conveying that the human couple are to participate in the sexual act and go with God's creative purposes in filling up the earth instead of against it. This is conveyed by the contextual ideas of reversal from the chaotic state in chapter 1 and the literary context of the entire book as a whole. Jordan cannot make the same claim legitimately, since his context is modern philosophic naturalism instead of a Biblical understanding that God is the one who creates life through Eve and her children. Hence, the human couple has no ability to have "as many children as possible."[5] They only have the ability to participate in the sexual act and to do so unhindered by any purposeful human opposition. In the end, God has decided how many children a couple will have, and a couple is to be open to that in obedience to this command.

Argument 3

He then argues that widows should get remarried or they are in sin; and people should marry young and try and have as many children as possible, or they are in sin.[6] Of course, both of these assume that the command is for individuals rather than for couples. This, however, is not a viable interpretation of Genesis 1:28.

Jordan himself admits that if the couple in Genesis 1:28 are being commanded as the married couple in 2:24 then his argument fails. He states:

> Provan might respond that in Genesis 1:27–28, the man and the woman are being addressed as a married couple, so that my points fail to touch him. But this is not the case. Marriage does not come into view until Genesis 2:18–25. We should notice about this latter passage that the woman is given to the man as his helper, but

5. Ibid.
6. Ibid.

nothing is said about multiplying. The man and woman are said to become one flesh, but again nothing is said about multiplying.[7]

One can only assume that Jordan is taking Genesis 1 and 2 as separate chronological events. This is neither a plausible reading of the texts nor is it the view of the Lord in His interpretation of the event as it is displayed throughout the Bible.

Genesis 1 and 2 display complementary theological viewpoints of the same event. They are not two separate events. Chapter 2 plays off of chapter 1 and vice versa. Hence, the command states that God said to *them*, "be fruitful and multiply, etc." The couple is addressed as a couple, and this is the same couple that we see in chapter 2. The reason given, therefore, for marriage is that the male and the female who were created must become one flesh. Why must they become one flesh? Because they are to be fruitful and multiply. Why are they to be fruitful and multiply? Because it is not good for the man to be a single unit, but instead to be united to the larger group of humanity that will be his children. Hence, the woman has been made to be his helper, so that he is no longer the only human, and God can reverse the state of Genesis 1:2, where the earth is uninhabited. The original texts refute Jordan's claim that the command is to individuals (as though it were possible for an individual to have children apart from coupling with another individual of the opposite sex anyway).

The Lord Jesus helps us understand that the creation of humanity is not the creation of individuals, but of couples. The command is, therefore, given to the couple, not to individuals apart from this coupled relationship. When speaking of divorce, the Lord states that God made them male and female for the purpose of the one flesh union. In other words, the couple in 1:28 is linked to the married couple in 2:24 (Matt 19:4–6).

However, according to Jordan's logic, this would be the equivalent of Jesus saying that God made them male and female (v. 4); therefore, unmarried, single individuals should not get a divorce. Of course, Jordan's interpretation has created an impossible situation, as single individuals cannot get divorces precisely because they are not married in the first place. Jesus has appealed to the passage to show that *married couples*, not singles, ought not be divorced. He is the one who interprets the couple in 1:28 as the couple in 2:24. Jordan's disagreement, concerning the in-

7. Ibid.

tended audience in Genesis 1:28, ignores both the language of the passage as well as its divine interpretation by the Lord who originally spoke it. The command, therefore, does not directly apply to individuals, but to married couples. Therefore, Jordan's argument, that the command must be collective based on the fact that not every individual is obligated to fulfill it, is refuted by both the original texts and the Lord's interpretation thereof. His arguments, as he himself has observed, fail to refute Provan's assertion.

Argument 4

Jordan states, "A missionary might take a wife as a helper, but not to have children."[8] Of course, one might respond, "Why can't the missionary take another man as his husband to help him if there is no procreative intention?" Jordan may argue a biological and psychological differentiation argument, but this would not be a Biblical or theological argument. The theological argument made is that the helper to the man must be female because only she is able to help him become more numerous, no longer separated from his human family, which is the true meaning of the text when it says that it is not good for him to be *l'bad* "alone." Jordan has misconstrued the text of Genesis 2 to be dealing with the issue of companionship. It is true that the woman is to be the man's helper in ministry, but the ministry in Genesis 1–2 is to their children.

Secondly, this statement does not contribute to Jordan's argument in any way. It is a descriptive example of what someone may do, but does not tell us prescriptively what should be done. Instead, it begs the question as to whether this missionary is morally right for doing A for purpose C, rather than doing A for purpose B. Jordan has not answered this question, so his descriptive example is irrelevant.

Argument 5

Jordan asks the question, "If God wants us to keep having children, why does He cause women to outgrow the childbearing stage?"[9] It is interesting to note that Jordan so disparages the argument from *lex naturalis* that he here makes the same argument to support his position. Of course, Jordan's argument is the real Stoic *lex naturalis* argument, where what

8. Ibid.
9. Ibid.

occurs in nature is subjectively applied to a moral issue. There are three fallacies that I can perceive right away in this statement.

1. That the woman getting old and her body breaking down, so as to not allow childbearing to occur at some point is a direct act of God, rather than a consequence of the Fall;

2. That God wants us to keep having children, as though that was in any way the implication of a non-naturalistic reading of Gen 1:28; and

3. That what is empirically observable in nature can be a guide to conclude one way or the other about a moral issue's viability.

All three of these presuppositions are false, and therefore, make this single argument absurd. Therefore, the idea that it is impossible to take the command as distributive and must be taken as collective is based upon certain false assumptions that should be categorically rejected.

THE COMMAND IS FOR THE COVENANT COMMUNITY

Jordan argues that the command of Genesis 1:28 is for the covenant community, not for the whole world. He argues that the command is given to righteous humanity, not to the unrighteous.[10] Ultimately, Jordan is correct, and this is what I have consistently argued within this book. However, although I would agree that God desires the righteous to multiply and that His goal is to fill up the earth with covenant children, that does not mean that God's moral commands are not given to the wicked. If that were true, then how could God judge them for not obeying what He never commanded them to obey? Ultimately, Jordan is right in that the command is meant to increase the righteous upon the earth; but I fail to see how this contributes anything substantive to his argument against Provan.

WOMEN AREN'T SAVED THROUGH CHILDBEARING

Jordan also denies that 1 Timothy 2:15 makes a connection between the woman's salvation/sanctification and the act of childbearing. Jordan essentially argues that the statements concerning the method through which women are saved is speaking only about Eve, and no one else. He follows Meyers in arguing that the grammar of *sōthēsetai*, a third person singular,

10. Ibid., 3–4.

should read "she will be saved," and hence, only refers to Eve being saved by *the childbirth* (i.e., the birth of Christ). Hence, when the text is seen in this way, it says nothing toward the idea that a woman is saved through childbearing.[11] This, of course, is a completely acceptable translation of *sōthēsetai*. The problem is that the third person here is clearly a collective. The first woman, Eve, is seen as representative of all women in the context. Hence, because the first woman was placed in a subjective role to the first man, Paul argues that no woman should be placed in authority over a man. This collective use is made definitive in the context by the next verb *meinōsin*, a third person plural, "they remain."[12]

Jordan argues that the women in v. 15a are different than the woman in v. 15b, but this does not seem theologically correct. The two clauses are connected together in a apodosis-protasis relationship. In other words, X will occur if Y occurs, but if not Y, then neither X.[13] The text would then say that the woman (i.e., Eve) would only be saved if women in general remain in faith, love and holiness with self-control. So Eve's salvation is dependent upon other women? This absurdity is avoidable by simply understanding the verb *sōthēsetai* as a collective, as the context clearly indicates.

Jordan, also following Meyers, makes the observation that the noun *teknogonia* has an article in front of it. They erroneously conclude that this somehow means that the phrase must be translated as "the childbirth," referring to the birth of Christ. There are two problems with this analysis.

First, the noun *teknogonia* is an abstract noun, something indicated by the *ia* ending in Greco-Latin morphology, and does not mean "childbirth" in a concrete sense, as would be needed in the designation of a specific event (i.e., like the birth of Christ). The list of abstract nouns in the context (i.e., *pistei, agapē, hagiasmos*, and *sōphrosunē*) also bears this out.

---

11. Ibid., 7–8.

12. Schreiner, "An Interpretation of 1 Timothy 2:9–15," 146–53.

13. The attempt to divorce the two clauses, but then to insert the verb of v. 15a into v. 15b is a grammatically unacceptable twisting of the text. The verb of v. 15a is implied because the subject of the verb in both cases refer to the same group of people (i.e., she [the woman as a generic collective] and they [women as distributive] will be saved through . . .). This is in the context of every Christian woman represented by Eve in her relationship to every Christian man, represented by Adam.

Second, the presence of the definite article on an abstract noun does not mean it should be translated as "the childbirth," as though the article made the abstract a more concrete substantive. As *per* basic Greek syntax, abstract nouns appearing with or without the article carry the same meaning. The only thing the article with an abstract noun may indicate, when the author chooses to employ it, is grammatical "markedness," and therefore, it may place an emphasis on the word(s) chosen.[14]

Meyer's and Jordan's interpretation, therefore, has no foundation to it. The text is speaking of the woman's role generically, not specifically of Eve; and the means to the restored fulfillment of the woman's role is through childbearing when accompanied by faith, love, holiness, and self-control. Paul's statement, therefore, counters both the Gnosticism of his own day and of ours by not only placing spiritual characteristics, but also her physical biological purpose as participatory in her sanctification.

STRANGE INTERPRETATIONS OF SEMEN

Jordan continues his analysis by arguing against Provan's strange idea that sperm are children.[15] What is interesting about this exchange is that both Provan and Jordan at this point make numerous illogical assumptions that can only be explained by unreasonable dogmatism.

Provan argues that the Bible tells us that semen consists of living humans. I do not agree with Provan at this point, as he has misunderstood that the "seed," which is the Bible's way of referring to semen, also refers to children, not because semen is children, but because it is the substance from which children are made. It is therefore a causal metonymy (i.e., the cause is stated for the effect it produces).[16] It is like saying that "on the day of battle, raw iron shall clash in fury." The raw iron from which swords/weapons are made is used to refer to those weapons. It does not mean that if one found a clump of raw iron that he could say that he now owned a sword. Therefore, X may be used to create Y, but X does not equal Y. Provan is mistaken here.

14. For example, 1 Cor 13:4, Ἡ ἀγάπη μακροθυμεῖ, χρηστεύεται ἡ ἀγάπη, οὐ ζηλοῖ, etc., should be translated "love is patient, love is kind, it is not jealous, etc., not "*the* love is patient, *the* love is kind, it is not jealous . . ." Here we have one of *many* examples where the article functions to emphasize the prominent abstract word, but in no way is to be viewed as making that noun concrete.

15. Jordan, "The Bible and Family Planning," 6–7.

16. Bullinger, *Figures of Speech*, 540–60.

However, Jordan's attempt to counter Provan by stating that the milk in Job 10:10–11 refers to the Holy Spirit[17] is an eisegesis to be equaled only to that of the likes of Origen's wildly allegorical interpretations of Scripture. There is absolutely no hint of anything Jordan suggests in his alternate interpretation of this passage within the passage itself.

Jordan wants to argue that because the text says that God is the one who pours out the man like milk, and Provan interprets the milk as semen, then it would refer to God's semen.[18] He then argues against the absurdity of such a thing. Indeed, it is quite absurd; but that is not what is being said. God is causing the pouring out of the semen through another human being.[19] No one would think that because God causes the bodily functions to bring forth the material He uses to make a child through the sexual act, that the fluid comes from God Himself. By Jordan's logic, Job's statement that God has brought him out of the womb (10:18) would mean that it was God's womb. This argument simply presents an ignorance of the cosmology presented in the book of Job, and replaces it with an assumed naturalistic cosmology of the conception event.[20]

Jordan then goes on to argue that this really just refers to the Spirit who gave life to Adam at creation. Of course, the context screams otherwise. Job is crying out to God and wondering why God made him personally if all He intended to do was destroy him. He is not talking about God pouring him out of himself at all. The text is clearly talking about the creation of a human being inside the womb. He is asking God why He took such great effort in every aspect of his creation through the sexual act if His only intention was to bring him to nothing. Jordan's attempt to make this text say otherwise can only be attributed to his naturalistic

17. Jordan, "The Bible and Family Planning," 6.

18. Ibid.

19. Not only is this the obvious meaning of the Hiphil verb used here, but is also consistent within the larger Israelite cosmology of Job, where God is the one who causes nature to perform in the way that it does.

20. What Jordan fails to realize is that God gives the gift of conception to the couple in each instance of the sexual act, so that it is God causing the conception of a human being to take place through the sexual act. See Ruth 4:13, "And Boaz took Ruth and she became his wife. He went into her and YHWH gave conception to her and she bore a son." Jordan's "either the father is pouring out semen or God is" argument is a false dichotomy only to be attributed to Jordan's natural/supernatural, neo-Platonist distinction of the conception event.

understanding of the conception event, against which this text speaks volumes.

Jordan continues:

> Provan writes, "If it is wrong to destroy life in the womb, then it is wrong to deliberately kill semen" (Provan, p. 26). This is an incredible statement! Having sex with your wife at any time except when she might conceive is sure to kill semen, so it would be sinful. Having sex with your wife if she is sterile or past menopause is sure to kill semen, so it would be sinful. Having sex with your wife in the early months of pregnancy would be sinful.[21]

Although, I do not necessarily agree with Provan at this point, I do want to point out Jordan's equally illogical argument against him.

Half of all conceptions spontaneously abort. According to Jordan's logic, if an involuntary act equals a voluntary one then every woman who conceives and loses a child would be guilty of abortion/murder. Jordan cannot have it both ways. If his argument that voluntary and involuntary waste, or "death," of semen is valid then he must also either conclude that abortion is morally acceptable or that all women who have had a miscarriage are murderers.

Of course, this absurd conundrum is solved by denying Jordan's argument that voluntary and involuntary acts are morally equivalent. As stated before, morality is in the purposeful act, not in the unintentional.[22]

PREVENTING CHILDREN FROM EXISTING IS MORALLY ACCEPTABLE BECAUSE THEY DON'T YET EXIST

Finally, Jordan argues against an argument that both Provan and the historic Church make against the contraceptive mindset: that the use of contraception is the attempt to prevent a future person from existing. Here Jordan commits cognitive suicide in attempting to dismiss this argument.

He argues that no one can prevent a human being from existing because a human being does not yet exist.[23] Within this assumption seems to be the idea that someone or something in the future cannot be harmed by something in the present because it does not yet exist to harm. He

21. Ibid., 6.

22. See Geisler, *Christian Ethics*, 152.

23. Jordan, "The Bible and Family Planning," 6–7.

confuses Provan's argument with the Mormon argument by stating that this implies there are babies up in heaven waiting to be born. Of course, it does not imply this at all; but Jordan's strange logic that what is future cannot be harmed by what is present seems to interfere with his grasp of the argument.

For instance, if I go to the doctor with a concern that I may get skin cancer, since it runs in my family, he does not tell me, "There's nothing you can do about it because it does not yet exist. Go play in the sun twenty-four/seven and enjoy because a present action cannot prevent a future thing." Instead, since I can in fact harm my chances of getting skin cancer (and hence, possibly prevent its existence in me) by staying out of the sun (which is a good thing), he tells me to stay out of the sun and use heavy-duty sun block in an effort to *prevent* a future thing from existing. It is not through direct contact that a present action can affect a future person, therefore, but it is through prevention that a future being can be harmed.

Jordan's argument here is just absolutely amazing in that he then continues to argue from the sovereignty of God that nothing future can be thwarted through an action, since God's plans are always accomplished. As I have argued here, however, God's decretive plans are always accomplished. However, to say that because God's decretive plans are always accomplished is not the same as saying that His moral desire to create a future child through the sexual act cannot be thwarted according to His own decretive allowance. Surely, even Jordan would argue that it was God's moral will that Onan let a future child come into existence through his sexual act with Tamar even though God's decretive will was that another future child and heir would be born through the prostituted sexual act between Tamar and Judah.

Furthermore, if a person cannot prevent a future person from being born through the use of birth control, then why would anyone use it? Is not its very purpose the prevention of a future child being born? Why participate in such an impossible endeavor? Jordan is either playing word games here, or he has really banished logic from his argument at this point.

We might further ask why God thought it necessary to command the man and woman to have future children if in fact they were unable to do anything about it anyway.

We might go even further to state that ultimately, even if no future person is set to come forth from a sexual act, that contraception is still an act of murder because of the intent on the part of the practitioners to wipe out the existence of a future human being. Attempted murder and murder in the Bible is a part of the same sin. The only difference is that one misses the mark and the other does not.

Instead, Jordan seems to be functioning off of the idea that a person does not need to worry about using contraception because God's will cannot be thwarted anyway (but then why use birth control?) and because a future person does not yet exist, and therefore, cannot be harmed by a present action.

Jordan's strange argument, every bit as strange as Provan's previous "seed" argument, should be abandoned on the basis that a present action is in fact capable of harming the existence of a future person through preventative measures (which is in fact what contraceptive practices are), and this intention in the act of contraception has nothing to do with God's decretive, but rather His moral will. It runs contrary to the perpetuation of creation, contrary to the preservation of future life, and contrary to the moral will of God.

Jordan argues:

> If birth control eliminates future people (Provan, p. 24), then who are these future people who have been eliminated? What are their names? What is their ontological status? Asking these questions shows how illogical this argument is. If you use birth control, then there are no future people to be eliminated. You cannot eliminate people who don't exist.[24]

Does Jordan intend this to be a serious argument? What are their names? If we were attempting to argue to Adam why he should not practice contraception, do we really need to supply all of the names of people who would not exist because of his disobedience? Is the existence of a future person contingent upon the perfect knowledge of him or her by his or her parents?

Jordan argues that one cannot eliminate people who don't exist. But they do not exist because of an action taken by humans who presently exist. The question then is, "Is what those humans have done, in intending to prevent other humans from existing, wrong?" Jordan wants to have it

24. Ibid., 7.

both ways. He wants to argue that everyone who exists is supposed to exist and humans cannot thwart that; but then he wants to argue that the use of birth control, which is performed solely for the purpose of thwarting future human existence, is permissible because it is not really preventing future persons from existing at all. But if this is true, then why use it?! If a present action has no bearing on the future of human persons, then why pay the money to buy birth control pills or have a vasectomy? If anything, Jordan's absurd argument lays the foundation for us to argue that no one should ever use birth control because it is a waste of time and money, and therefore, a case of bad stewardship, since the same result will occur either way.

What Jordan has confirmed here, however, is that the argument, concerning what is obvious in the intent to prevent the existence of future persons, is so logical that one must resort to intellectual suicide in order to deny it. This illogical argument breaks down as follows:

1. Person A cannot prevent Person X from existing.

2. It is therefore permissible for Person A to use contraception in order to prevent Person X from existing.

The self refutation is evident in that this is the equivalent of arguing that it is permissible to drink a glass of milk because glasses of milk do not exist to drink.

Perhaps it is true that all whose existence is blocked by means A will come about through means B. In other words, it may be that all of the children who would be born to a particular couple will now be brought about by God through another couple in the world, so that no one's planned life is ever thwarted. Jordan, of course, has not even proven that this would be the case with his argument (he seems only to assume it), but let's grant it for the moment for argument's sake. This still has nothing to do with whether the original couple has sinned and committed an act of anti-life/murder. I could argue the same thing in the case of abortion, and say that all of the souls that would have been given to the unborn are transferred to others who are born. This still does not justify an act of abortion by classifying it as a "non-murder." Jordan has failed to understand the moral will of God in the argument presented. The question is not what will ultimately happen to aborted or "contracepted" individuals, but whether the acts that abort and contracept them are moral or immoral. Jordan seems to be switching from one question to the other, and as a result, is able to answer neither of them adequately.

IS PSALM 127 TALKING ABOUT A FAMILY OR A CITY?

Jordan further attempts to undermine Psalm 127's contribution to the discussion by stating the following:

> If we read Psalm 127 carefully, we have to ask if the nuclear family and its children are primarily in view at all. The first three verses are speaking about the city, not the family. The last verse speaks of enemies at the gate of the city. By way of contrast, Psalm 128 speaks of the family from start to finish. It seems to me that the children of Psalm 127 are those of the city, not of the nuclear family. We are talking about a clan, or a town, in this Psalm. The Psalmist is not saying that each and every marriage must have loads of children, but rather is celebrating the blessings of many children in a community. There may be some marriages that contribute to society in ways other than producing lots of children.

The attempt to dismiss the Psalm, by arguing that it speaks only to the city instead of the family unit, fails in a few areas. The first of which is that even if the Psalm were primarily, or even completely, speaking of a city, its applicatory comments pertaining to the stability of a communal unit (such as a family) would still remain intact. Here Jordan is following a good amount of modern commentaries on the passage.

However, there has been a fundamental mistake made by those commentators who take the Psalm's comments to be directed toward the urban center, and that is the confusion between the theme and the thematic metaphor. The theme is clearly a man's household, but the thematic metaphor utilized to exemplify it is the city.

The city is an example of habitation, not the intended subject matter. The security of habitation is the intended subject matter, and the house, is clearly the primary habitation in view.[25] In fact, a secure habitation is the first element of an ordered creation/society. The city, therefore, simply macrocosmically represents the household which is its microcosm. This

---

25. The city as an expansion of the household is not ruled out of the equation, but neither can one use it as a way to undermine the intention of the Psalmist to convey that even the smallest unit of society is secured, not by human achievements, but by the hand of the Lord.

is made clear by the opening statement: "If YHWH does not build the household,[26] those who build it labor in vain."

One cannot, therefore, take what represents as the intended subject matter of discourse for that which is represented. For example, "sons" in v. 3a is parallel to "fruit" in v. 3b. One cannot make the argument that the passage is really about fruit instead of sons based on the parallel. Sons are also likened to arrows (v. 4), but sons, not arrows, are the intended subject matter. Hence, the theme in the latter half of the Psalm is the reward of offspring, not fruit and arrows.

What certain commentators will then say is that the reference to the house is either metaphoric of the city or that it speaks of the temple (the *bêth* referring to the *bêth YHWH* "house of YHWH"). Hence, the intended subject matter is the city. The mention of the city gate at the end of the Psalm ties in nicely with this view due to the fact that the Psalmist will have provided an overview of the city from its innermost part (i.e., the temple) to its outer walls. The military metaphor, referring to sons as arrows,[27] would also make sense here.[28]

The problem with this view is that the phrase, as is the case with the entire Psalm, typical of the genre of wisdom literature, is gnomic and does not refer to a specific situation or structure. It is too much of a stretch to suggest that the generic *bêth* is meant to refer to a special phrase designat-

26. The word *bêth* can refer either to the physical structure of the house or the household/family as a whole. The addition of *bô*, referring to those who build it up from "inside of it," may indicate that the family itself, rather than a physical structure is being viewed as the necessary habitation that must be created for further covenant children to thrive.

27. Some have argued that "sons," not daughters are mentioned here because they are the ones who are needed in warfare. Although sons are prized in the ancient world for defense of the household and their ability to pass on the inheritance of a family, it is not likely that the text is making a military reference here; and daughters are also able to inherit in the ancient world when a son is absent. Furthermore, the term should be taken as a reference to all children, not only because the New Testament expands the rights of the sons to the daughters as well, but also because the very Psalm itself seems only to use the term as a case of poetic paronomasia holding its strophic structure together. See Allen (*Psalms 101–150*, 237) who states that the text exhibits "an initial wordplay, בוניו, 'its builders,' and בנים, 'sons.' There are further parallel features between the strophes. The repetition בוניו, 'its builders,' and יבנה, 'he builds,' in v 1 corresponds to בנים/בנו 'sons.'" It is more likely then that word choice is not due to the author's limitation of the blessed offspring to a particular gender, but to poetic diction.

28. Some have attempted to amend the text in v. 5 to read *gibbōr* "warrior" instead of *geber* "man." Dahood (*Psalms III*, 224–25) rightly states such a repointing of the text as "unsatisfactory."

ing the temple apart from any contextual elements indicating such, much less its usual collocation with the name YHWH when referring to the temple. Any accompanying language of the cultus is also absent, further indicating that the temple is not in view here.

It is also important to note that the *geber* "man," who is usually the representative of the smallest unit of the family (cf. Josh 7:14), and is clearly a reference to the father here, is the one who is directly blessed, not the king or military general or city. The "fruit of the womb" in v. 3 is a reward (i.e., not a gift, but a commendation of piety) for an individual *geber*'s fearing God (cf. Ps 128:3).[29]

Furthermore, if one understands that the intended subject of vv. 1–2 is YHWH securing habitation for those who trust in Him (cf. Gen 1:3–25), and the intended subject of vv. 3–5 is YHWH rewarding His faithful with children/inhabitants (cf. Gen 1:26–31), then applications to both household and the city can be drawn from the text. The larger community is blessed by the blessings bestowed upon its individual family units. In fact, the hypothetical claim that might be made against a man's covenant participation, by the family's domestic opponents, is refuted by his having raised children.[30]

What cannot be done is to attempt to draw a false dichotomy by replacing the macrocosm for the microcosm, as though the blessing of the smaller unit does not spill out and become the blessing of the larger in which it resides.

The Psalm, therefore, is to be interpreted as primarily teaching that the reward of a godly man is "pro-creation" (i.e., secure order of habita-

---

29. Psalm 127 and 128 are meant to mirror one another. Like Psalm 127, Psalm 128 breaks down the reward of those who fear YHWH as security of resources (i.e., a key element of habitation) with which to live and the reward of children (i.e., inhabitants).

30. The city gate is a reference to the court where disputes are brought against fellow members of the community. The attempt to posit a military reference is unlikely here. As Allen (*Psalms 101–150*, 236) concludes, "Heb אֶת דַּבֵּר, lit. "speak with," has a forensic connotation, as in twelve other cases in the OT (cf. D. J. Estes, *VT* 41 [1991] 308 n. 27): cf. NJB 'dispute,' NJPS and RNAB 'contend.' This sense fits the function of the city gate in the OT as a place of judgment. However, Lipiński (*RB* 75 [1968] 351 n. 130), Dahood (225), Watson (*Classical Hebrew Poetry,* 286, 361), D. E. Fleming (*ZAW* 107 [1995] 442), Crow (*Songs of Ascents,* 67–68), and HALOT, 209b, relate to the other root, דָּבַר, "repulse (adversaries)." A military reference would nicely match the urban defense of v 1b by way of inclusion, but the use of the sign of the definite obj. before אֹיְבִים, "adversaries," would be awkward, and the metaphorical nature of the military reference to arrows in vv 4–5a suggests that a literal military sense is not to be found in v 5b."

tion and multiplying of inhabitants). The attempt to do otherwise does not take into account the distinction between the theme of reward as security of habitation and inhabitants in the microcosm and the thematic metaphor that displays the need for the Lord to secure the macrocosm of the city, the theology of creation/order as divine blessing in ancient Israelite society, the immediate context within the Psalm that displays numerous references to the individual family unit, or the context of the following Psalm that mirrors its subject matter.

JORDAN'S SKEPTICISM OF HISTORICAL FACT

Jordan argues against Provan's use of the historical Protestant argument by calling into question a couple of works quoted by Provan.[31] The two cited works are those of the Puritan court case against an adulterer and Arthur Pink's comments against, what is most likely, artificial contraception.

The Puritan case consists of a mixture of sexual improprieties practiced by the defendant. As such, Jordan may be right to conclude that this cannot be used as evidence that the Puritans were against such practices. The mountains of other writings indicating Puritan opposition to the practice, along with their large families, is enough evidence to substantiate the claim without having to bring ambiguous evidence into play.

The quote by A. W. Pink (1886–1952), a pastor who lived during the transition stage between the historic view and the modern view, is equally ambiguous. It is difficult to say whether Pink condemns all forms of contraception when he says "we do not believe in what is termed birth control,"[32] and is advocating that Christians also use control of their sexual appetites; or if he is in fact suggesting the limiting of children through abstention from sexual activities, as would be the case in the practice of the rhythm method of his day.

The real issue is why Jordan insists on using two bad examples as dismissive of Provan's larger argument. He seems to do this to undermine the argument that Christians have been against the practice of limiting children for nearly two millennia. I could easily cite numerous Puritans who represent the Puritan position against contraception. Conversely, challenging Provan based on a twentieth century author like Pink simply proves Provan's point that Protestant opinion turned against the historical

31. Ibid., 8–9.

32. Comment on 13:4 in *An Exposition of Hebrews*.

view in that century. Jordan seems to bring these up, however, to plant some sort of doubtful seed in the mind of his readers that might suggest that historical Christians thought the use of contraceptive methods were morally acceptable. Unfortunately, the mountain of evidence speaks otherwise, and this is possibly why Jordan does not spend much time on this argument. He does not stay long on this argument for good reason (i.e., he doesn't seem to really know a tremendous amount of the historical data).

He further back-peddles by stating that the Church has to be in the mode of *semper reformanda* anyway. In other words, even if the entire Church condemned the use of contraception and saw the sexual act as primarily procreative, the true reformation spirit is to always be reforming. Hence, one is justified in rejecting the historic position.

Like other cultic and apostate movements throughout the Church's history, however, Jordan has failed to realize that genuine reformation always returns a wayward church or movement to the historic orthodoxy and orthopraxis of the historic Christian position. This is why the reformers quoted the Bible alongside the Church Fathers. Their point was not that they were conjuring up a new view of Christianity, but that their views were consistent with the teachings and presuppositions of the early Church (specifically those of an anthropological orthodoxy as seen in its affirmation of Augustinian, rather than Pelagian and Semi-Pelagian, presuppositions). What cultic movements do is to use this same banner of the reformation in order to give credence to a theology or practice that disconnects itself from historic orthodoxy or orthopraxis. The difference is night and day. Reformation returns and restores the historic Christianity that was lost. Apostasy turns away from the views of historic Christianity. Those are two different animals altogether. If, therefore, Jordan's ethical views of sex turn away from the orthopraxis of historic Christianity, is it reformation or apostasy?

THE OLD HAS BECOME THE FEARED NEW: NEO OR PALEO-PHOBIA?

Jordan then presents his "neo-phobia" argument that presents the condemnation of contraception as a mere fear of what is new.[33] Jordan's neo-

---

33. Jordan, "The Bible and Family Planning," 10.

phobia argument, of course, is nonsense, as neither contraception, nor its availability, is anything new.

Secondly, this is very similar to the argument presented against Christians who oppose homosexuality. It is easier to say that someone is homophobic than to simply deal honestly with their reasons for denying that homosexual sex is morally acceptable.

Jordan completes his absurdity by citing the Amish as his prime example, as though that group was somehow representative of the larger Christian community today. Of course, the larger group of Christians who are opposed to contraception still drive cars, own computers, take all sorts of medication, even participate in reproductive technologies. This willingly seems to escape Jordan's notice, as he pretends that an acceptance of a God-directed life, rather than one in which we take control, is somehow the fearful stance in this whole debate.

Thirdly, what is fascinating about this claim is that in reality the "new" to most evangelicals today is not the use of birth control, but the condemnation of it. In other words, the new is the old. What we have witnessed to a much larger degree than the ghost of Jordan's anti-contraception advocates who huddle in their caves, fearing technology, is that the fear belongs to those who are afraid to have their lives change with children who interrupt the lives of those who have them planned out already. Jordan can call the kettle black all he likes, but in the end, those who risk their plans for the sake of the divinely created interruptions of children are anything but the more fearful of these two positions.

FEARING PLEASURE OR FEARING GOD WITH OUR USES OF PLEASURE?

Jordan argues that the Fathers, as well as historic Christianity that often follows them, banned these things because they feared pleasure.[34] Anything that has the potential for giving pleasure, therefore, was seen in a bad light. On the subjects of food, drink, sex, dancing, etc., therefore, historic Christianity is unreliable.[35]

34. Ibid., 10–11.

35. Of course, the fact that we live in an atheistic and hedonistic culture, which would render our views of pleasure skewed, is not considered. Within Jordan's statement is the assumption that our assessments of pleasure are reliable. Hence, we ought to trust ourselves rather than believing that the Church had any sort of divine guidance throughout the centuries.

Jordan's absurd argument that the Fathers "feared pleasure" can only be described as an assessment lacking any real interaction with Patristic theology. The Fathers did not fear pleasure, nor did they consider the eating of food or drinking of wine a sin, as Jordan suggests.[36] (See Appendix D.) However, they would conclude that Jordan's hedonistic understanding of pleasure ought to be scrutinized for what it is. We'll let the Bible decide who has the correct appropriation of the pleasures.

The Bible: "Whether, then, you eat or drink or whatever you do, do everything *for* the glory of God" (1 Cor 10:31, italics added).

Jordan: "It is fine to eat food *for* its taste."

"Music feels good and sounds good, and the Bible shows us this as well. It is fine to make music *even if you are not in a worship service.*"

"Sex feels good, and it is fine to have sex *for* fun."[37]

No one, of course, suggests that music is only to be made in a worship service, but should it not be made in worship? Food tastes good and sex is pleasurable, but should they be used solely for our personal pleasure, even if this makes up only an occasional use? Does not the Scripture here tell us that whatever we do, do *everything* for the glory of God?

The pagan festivals Paul is addressing here engage in the eating of meat and drinking of wine and merry-making that all *feel* good. The point is that whatever we do we are to do for God's pleasure first. Our pleasure should be secondary to that which glorifies Him. Pleasure *for* pleasure's sake is hedonism, not Christianity. It is worship of the self that says, "It is fine to eat food *for* its taste," rather than saying, "It is good to eat food *for* the glory of God." Pleasure is already an assumed result of the act. The theological and ethical question becomes, "Is the participation in practice X meant to be used for more than the pleasure that will automatically result from that practice?"

36. Cf. the comments made by Cyril of Jerusalem, *Catacheses* 4.27: "For we fast abstaining from wine and meat, not because we abhor them as abominations . . . Do not despise therefore those who eat . . . nor accuse those who use a little wine for their stomachs . . . neither condemn the men as sinners, nor abhor meat as unclean food; for the Apostle knows some people who are like this, when he says: 'forbidding to marry, and commanding to abstain from meats, which God created to be received with thanksgiving by those who believe.'" The Fathers, therefore, understood the distinction between issues of conscience and issues of morality in the use of those things that give pleasure.

37. Ibid., 11, italics added.

Jordan wants to assume that our pleasure is God's pleasure, but if that were true there would be no need for Paul's exhortation. What we enjoyed, God would enjoy automatically. Instead, we need to ask the question, together with the Corinthians, "Is God pleased with the way I am using X?" or even, "Is God pleased with my being pleased with the use of X?"

THE SONG OF SOLOMON

I did have to comment on something that I thought was a bit humorous in Jordan's argument. He exaggerates that "the Bible celebrates the pleasure of sex from start to finish." He then goes on to cite the Song of Solomon as proof of this. Apparently, to Jordan, the little eight chapter love poem, along with a few proverbs, constitutes the entire Bible from start to finish. The most common pleasure of the sexual act celebrated throughout the Bible, of course, is linked to the joy of children.

But what is interesting about the Song is that its title is actually "the Song of Songs," which is a superlative in Hebrew that means "the Greatest Song." Now, are we to believe that the greatest song, written by a king who wrote around a thousand love songs, is all about two swimsuit models who want to have sex with one another? Or is it, as is the case with every other ancient genre utilized by the Bible, that the Song really is ultimately meant to convey something about our relationship with God. Does it not convey God's desire and aggressive pursuit of us and our desire and aggressive response to His pursuit of us? What is a more perfect genre in which to display our passionate relationship with God than ancient Near Eastern love poetry? What stronger desire than sexual desire is there to convey the desire that God has for us and that we, in return, have for God? Jordan, and many modern interpreters today, want to interpret the Song literally. Of course, as I have argued already, whether one takes the Song as literal or figurative is irrelevant to any prescriptive idea that might be assigned to the sexual act.[38] If one takes it as literal (rather than making

38. Elements that indicate that the procreative purpose is not divorced from pleasure in the Song: (1) Love poems do not indicate one's view of the sexual act, but instead the desire to have enjoyable sex with another person. They, therefore, cannot substantiate what view the author had of the ultimate purpose of the sexual act. There is no need to even show, therefore, that the author talks about procreation in the Song. That is like saying that Jesus told us to worship God in spirit and truth and therefore does not believe that action is a part of our worship toward God. These are arguments from silence. The

it a romantic allegory about intimacy[39]), one must simply conclude that sex with pretty people is something to be desired. What a fantastic revelation this is to humanity! Although it is true that a couple will desire one another if they are faithful to their Pilates classes and maintain their six pack abs, it is doubtful that the Holy Spirit included the book in the canon of Scripture as "the Greatest Song" for this reason.

Instead, the "Greatest Song" is God/Christ, our Bridegroom pursuing us, His bride, with the passion and desire of the king in the book, along with our reciprocated pursuit of Him in desire. We really do need this revelation to help us understand the type of vital relationship we can have with God, but do we really need to know that pretty people are attractive? I guess, I just think it is ironic that the ancient interpretation of the text is seen as the absurd interpretation and the literal the more sane when the former makes perfect sense in the context of Scripture and the latter seems rather irrelevant and out of place. Either way, however, the Song holds no threat to the procreative argument unless a person attempts to draw a false dichotomy from it, as Jordan erroneously does.

Biblical view of procreation must be gained from the whole of Scripture then not one part of it that is not even discussing the purpose of the sexual act. (2) the עלמות are women who are eligible to have children, not unmarried virgins alone. To express this in the Song tells us that the writer views his options for having sex is with someone who is eligible to have a child; (3) the dove is a symbol of "procreation" in the sense that it represents what is beneficial for perpetuating life (cf. Noah's sending of the dove out, it returning with an olive branch to indicate that the earth can again be inhabited, and the command to procreate to follow; also cf. the Holy Spirit—the Spirit who creates life in Genesis—who descends as a dove). (4) Mandrakes (7:13) are often associated with fertility. (5) The idea that an ancient Israelite would really see the pleasure of sex as separate from its procreative possibilities is really stretching it beyond what is said. If, in fact, the Israelites viewed non-procreative sexual acts as abominable forms of sexual immorality, it would be absurd to suggest, that because our author only discusses how enjoyable sex would be with this woman, that this somehow means he no longer believes that sex must have procreative possibilities. (cf. Ps 128:3 with Song 6:11; 7:8, 12.)

39. Most modern interpreters attempt to force psychological principles into the Song in order to make it more spiritual, but in the end, if the Song is to be taken literally, then the Song must be taken for what it says rather than what our modern glasses of romanticism want to make it. The attributes described by the couple are mainly physical (seventy seven physical attributes are mentioned as the source of attraction) with sexual aggressiveness spoken of thirteen times, and a single moral attribute assigned only four times to the woman; none are assigned to the man. It might be possible to squeeze one or two other attributes out of the text, but as a whole, the literal text celebrates the physical attractiveness and sexual relations between two beautiful people.

CONTRACEPTION AND THE USE OF PAGAN INVENTIONS

Jordan's "Enoch Factor" essentially argues that anything pagans manufacture for evil can be used by Christians in a godly manner.[40] This, of course, is true, but not relevant to our discussion, as Jordan attempts to make an analogy between created objects and their uses. One may find that contraceptive drugs kill off black widow spiders. Great! The point is that "contracepting" a child is immoral. The method, whether with a pagan instrument or not, is irrelevant to the use. The question concerns whether the use is moral or immoral.

This is a false analogy, then, because one cannot compare the permission to use a created object with the right or wrong use of that object. This is like saying that because certain knives, which were developed originally in violent warfare, can be used by Christians to cut their food, this somehow means that Christians can also use them to kill their neighbors. *Freedom* to use an object is not the same as the *free use* of an object. We are to use all created objects for the glory of God in obedience to His desires. We are not free to use that object in whatever way we wish. The question, therefore, is, "What is God's desire in the sexual act, and should it be hindered by the use of a foreign object?" Jordan has assumed the answer to this question rather than attempting to discuss it with any sophistication.

Jordan then proceeds to lay out his situational ethics. He is only able to do so because he has begged the question, and assumed that contraception is morally acceptable. He, therefore, believes it to be a matter of conscience and gifting. This assumption, of course, has been dismantled by this present work. Hence, Jordan's argument here is null and void.

JORDAN ENDS WHERE HE BEGAN

Jordan's last few arguments consist of ad hominem attacks. He asserts that everyone he has read, who opposes the use of contraception by Christians, is a "novice to the Christian religion who has little feeling for the theology of Reformation Christianity" and that "every writer is an ideologue rather than a pastor."[41] Of course, Jordan must have forgotten all of those pastors and teachers of the Christian Church for the past two thousand years. I'm not sure one can consider John Calvin a "novice to the Christian religion

40. Ibid.
41. Ibid., 12.

who has little feeling for the theology of Reformation Christianity," or call Spurgeon "an ideologue rather than a pastor." Jordan wants to limit his comments, of course, to recent lay works, such as those by Provan and Pride; but he forgets that their theology stems from the massive cloud of witnesses throughout Church history that dwarfs Jordan's claims of doctrinal and moral maturity by the span of two millennia and beyond.[42] In Jordan's mind, those who advocate for the historical position are to be demeaned by name-calling;[43] but this sort of argument just doesn't belong in a reasonable discussion of this topic. In the end, ad hominem may make the user "feel good" about him or herself by debasing another's position, intelligence, or character; but it accomplishes nothing but the spread of more heat than light.

Jordan ends his argument with a plea to preach the Bible, assuming that the Bible does not speak directly to this subject, and God will take care of those things not explicitly dealt with in Scripture. While I do not disagree with Jordan, that the Bible ought to be preached, since it delivers a mindset within God's people instead of a list of rules, the method for how one goes about preaching that mindset does not need to be divided between explicit commands and implicit principles. The implicit is taught through the explicit examples. The Scripture itself teaches this way. The true solution to all forms of legalism is to teach that the explicit commands of law are not exhaustive, but are instead applications of larger principles. This is the way Jesus and the Apostles taught the Scripture, and it is the duty of the Church, therefore, to reclaim this hermeneutic by teaching both the examples and the principles that stand behind them.

CONCLUSION

Jordan's analysis of Provan's work is made up of the worst forms of argumentation; and yet, it is the best defense the opposition can provide for their position. It begs the question of naturalism in the conception event, makes self-refuting arguments about the possibility of affecting the existence of future persons, uses genetic and *ad hominem* fallacies in its attempt to dismiss the historical argument, uses the *ad hominem* fallacy

---

42. Of course, he makes it well known that he is not above attacking the integrity of the Church's greatest theologians in order to advance his position (cf. his comments concerning Augustine).

43. For example, Jordan calls the anti-contraceptive view "quackodoxy" in an effort to convey that this view is crazy and is not worthy of intelligent engagement.

when dismissing the books written by lay authors in the late twentieth century, misinterprets Scripture with faulty hermeneutics and an understanding of lexicography and grammar that is to be considered novice at best, and it employs the use of straw men, *reductio ad absurdum*, and non sequiturs.

There is no doubt that Jordan has made points against Provan's work that are true. Provan equates seed with people rather than seeing the seed as a potential person only because it may be used by God to make a person through the sexual act. Provan uses quotes from a few authors and groups that may or may not refer to contraception in the way Provan refers to it in his book.

However, for the few flaws that can be seen in Provan's arguments, there is much more that remains unaffected by Jordan's "refutation." In fact, there are far more fallacies utilized by Jordan, in his attempt to undermine Provan's arguments, than there actually are in Provan's arguments themselves. What this tells us, once again, is that the opposing viewpoint is incapable of producing a validly biblical argument that is capable of withstanding the scrutiny of exegetical analysis, basic logical principles, and the discernment of historical orthodoxy.

Recommendations for Further Reading

IN AN EFFORT TO further reflection, as well as to achieve a more comprehensive view of the issue, I would like to suggest some excellent works for the lay reader.

Bayly, Tim. "The Place of Childbirth in Christian Marriage: Raising Up a Godly Seed," *Journal of Biblical Manhood and Womanhood* 3 (1998) 1. This article is also available online at http://www.cbmw.org/Journal/Vol-3-No-4/Shepherd-s-Pie.

Carlson, Allan. "Children of the Reformation: A Short and Surprising History of Protestantism and Contraception," *Touchstone*, May, 2007. Carlson's article can be viewed online at http://www.touchstonemag.com/archives/article.php?id=20-04-020-f.

Hess, Rick and Jan. *A Full Quiver: Family Planning and the Lordship of Christ*. Brentwood, Tenn.: Wolgemuth & Hyatt Publishers, Inc., 1990.

Marshall, Robert G., and Charles A. Donovan, *Blessed Are the Barren: The Social Policy of Planned Parenthood*. San Francisco: Ignatius, 1991.

Patterson, Dorothy. "The High Calling of Wife and Mother in Biblical Perspective," in John Piper and Wayne Grudem (eds.), *Recovering Biblical Manhood and Womanhood: A Response to Evangelical Feminism*. Wheaton: Crossway Books, 1991, 264–77. Patterson's article can be read online at http://www.cbmw.org/Recovering-Biblical-Manhood-and-Womanhood/. Readers might also want to read: Mary Pride, *The Way Home: Beyond Feminism, Back to Reality* (Wheaton: Crossway, 1993).

Wilson, Doug. *Standing on the Promises: A Handbook of Biblical Childrearing*. Moscow, ID: Canon Press, 1997.

Bibliography

Allen, Leslie C. *Psalms 101-50*. Revised. Word Biblical Commentary. Dallas: Word Press, 2002.

Allen, Thomas W., ed. *Homeri Opera*, vol. 5. Oxford: Oxford University Press, 1919.

Alter, Robert. *Genesis: Translation and Commentary*. New York: W.W. Norton and Co., 1996.

Aquinas, Thomas. *The Summa Theologica of St. Thomas Aquinas*. 5 volumes. Translated by the Fathers of the English Dominican Province. Notre Dame, IN: Thomas More, 1981.

Aristotle. *Politics*. Loeb Classical Library 264. Translated and edited by Peter Simpson. Cambridge, MA: Harvard University Press, 1932.

Augustine. *Augustine's Commentary on Galatians*. Introduction, Text, Translation and Notes by Eric Plumer. Oxford: Oxford University Press, 2006.

Batto, Bernard. *Slaying the Dragon: Mythmaking in the Biblical Tradition*. Louisville: Westminster, 1992.

Balz, Horst, and Gerhard Schneider, eds. *Exegetical Dictionary of the New Testament*. 3 vols. Grand Rapids: Eerdmans, 1991.

Bauer, Walter et al., ed. *A Greek-English Lexicon of the New Testament and Other Early Christian Literature*. 3rd ed. Edited by Frederick William Danker. Chicago: University of Chicago Press, 2001.

Barlow, Claude W. *Martini Episcopi Bracarensis Opera Omnia*. Papers and Monographs of the American Academy in Rome, XII. New Haven, Yale University Press, 1950.

Beale, G. K. *The Book of Revelation*. New International Commentary on the Greek New Testament. Grand Rapids: Eerdmans, 1999.

Beckwith, Francis J. *Politically Correct Death: Answering Arguments for Abortion Rights*. Grand Rapids: Baker Books, 1998.

Bercot, David W., ed. *A Dictionary of Early Christian Beliefs*. Peabody, MA: Hendrickson, 2000.

Biggs, R. D. "Conception, Contraception and Abortion in Ancient Mesopotamia." In *Wisdom, Gods and Literature: Studies in Assyriology in Honor of W.G. Lambert*. Edited by A. R. George and I. L. Finkel, 1-13. Winona Lake: Eisenbrauns, 2000.

Black, Jeremy et al., ed. *A Concise Dictionary of Akkadian*. Wiesbadden: Harrassowitz Verlag, 1999.

Bonhoeffer, Dietrich. *Ethics*. Eberhard Bethge, ed. New York: Macmillan, 1955.

Botterweck, G. Johannes et al., ed. *Theological Dictionary of the Old Testament*. 15 vols. Translated by John T. Willis et al. Grand Rapids: Eerdmans, 1977-2006.

Brennan, Tad. *The Stoic Life: Emotions, Duty & Fate*. Oxford: Oxford University Press, 2007.

Brown, Colin, ed. *New International Dictionary of New Testament Theology*. 4 vols. Grand Rapids: Zondervan, 1975–1985.

Bullinger, E. W. *Figures of Speech Used in the Bible: Explained and Illustrated*. Grand Rapids: Baker Books, 2003.

Calvin, John. *Commentaries on the Epistles of Paul to the Galatians and Ephesians*. Translated by William Pringle. Grand Rapids: Baker, 2003.

———. *Commentaries on the Book of Genesis*. Translated by John King. Grand Rapids: Baker, 2003.

———. *Institutes of the Christian Religion*. Translated by Henry Beveridge. Grand Rapids: Eerdmans, 2001.

Charlesworth, James H., ed. *The Old Testament Pseudepigrapha: Volume 1: Apocalyptic Literature and Testaments*. The Anchor Bible Reference Library. Garden City: Doubleday, 1983.

———, ed. *The Old Testament Pseudepigrapha: Volume 2: Expansions of the "Old Testament" and Legends, Wisdom and Philosophical Literature, Prayers, Psalms and Odes, Fragments of Lost Judeo-Hellenistic Works*. Garden City: Doubleday, 1985.

Childress, James F. and John Macquarrie, eds. *The Westminster Dictionary of Christian Ethics*. Philadelphia, Westminster Press, 1986.

Christensen, Duane L. *Deuteronomy*. Word Biblical Commentary. Dallas: Thomas Nelson, 2002.

Clines, David J. A., ed. *Dictionary of Classical Hebrew*. 6 vols. Sheffield: Sheffield Academic Press, 1993–2007.

Colish, Marcia L. *The Stoic Tradition from Antiquity to the Early Middle Ages: Stoicism in Christian Latin Thought through the Sixth Century*. Leiden: Brill, 1985.

Cranfield, C. E. B. *A Critical and Exegetical Commentary on the Epistle to the Romans*. Edinburgh: T&T Clark, 1979.

Dahood, Mitchell. *Psalms*. 3 vols. Anchor Bible Commentary. Garden City: Doubleday, 1968.

Davis, John Jefferson, *Evangelical Ethics: Issues Facing the Church Today*. 2nd ed. Phillipsburg, NJ: P&R Publishing, 1993.

———, "Theologically Sound." In *The Sterilization Option: A Guide for Christians*. Edited by David Biebel. Grand Rapids: Baker, 1995.

Dearmen, J. Andrew. "Marriage in the Old Testament." In *Biblical Ethics and Homosexuality: Listening to Scripture*. Edited by Robert L. Brawley. Louisville: WJK Press, 1996.

Desiring God staff, "Does the Bible permit birth control?" In *Questions and Answers*. Minneapolis, MN: Desiring God Ministries, 2006. Online: http://www.desiringgod. org/ResourceLibrary/Articles/ByDate/2006/1440_Does_the_Bible_permit_birth_ control/.

Driver, S. R. *The Book of Genesis with Introduction and Notes*, 11th ed. London: Mathuen & Co., 1920.

Dunn, James D. G. *Romans*. 2 vols. Word Biblical Commentary. Dallas: Word Books, 1988.

Erickson, Millard. *Christian Theology*. Grand Rapids: Baker, 1985.

Feinberg, John S., and Paul D. Feinberg, *Ethics for a Brave New World*. Wheaton, IL: Crossway, 1993.

Finkel, I. L. "On Late Babylonian Medical Training." In *Wisdom, Gods and Literature: Studies in Assyriology in Honor of W. G. Lambert*. Edited by A. R. George and I. L. Finkel 137–223. Winona Lake: Eisenbrauns, 2000.

Fitzmeyer, Joseph A. *To Advance the Gospel.* Grand Rapids: Eerdmans, 1998.

———. *Romans: A New Translation with Introduction and Commentary.* Anchor Bible Commentary. New York: Doubleday, 1993.

Frame, John. *Pastoral and Social Ethics* (Course Outline). In "Christians and Contraception: Convenience or Kingdom Thinking?" Barth Garrett, 228. No pages. *IIIM Magazine Online* 3 (June 2001).

Fredrickson, David. "Natural and Unnatural Use in Romans 1:24–27: Paul and the Philosophic Critique of Eros." In *Homosexuality, Science, and the "Plain Sense" of Scripture.* Edited by D.L. Balch. Grand Rapids: Eerdmans, 2000.

Frymer-Kensky, Tikva. "The Atrahasis Epic and Its Significance for Our Understanding of Genesis 1–9." *BA* 40 (1977) 147–55.

Garrett, Barth. "Christians and Contraception: Convenience or Kingdom Thinking?" *IIIM Magazine Online* 3 (June 2001) 1–12.

Geisler, Norman L. *Christian Apologetics.* Grand Rapids: Baker, 1976.

———. *Christian Ethics: Options and Issues.* Grand Rapids: Baker, 1989.

Glazier-McDonald, Beth. *Malachi: The Divine Messenger.* SBL Dissertation Series 98. Atlanta: Scholars Press, 1987.

Gesenius, Wilhelm. *Gesenius' Hebrew Grammar.* 1910 ed. Edited and enlarged by Emil Kautsch. Translated by Arthur Ernest Cowley. 2nd English ed. Oxford: Oxford at the Clarendon Press, 2003.

Goodson, Patricia. "Ethics of Contraception: A Recurring Debate." *Presbyterion: Covenant Seminary Review* 18 (1992) 34–49.

Grenz, Stanley. "Family Planning and the People of God." *Christianity Today* 35 (November 1991) 34–45.

Gruber, Mayer. "Breast-Feeding Practices in Biblical Israel and in Old Babylonian Mesopotamia." *JANES* 19 (1989) 61–83.

Hahn, Scott. *The Scott Hahn Conversion Story.* Powell River, BC: The Catholic Education Resource Center. No pages. Online: http://www.catholiceducation.org/articles/apologetics/ap0088.html.

Hamilton, Victor P. *The Book of Genesis.* 2 vols. Grand Rapids: Eerdmans, 1990, 1995.

Harakas, Stanley. *Contemporary Moral Issues Facing the Orthodox Christian.* Minneapolis, MN: Light and Life Publishing, 1982.

Harrison, Brian W. "The Sin of Onan Revisited." *Living Tradition* 67 (1996) 1.

Hartley, J. E. *Leviticus.* Word Biblical Commentary. Dallas: Word, 2002.

Henry, Matthew. *Matthew Henry's Commentary on the Whole Bible.* Unabridged ed. Peabody, MA: Hendrickson, 2008.

Herrin, Judith, and Alexander Kazhdan, "Contraception." In *The Oxford Dictionary of Byzantium,* vol. 1. Edited by Alexander P. Kazhdan et al. Oxford: Oxford University Press, 1991.

Herlihy, David, and Klapische-Zuber, Christiane. *Tuscans and Their Families: A Study of the Florentine Catasto of 1427.* New Haven: Yale University Press, 1985.

Hess, Richard S. *The Song of Songs.* Baker Commentary on the Old Testament Wisdom and Psalm Series. Grand Rapids: Baker, 2005.

Hess, Rick and Jan. *A Full Quiver: Family Planning and the Lordship of Christ.* Brentwood, TN: Wolgemuth & Hyatt Publishers, Inc., 1990.

Holmes, Michael W., ed. *The Apostolic Fathers: Greek Texts and English Translations.* Grand Rapids: Baker, 1999.

Horn, Joyce. "Joseph Hall." In *The New International Dictionary of the Christian Church*, 447. Edited by J. D. Douglas. Grand Rapids: Zondervan, 1978.

House, H. Wayne. "Should Christians Use Birth Control?" Charlotte, NC: Christian Research Institute, 2009. No pages. Online: http://www.equip.org/articles/should-christians-use-birth-control-.

Hubbard, David A. *Ecclesiastes/Song of Solomon*. The Preacher's Commentary, vol. 16. Nashville, TN: Thomas Nelson, 2002.

Inwood, Brad and Lloyd P. Gerson , eds. *The Stoics Reader: Selected Writings and Testimonia*. Indianapolis, IN: Hackett Publishing, 2008.

Irmischer, Johann K., ed. *Martin Luther's Definition of Faith: An excerpt from "An Introduction to St. Paul's Letter to the Romans."* Vol. 63. Translated by Robert E. Smith. Erlangen: Heyder and Zimmer, 1854.

Jaeger, Werner. *Early Christianity and Greek Paideia*. London: Oxford University Press, 1961.

Jenni, Ernst, and Claus Westermann, eds. *Theological Lexicon of the Old Testament*. 3 vols. Translated by Mark Biddle. Peabody, Mass: Hendrickson, 1997.

Jewett, Robert. *A Commentary on the Book of Romans*. Hermeneia. Minneapolis: Fortress Press, 2006.

Johnson, Phillip. *The Wedge of Truth: Splitting the Foundations of Naturalism*. Downers Grove: Intervarsity Press, 2000.

Jones, A. H. M. *The Later Roman Empire, 282-602: A Social, Economic, and Administrative Survey*. 2 vols. Baltimore: Johns Hopkins University Press, 1986.

Jordan, James B. "The Bible and Family Planning: An Answer to Charles Provan's 'The Bible and Birth Control.'" *Contra Mundum 9* (1993), 2–14.

Keil, Carl Friedrich and F. Delitzsch. *The Pentateuch*. Biblical Commentary on the Old Testament, volume 1. Peabody, MA: Hendrickson, 1996.

Kidner, Derek. *Genesis: An Introduction and Commentary*. Tyndale Old Testament Commentaries. Downer's Grove, IL: Intervarsity, 1967.

Kikawada, Isaac M., and Arthur Quinn. *Before Abraham Was*. Nashville: Abingdon, 1985.

Kilmer, Anne. "The Mesopotamian Concept of Overpopulation and Its Solution as Reflected in Mythology." *Or* 41 (1972), 160–77.

Kinlaw, Dennis F. "Song of Songs." In *The Expositor's Bible Commentary: Psalms, Proverbs, Ecclesiastes, Song of Songs*. Volume 5. Grand Rapids: Zondervan, 1991.

Kittel, G. and G. Friedrich, eds. *Theological Dictionary of the New Testament*. Translated by G.W. Bromiley. 10 volumes. Grand Rapids: Eerdmans, 1964–1976.

Knight, George W., III. *The Pastoral Epistles: A Commentary on the Greek Text*. The New International Greek Testament Commentary. Grand Rapids: Eerdmans, 1992.

Koehler, Ludwig, and Walter Baumgartner. *The Hebrew and Aramaic Lexicon of the Old Testament*. 2 vol. study edition. Translated by M. E. J. Richardson. Leiden: Brill Academic, 2002.

Lambert, W. G., and A. R. Millard. *Atra-ḫasīs: The Babylonian Story of the Flood*. Winona Lake: Eisenbrauns, 1999.

Lampe, G. W. *A Patristic Greek Lexicon*. Oxford: Oxford University Press, 2004.

Laney, J. Carl. "The Abortion Epidemic: America's Silent Holocaust." *BibSac* 139 (1982) 342–353.

LDS Church, *Church Handbook of Instructions, Book 1: Stake Presidencies and Bishoprics*. Salt Lake City, Utah: LDS Church, 2006.

Leupold, H. C. *Exposition of Genesis*, vol. 1. 11th Printing. Grand Rapids: Baker, 1971.

Levenson, Jon D. *Creation and the Persistence of Evil: The Jewish Drama of Divine Omnipotence*. Princeton, NJ: Princeton University Press, 1988.

Lewis, C. S. *The Abolition of Man*. New York: Macmillan. 1965.

———. *Mere Christianity*. New York: Macmillan. 1960.

Ley, John. *The Westminster Annotations and Commentary on the Whole Bible*. London, 1657.

Liddell, Henry George, and Robert Scott. *A Greek-English Lexicon*. 9th ed. Edited by Henry Stuart Jones. Clarendon: Oxford University Press, 1995.

Liederbach, Mark. "Contraception," in Andreas J. Köstenberger with David W. Jones, eds. *God, Marriage and Family*. Wheaton: Crossway, 2004.

Long, A. A. *Stoic Studies*. Cambridge: Cambridge University Press, 1996.

Louw, Johannes P., and Eugene Nida, eds. *Greek-English Lexicon of the New Testament Based on Semantic Domains*. 2 vols. 2nd ed. New York: United Bible Societies, 1989.

Luneburg, H. *Die Gynakologie des Soranus von Ephesus*. Munchen: Lehmann, 1894.

Luther, Martin. *Luther's Works*. 55 vols. Jaroslav Jan Pelikan, ed. Minneapolis, MN: Fortress Press and Concordia, 1957–76.

MacArthur, John F. "What does the Bible teach about birth control?" *Issues & Answers*. Panorama City, CA: Grace to You, 2008. No pages. Online: http://www.biblebb.com/files/macqa/birthcontrol.htm.

MacArthur, John F. et al. *Right Thinking in a World Gone Wrong: A Biblical Response to Today's Most Controversial Issues*. Eugene, OR: Harvest House, 2009.

Mather, Cotton. *The Pure Nazarite*. Boston, 1723.

Mathison, Keith A. *The Shape of Sola Scriptura*. Moscow, ID: Canon Press, 2001.

McCarthy, Dennis J. "Creation Motifs in Ancient Hebrew Poetry." in Berhard W. Anderson (ed.) *Creation in the Old Testament*. Philadelphia: Fortress Press, 1984.

McLaren, Angus. *A History of Contraception from Antiquity to the Present Day* Cambridge: Blackwell, 1990.

Migne, Jacques Paul, ed. *Patrologiae Cursus Completus: Series Graeca*. 161 vols. Paris: Imprimerie Catholique, 1857–68.

———. *Patrologiae Cursus Completus: Series Latine*. 217 vols. Paris: Imprimerie Catholique, 1844–55.

Milgrom, Jacob. *Leviticus*. 3 vols. Anchor Bible Commentary. New York: Doubleday, 1991.

Miller, James "The Practices of Romans 1:26: Homosexual or Heterosexual?" *NovTest* 37 (1995), 1–11.

Mitchell, Christopher Wright. *The Meaning of BRK "to Bless" in the Old Testament*. SBL Dissertation Series 95. Atlanta: Scholars Press, 1987.

Mitchell, Hinckley G. et al. *A Critical and Exegetical Commentary on Haggai, Zechariah, Malachi and Jonah*. Edinburgh: T&T Clark, 1999.

Mitsis, Phillip. "The Stoics and Aquinas on Virtue and Natural Law." *The Studia Philonica Annual* 15 (2003) 35–53.

Moo, Douglas. *The Epistle to the Romans*. New International Commentary on the New Testament. Grand Rapids: Eerdmans, 1996.

Moulton, James Hope, and G. Milligan. *Vocabulary of the Greek New Testament*. Peabody, MA: Hendrickson, 1997.

Noonan, John T., Jr. *The Church and Contraception—The Issues at Stake*. New York: Paulist Press, 1967.

————. *Contraception: A History of Its Treatment by the Catholic Theologians and Canonists.* Cambridge, MA: Harvard University Press, 1967.

Noth, Martin. *Leviticus.* Old Testament Library. Philadelphia: Westminster Press, 1977.

Orr, Robert D. "Ethically Defensible." In *The Sterilization Option.* Edited by David B. Biebel. Grand Rapids: Baker Publishing Group, 1995.

Owen, John. *Hebrews.* 7 vols. Edinburgh: Banner of Truth, 1996.

Paris, Jenell Williams. *Birth Control for Christians.* Grand Rapids: Baker, 2003.

Parsons, Greg W. "Guidelines for Understanding and Utilizing the Song of Songs." *BibSac* 156 (1999), 399–422.

Pedersen, Nils Arne. *A Study of Titus of Bostra's Contra Manichaeos: The Work's Sources, Aims, and Relation to Its Contemporary Theology.* Nag Hammadi and Manichaean Studies 56. Boston: E. J. Brill, 1959.

Peterson, David L. *Zechariah 9–14 and Malachi.* Old Testament Literature. Louisville, KY: WJK, 1995.

Pink, Arthur W. *An Exposition of Hebrews.* Swengel, PA: I.C. Herendeen, 1954.

Poole, Matthew. *Matthew Poole's Commentaries*, Vol. 1. Peabody, MA: Hendrickson, 1982.

Provan, Charles. *The Bible and Birth Control.* Monongahela, PA: Charles Provan, 1989.

Quinn, Jerome D., and William C. Wacker. *The First and Second Letters to Timothy.* Eerdmans Critical Commentary. Grand Rapids: Eerdmans, 2000.

Rice, John R. *The Home: Courtship, Marriage and Children: A Bible Manual of 22 Chapters.* Murfreesboro, TN: Sword of the Lord, 1987.

Roth, Martha et al. *The Assyrian Dictionary of the Oriental Institute of the University of Chicago.* 21 vols. in 26 parts. Chicago: University of Chicago Press, 1956–2006.

Riddle, John. *Contraception and Abortion from the Ancient World to the Renaissance.* Cambridge: Harvard University Press, 1994.

Schaff, Philip. *The Creeds of Christendom.* Grand Rapids: Baker, 1996.

Schofield, Malcolm. "Stoic Ethics." In *The Cambridge Companion to the Stoics.* Edited by Brad Inwood. Cambridge: Cambridge University Press, 2003.

Schreiner, Thomas. "An Interpretation of 1 Timothy 2:9-15: A Dialogue with Scholarship." In *Women in the Church: A Fresh Analysis of 1 Timothy 2:9-15.* Edited by Andreas J. Köstenberger et al., 105–54. Grand Rapids: Baker, 1995.

Sellars, John. "Neostoicism." In *The Internet Encyclopedia of Philosophy.* Edited by James Fieser et al. 2005. No pages. Online: http://www.iep.utm.edu/n/neostoic.htm.

Ska, Jadwiya Lekczyn. "'Je vais lui faire allié qui soit son homologue' (Gen 2,18). A propos du terme *)ezer*—'aide.'" *Biblica* 65 (1953) 188–204.

Smith, Ralph L. *Micah–Malachi.* Word Biblical Commentary. Dallas: Word Books, 1984.

Spicq, Ceslas. *Theological Lexicon of the New Testament.* Translated and edited by James D. Ernest. 3 vols. Peabody, MA: Hendrickson, 1994.

Spurgeon, Charles H., *The Treasury of David.* 3 vols. Peabody, MA: Hendrickson, 1876.

Stahl, Nanette. *Law and Liminality in the Bible.* JSOTsup 202. Sheffield: Sheffield Academic Press, 1985.

Striker, Gisela. *Essays on Hellenistic Epistemology and Ethics.* Cambridge: University of Cambridge, 1996.

Strong, John T. "Shattering the Image of God: A Response to Theodore Hiebert's Interpretation of the Story of Babel." *JBL* 127 (2008), 625–34.

Thayer, Joseph Henry. *The New Thayer's Greek-English Lexicon.* Peabody, MA: Hendrickson, 1981.

Thielicke, Helmut. *Theological Ethics*. 3 vols. Grand Rapids: Eerdmans, 1979.

Tigay, Jeffrey H. *Deuteronomy*. JPS Torah Commentary. Philadelphia: JPS, 1996.

Tozer, A. W. *"The Waning Authority of Christ in the Churches: Is He Lord or Merely a Beloved Symbol?"* *The Alliance Witness* May 15, 1963.

Tsumura, David T. *The Earth and the Waters in Genesis 1 and 2: A Linguistic Investigation*. JSOTsup 83. Sheffield: Sheffield Academic Press, 1989.

VanGemeren, Willem A. (ed.), *New International Dictionary of Old Testament Theology and Exegesis*. 5 vols. Grand Rapids: Zondervan, 1997.

Van Leeuwen, Raymond C. "Breeding Stock or Lords of Creation." *Christianity Today* 35 (1991), 34–45.

Waltke, Bruce K. "Old Testament Texts Bearing on the Problem of the Control of Human Reproduction." In *Birth Control and the Christian*, Edited by Walter O. Spitzer and Carlyle L. Saylor. Wheaton: Tyndale House Publishers, 1969.

———. "The Old Testament and Birth Control." *Christianity Today* 13 (1968), 3–6.

———. and M. O'Connor. *An Introduction to Biblical Hebrew Syntax*. Winona Lake, IN: Eisenbrauns, 1990.

Walton, John H. *Genesis: The NIV Application Commentary*. Grand Rapids: Zondervan, 2001.

Ware, Kallistos. *The Orthodox Church*. Revised. New York: St. Vladimirs Seminary Press, 1993.

Wenham, G. J. *Genesis*. 2 vols. Word Biblical Commentary. Dallas: Thomas Nelson, 2002.

Wesley, John. *Notes on the First Book of Moses Called Genesis*. Nampa, ID: Northwest Nazarene University: Wesley Center for Applied Theology, 2009. No pages. Online: http://wesley.nnu.edu/john_wesley/notes/genesis.htm#Chapter+XXXVIII.

Westermann, Claus. *Genesis 1–11*. Minneapolis: Fortress, 1994.

Williams, Ronald J. *Hebrew Syntax: An Outline*. Toronto: University of Toronto Press, 1978.

Wolde, Ellen van. *Words Become Worlds: Semantic Studies of Genesis 1–11*. Leiden: E. J. Brill, 1994.

Wolfgram, Ann F. *Population, Resources and Environment: A Survey of the Debate*. Washington, DC: Catholic University of America, 2005. No pages. Online: http://www-rohan.sdsu.edu/faculty/dunnweb/rprnts.2005.10.10Malthus.pdf.

Young, E. J. *Studies in Genesis One*. USA: Presbyterian and Reformed Publishing Co., 1973.